Strategic Carp Fishing

STRATEGIC CARP FISHING

The Crowood Press

First published in 1997 by
The Crowood Press Ltd
Ramsbury, Marlborough
Wiltshire SN8 2HR

www.crowood.com

This impression 2005

British Library Cataloguing-in-Publication Data
A catalogue reference for this book is available from the British Library

ISBN 1 86126 092 X

Line illustrations by Helen Newell.

Photographs by the authors and contributors.

Dedication
For my mum Stella, and for Cath.
Rob

For my mum.
Simon

Typefaces used: text, M Plantin; labels, Helvetica.

Typeset and designed by
D & N Publishing
Membury Business Park, Lambourn Woodlands
Hungerford, Berkshire.

Printed and bound in Great Britain by CPI Bath.

CONTENTS

ACKNOWLEDGEMENTS

Our wholehearted thanks go out to the following: to Tim for all the help and encouragement he has given us over the years; to Chilts for all the Kryston gear he has given us over the years; to those close to us for putting up with us over the years; and to Kev Clifford and Helen Newell at *Carp Talk*, without whom this book would never have been completed on time. To Marg Nicklin for the artwork, and to Jonathan Higton for putting to rights Rob's mistakes on the computer.

An extra big thanks again to Helen for deciphering Simon's writing and Rob's rig drawings; to Cath for holding the tape measure, and to Sush for wanting to; to all the Nottingham 1996 crew for putting up with the occasional grumble, especially Callum, Bec and Liz, Nik, Lex and Deb; and finally to Eagle and Wicko, just for being a pain in the ....

Last, but certainly not least, to Nashy and Bayesy, not just for our sponsorship, but for being good mates.

We cannot conclude without a mention in dispatches for the following: Clive Deidrich, Mary and Pip, Chris Ball, John Lilley, Tim Kay, Brian Atkins, Korda Leads, Angling Technics, Nina Sansome, Franck Martin, Neil Bannister, Phillip and Ronnie, Raphael Farraggi, Paul Bray and his bad back, John Thacker, Ludovic Dyevre, Simon Horton, Prezmyslaw Mroczek, and Ant and his mum and dad.

You only live once, but if you live right,
once is enough.

Rob Hughes & Simon Crow, 1997

FOREWORD

As the editor of a monthly carp magazine I receive a great deal of material from new writers. Much of the first attempt material is returned, and the writers never heard from again. Some writers have one good piece of writing in them, then never follow through. Others clearly have what it takes to become regular contributors right from the beginning, and when I first received material from Rob and Simon I knew that they fell into this category. They did not just want an article published, they wanted to contribute on a regular basis – and they have done ever since their first feature appeared some years ago.

The carp writing arena is a very competitive one, and successful writers need a number of things going for them to catch the eye first of the editors, and then the publishers. My two friends from Wolverhampton carved out a niche for themselves in *Carpworld* through their ongoing day ticket series, and then in *Carp-Talk* with their regional and young carpers material. Happily for all of us they have now caught the attention of Crowood, and this, their first book, is the end result.

I doubt it will be their last. They are addicted carp anglers who understand that writing is based on experience, and like all the successful ones, they gain it the hard way, by getting out on the lakes and rivers, both in Britain and abroad, as often as possible. They are experienced, talented, enthusiastic and successful, and are able to translate their practical expertise and knowledge into very readable, informative material.

For all their writing prowess, and however successful they may ultimately become as anglers and writers, my outstanding memory of Rob and Simon will always centre on the World Carp Cup at Fishabil, Brittany in May 1996. They won deservedly and handsomely from an unfancied swim against the best that Europe could throw at them, and proved that they can practise what they preach in the full glare of publicity and in the heat of competition. I know of very few other carp angling writers who can make that claim, and I enjoyed sharing that memorable experience with them. They deserve to have a carp book published, and I am delighted that Crowood has had the necessary belief in them to make this one possible.

Tim Paisley

Time for celebration and one in the bag for England.

INTRODUCTION

For some while we both contemplated writing a book that detailed our ideas, methods and approach to carp fishing. We have been writing articles for the top carp angling magazines since the early 1990s, but have always felt somewhat restricted as to what we were able to write. This is because a great number of our articles have been for a specific niche in the market, aimed at the novice rather than the advanced carper, and this has limited much of what we have wanted to say. Unfortunately this is one of the hurdles that regular writers encounter and it is often unavoidable, as the customer's demands have a far greater effect on magazine content than those of the contributors. It is also very difficult to keep finding enough time both to write new material for the weekly features *and* actually to go angling on a regular basis!

As most anglers, we both prefer practising the sport before anything else; but from a writing perspective we also enjoy a new challenge, and this book has certainly fulfilled this need. Although we have both contributed to other people's books, neither of us has written one of our own – and it was certainly every bit as difficult as we imagined it might be! Nevertheless, we knew that we would never be able to commit to paper everything that we wanted to just through the columns of the angling magazines.

The main theme of the book is choosing the correct strategy for angling. We both believe that there is a great deal more to successful carp fishing than has been written in the past. There is too much information on how to do it, instead of how to *think* about doing it. Merely knowing about specific techniques and methods is not enough for anglers to rely on in a real fishing situation: in fact what we need is to know *when* to put certain methods into practice, and when to withdraw them, and *this* is the message we are trying convey in this book.

The contents are not aimed towards any specific part of the market: we have tried to keep the book open to all and to include items related both to the advanced and to the novice carper. Likewise the topics covered have not necessarily been focused on the British angler: we have offered advice and information to the growing number of carp anglers in other countries, too.

The book covers what we believe to be the issue fundamental to strategic carp fishing: choosing a strategy for success. To this end we first take a detailed look at a strategy, and at how its formulation gives essential advantages to the angler. We then consider some of the methods and techniques that are required within this angling strategy and how they fit specific situations. The next section investigates scientific details regarding the carp and its environment; and finally we undertake a series of detailed experiments connected to typical carp angling situations: this technical information, if read and used in the right context, we hope will educate carpers and specialist anglers alike.

The exact sequence of chapters should be followed. Many readers (and we are no exception) have a habit of opening a book at random and of commencing to read from there – usually close to where the attractive and colourful pictures are. However, we do advise everyone to read this book through in order because we have written each passage with an intention, and have attempted to link them together so that they come across clearly and logically.

We hope you enjoy reading the text as much as we have enjoyed writing it, but most of all we hope that you gain something from it and that the information we provide will enable you to put a few extra fish on the bank. If we help you to do this, then we know that we have served our purpose and that all our hard work and effort has paid off.

Carpe diem – seize the day!

1 FORMING A STRATEGY

Carp fishing has often been described as a drug to which anglers become addicted, and if we each took a few minutes to consider this statement, surely very few of us would disagree. As far as we are concerned even after many years of involvement we have absolutely no idea what it is that keeps persuading us to sit through the most dreadful weather conditions just to catch a carp – and probably most carp anglers experience similar lines of thought.

If we had to give a reason *why* we felt constrained to return to the lakeside time and time again we would probably say that it had something to do with a desire to achieve. Certainly in carp fishing the enjoyment factor is high on the list, but full enjoyment generally only comes through achieving a certain goal. Consider a lost fish as an example: where is the enjoyment in losing a personal best carp? Basically there is no pleasure, because the angler is denied the chance of fulfilling a specific goal or target.

It is the desire to reach a target that shapes an angler, and without this hunger the angling session would be devoid of meaning. For us, there is always an end result behind every visit to the water, whether it is a simple outcome such as fish, or a more complicated issue such as catching the biggest carp in a lake. Whatever the occasion there is always a challenge, and whatever this is, there is always an element of strategic planning helping us to achieve our goal. Strategy is an essential component of our fishing, as both minor and major, short- and long-term goals require purposeful, well researched, well planned and well resourced activity.

Everything in life requires a strategy. The boxer does not achieve World Championship status without an understanding of the basics,

a routine for training, a strict diet and a series of build up fights before the main event. The same can be said for the predator–prey relationship between the lion and the gazelle or the owl and the mouse, as neither wishes to lose out to the other. You will not accomplish anything in life without strategic decisions, and as far as carp anglers are concerned, the practice of strategy is the fundamental ingredient behind success.

Every time we visit a lake to fish, we all follow a certain set of decisions that can be described as a simple strategy. Thus the angler who makes the right decisions at a particular time will more than likely be the most successful on the water; whereas the angler who is not capable of determining the right strategy for the occasion will be one of those who fails. We have all fitted into both of these categories within our time, but it is the former that we all aim to achieve on every occasion we go fishing. Thinking in a strategic way is the first step to reaching this target, and its process is possibly one of the most overlooked areas of carp fishing.

Let us consider the angling achievement as a movement from one point to another. Getting from A (the starting point) to B (the end result) is no more than a calculation of events which should be planned in parallel with available data at a specific time. All angling situations possess such information, and this can be obtained very easily: facts such as whether the fish are affected by the weather, whether they are feeding, and where the other anglers are located. These are all important, and it is up to the angler to discover and to use them – in the right context and to their advantage – within a form of strategy. Likewise tactical considerations need to be matched perfectly to the occasion. In fact the whole process of getting from A to B can be viewed as a jigsaw puzzle, where items that do not fit properly cause complications along the way.

There is, in essence, only one way of moving successfully from A to B, and the angler has to calculate and find this passage. Each fishing situation has an exact route as its key and it is not enough merely to possess knowledge of basic components such as how carp are affected by weather conditions, or how we should approach fishing in the weed when pursuing carp. Successful carp fishing requires thought and understanding, and how much time you have available, plus your approach, methods and manoeuvres, are all primary elements for inclusion within a strategy.

The Strategic Approach

We have both been using a strategic approach (*see* Fig 1) in our fishing for a number of years and have seen our successes climb at a rapid rate. Taking a closer look at our method, there are eight main components: Stage 1 represents the starting block and Stage 7 the end result, and between these two there are five separate areas that need interpretation before a result is achieved. Stage 8 monitors and evaluates the whole process if the desired result is not accomplished.

Each time we arrive at a water we will always follow this sequence, and in that order. Once put into practice, analysis and control of any component, apart from the first two stages, may be necessary to ensure that we stay on equal, or better terms than the fish. Carp have a habit of changing their behaviour at any time – as indeed do all sporting fish – and anglers need to be aware of this fact if a blank session is to be avoided. Obviously it is possible to accomplish a result by not following such a path, but what we are trying to achieve with its use is some sort of consistency in our fishing. Methods such as 'chuck and chance' – throwing in any old bait and hoping something might take it – can be effective on occasions, but you are relying on luck if you are a regular practitioner of this form of angling. *We* believe that every stage of fishing

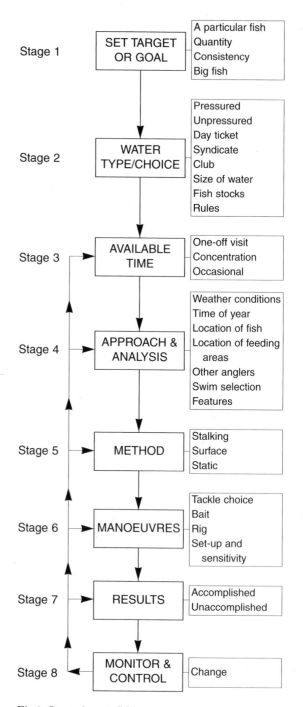

Fig 1 Strategic carp fishing.

needs to be broken down individually and analysed before being put into action. There needs to be some sort of meaning behind decisions and the strategic form of approach is the only way we can do this effectively.

Our reasons for selecting the different stages in the order given are mainly due to importance and relevance. An angler should not decide on a method of tackling a water before arriving there; and similarly, the type of bait should not be selected until he has chosen a method to pursue the fish, for several reasons. If you follow our sequence of events from Stages 1 to 8 you will always see the reasoning behind all our prescribed inclusions at any particular point. This can be understood more easily if we take a detailed look into each of the different stages.

Stage 1: Set Goal or Target

All anglers need a specific target or goal in their fishing: there is no point in turning up at a water just for the sake of it. If there is an absence of reason the fishing will become pointless and quite possibly boring. Moreover you can only have a result if you know exactly what you wish to achieve.

The goal or target may vary as the angler moves from water to water, or it may change on a daily basis according to the changing desires of the individual: may include the capture of a particular fish, the aim for consistency in the angling catch, the pursuit of the bigger fish in a water, or just the desire for a larger quantity of catch. It is vitally important to decide this stage of the strategy as any new target requires a different method of approach from that pursued previously. Thus a particular fish may be prone to capture on a specific length of rig or a special kind of bait, whereas a quantity catch of fish may only be achieved through the use of a universal rig, or by varying the way in which the bait is applied to the situation.

To summarize, different goals require different strategies, as all carp and all waters are different one from another. If you appreciate and understand this stage of the fishing process, then you are well on your way to reaching your goal.

Stage 2: Water Type

All waters are different, so each strategy should consider *water type* next. There are many of different variables that need to be considered: you need to know if the water you are fishing is pressured, unpressured, day ticket, how big it is, whether it is over-stocked, naturally productive, and so on.

If this analysis is carried out inefficiently, results can easily be adversely affected. Thus a pressured water may require something different or new, or the fish in a water may be of

A pressured water may require something different or new to the angling situation.

mixed race stock (which will affect rig selection); similarly, an overstocked water may require a line of approach that is quite different from that required for an understocked venue, or the rules at a fishery may forbid the use of certain baits.

Once all this information has been gathered, the angler must now consider the time he will have available at the water and how best to use it.

Stage 3: Available Time

Many anglers make mistakes at this point, as they often believe that time is irrelevant and that a single-day session should be treated in a similar fashion to a three-day session. How wrong they are! Obviously a great deal more work can be given to a fishing session lasting over several days: a one-off visit to a water needs to maximize a short space of time, and the angler is not able to draw on stored information about the venue because there is none. Instead it is necessary to make the most of what is available on the day, and to try to vary the approach in an attempt to ascertain the correct solution. There is simply no time for lengthy observation in such circumstances.

The angler who concentrates on a water on a regular basis undoubtedly has an advantage, because where time is unlimited for the angler the correct strategy will almost certainly be found eventually. There is time to calculate strategic decisions and then, if necessary, to put them into motion for longer periods, for instance as in baiting campaigns. Even so, available time still has to be used correctly to begin with, and this is why analysis of the situation fits neatly into the next step.

Stage 4: Approach and Analysis of Situation

Like waters, all situations are different one from another. The fish may be located at the opposite end of the lake today as compared with yesterday, or the weather may be having a completely different effect on the fish. Similarly, there may be more anglers on the water today, or they may be fishing different areas.

Situations vary so much at all times, and this is where so many of us make silly mistakes.

When you arrive at a lakeside, try not to be tempted into locking yourself away in the bivvy, or simply settling down at the first available and convenient swim on the water. Ask yourself questions such as how the time of year will affect the carp in your water: where are they at the present time, and where will they feed? And what about swim selection?

Never choose the method for tackling fish before you have analysed the situation thoroughly. Always be strict with this, and always consider very carefully the mood of the fish in conjunction with the situation you are confronted with. Break down the situation into information, and then make tactical decisions based on what you discover.

Stage 5: Method of Angling

Once you have located the fish – or, more important, their feeding areas and where you are going to fish – the angling method can be examined. Will the situation you are presented with be more suited to static bottom baits, surface fishing or stalking? What is your best line of attack, and what offers you the best chance of achieving your goal?

Is the particular fish you are after sitting in the upper layers of the water? If so, perhaps you should try surface fishing instead of static bottom baits. Successful carp fishing is about increasing your chances of catching fish, and there is nothing in the rules that says you have to sit behind three buzzers with a bag of boilies every time you go fishing. Is the water pressured? If so, why not try an element of surprise with your fishing? Stalking seems to be longforgotten as a method to use on pressured waters: it may not sound propitious, but all methods are worth considering.

Stage 6: Manoeuvres

This is possibly the most complicated stage of the whole strategy, as it involves such important decisions as tackle choice, bait selection, rig design and the sensitivity of your set-up. It is also the stage where many of our strategies tend to fail, and before any selections are made,

Which method should you pursue today?

thorough analyses of the previous stages are required. The tackle chosen should fit the situation and the method selected – thus it is inappropriate to use flimsy 6lb mainline in snaggy areas, or to expect to cast 100 yards with a 1oz lead and a 1lb test curve rod.

Be sensible about your choice, and always consider the type of situation and the water you are fishing. As with tackle, the bait and rigs also need to suit the situation: So, what type of bait are you going to use, and why? How is it going to be applied to the situation? How do the fish feed in this water, and how can you relate this to your rig design? Realistically, you can only make correct decisions concerning these areas once the previous stages of the strategy have been considered. All manoeuvres need to fit the occasion and they should never be pre-planned unless there is a justifiable reason for doing so.

Stage 7: Results

In this stage you analyse the results of your fishing strategy. If the desired target has been reached then a new purpose will be needed, and with it, a new strategy also. If it has not, then the current strategy will need some sort of evaluation and monitoring to try and sort out any problems which may be present. Simply ask yourself why you have not caught.

Stage 8: Monitor and Evaluate

Any problems present in the strategy will need to be identified and put right. Before any changes are made, however, it is important that plenty of time has been allowed for the current selection to have been tried, and shown to be inadequate. Constantly changing methods and manoeuvres can lead to serious problems – as can using the same method and manoeuvre for

What do you consider a result? Here's Luc Coppens with a Belgium fifty.

too long. The experience of the angler can only help at this stage, which is why so many experienced anglers are regularly successful: not only are they capable of analysing a situation well and matching the methods and manoeuvres to it, they can also judge whether or not enough time has been applied to a situation before a change should be made.

If a change *is* considered to be necessary, the angler then needs to recognize where it should be applied and when it should be carried out. In fact changes should always be made as soon as an angler has discovered a reason for doing so, and this is why any situation should be monitored continuously, taking into consideration not just the latest result, but all of the available information.

Out-thinking the Carp

As you can see from this step-by-step look at our approach to angling, there is a great deal that needs to be considered – but ours is a method which ensures that everything in an angling session is examined. Basically there is just too much information to evaluate at once, and whilst it would be nice to select winning strategies time and time again, unfortunately this is just not possible – even the very best anglers experience tough times in their fishing. How to overcome the problems is the key to successful angling, and evaluating the information available is the hardest part of the process. Nevertheless a strategic carping approach such as the one we have identified can be used effectively in virtually all types of situation, whether this is a one-off visit to a water for reconnaissance purposes, or a concerted effort to catch fish.

We are by no means claiming that our procedure is the only way in which the angling situation can be tackled: we are merely offering a course of stages that has worked, and is still working for us. Strategic planning is the basis of carp fishing and it is needed for all types of fishing scenario if success is to be achieved on a regular basis. Without strategy, the waiting game may be a long process because methods and manoeuvres will most certainly be selected haphazardly by the angler. All goals are reachable however, and you should never be led into believing that you cannot achieve the unthinkable. We are all quite capable of out-thinking carp: just use your mind in a strategic way and let your tackle and equipment do the rest!

We will now describe three different angling scenarios that we have faced recently, each requiring a different kind of approach to be successful, as each presented us with a specific situation. Even so, you can see how we broke down each scenario into stages and considered it analytically. We could then pinpoint the exact information that was available to us during the three occasions. More important, it is also clear how we used this information to our advantage, and how we arrived at our strategies for success.

Scenario 1 – Surface Fishing on a Pressured Water

Compared with most French lakes, L'Hermitage can be classed as a pressured water. It has been widely known on the French circuit for a number of years, and since the beginning of 1996 has been run as a holiday venue for budding carp anglers. Although limited to fifteen anglers a day, the venue is fished throughout the year so the carp within the water may be regarded as fairly clued up.

In the summer of 1996 we decided to pay this lake a visit for a few days; we had been fishing non-stop for over three weeks previously and we intended to have a rest here. Although we were principally at the water for a review for *Carpworld*, we were so tired that we wouldn't have minded not even seeing a fish. We did try fishing on the bottom in a relaxed manner for the first few days, but with no particular success, and we couldn't motivate ourselves enough to fish properly because we were so tired. It took us about five days to recover, during which time we watched other anglers trying their luck unsuccessfully on the surface near to a large snag tree at the southern end of the 16-acre (6.4ha) lake.

From our observations there were some hefty fish in this snag, the biggest probably about 45lb. They would quite happily cruise past your feet in this area – apparently in the full knowledge that

The picturesque L'Hermitage lake in central France.

anglers were watching them – and would even come up for floaters every now and again. However, pressure had put them off taking floaters from outside the snag; numerous anglers had sat there patiently waiting for carp to sample their hookbaits from this area throughout the week, but to no avail. Word kept getting back to us that it was hard going on the top, and that outside this snag the fish were very wary of anything that resembled a bait. It was starting to sound like a daunting challenge, but after five days of rest our enthusiasum for carping was beginning to shine through once again.

It was Simon who first felt inspired to try catching a carp off the surface from this area, and following a quick reconnaissance trip around the lake he was soon settled into the snag tree swim where plenty of big carp could be seen just below the surface. In theory, catching a fish off the surface from here looked an easy feat – we both knew it would be difficult in practice as the fish had certainly looked wary when we were observing the other anglers having a try for them. The water was also relatively under-stocked and contained only about a hundred carp, most of which to our knowledge had been caught before on several occasions. This was to be the last day of our stay at L'Hermitage, so if we were going to catch off the surface, it had to be now, and if it meant sitting in the tree all day and working for the fish, then so be it!

Simon was well hidden behind a bush near to the edge of the water, and he could almost reach out and touch some glorious fish. He had made his way to this position without a sound and was completely hidden from view, equipped with a bag of Chum Mixer. After about half an hour or so of feeding little and often, it was obvious that the fish were very wary of the baits, even when put directly into the snag. They were certainly interested, however, as they began a circular swimming motion around the snag looking quite excitable.

Eventually the trigger fish started to sample. This caused the other fish to show an interest, although like the trigger they too were very nervous. This was the situation as experienced by the other anglers who had tried surface fishing throughout the week, and obviously something needed to be done to overcome this shy behaviour. It was clear that they *wanted* to feed on the baits, but for some reason or another they were holding back. Maybe it was the smell of the bait? Simon went to get a bottle of salmon flavour and applied it to the mixers. The baits that had been fed to the fish by the other anglers were just plain and straight from the bag, and L'Hermitage owner Tim Kay had informed us that most of the anglers who decided to surface fish used them like this. It was hoped that by adding a dash of flavour, the fishes' greed would become so great that they would just *have* to try one.

Back at the swim, the fish could still be seen swimming in a cautious but interested manner. The mixers that had been thrown in previously were still there, and after a good soak in the bag, the first handful of the flavoured mixers went out alongside them. Immediately the fish began circling them, and after a short time the first one was taken, quickly followed by another, and very soon approximately ten fish were feeding confidently within the snag. They were obviously finding the flavoured mixers most appealing, and even started taking the unflavoured ones. Simon continued to feed the fish sporadically for almost two hours, and it appeared that the longer he did so, the more fish came into the swim.

There were two decent-sized fish among them, and we estimated that one was certainly about 40lb, with the other around 35lb. Both these fish really seemed to be intent on feeding on the mixers. It was getting to the point where a hookbait would need to be cast in, but Simon was still concentrating on nurturing the greed of the fish – one of the fundamental aspects of surface fishing. There was no way of fishing from within the snag itself as the branches were too numerous and tough, and to do so would not be in the best interests of the fish. To be successful, the fish had to be coaxed out of the snag towards the side where a rod could be used with ease. However, the fish were still very much within the snag and certainly did not look as if they would venture out by chance.

Fig 2 Plan view of L'Hermitage, France.

area where the fish was hooked

There was only one way of getting these fish out, and that was by obliging them to go out looking for more mixers. They obviously wanted the baits now – but would the strategy of depriving them of bait be the key to making them go out looking for it? Did they want the food that much? It had to be worth a try. Simon stopped applying the bait, and as soon as he did so, the fish started competing for the last few particles. As these disappeared, the fish began to look frustrated, swimming around in circles and sampling everything in sight. They kept circling for ten minutes, and at one point it looked as if they were not going to oblige Simon and move out of the snag. Slowly but surely however, after fifteen minutes of holding back, they did start to venture out and were soon well into their search.

They seemed very annoyed that their food supply had been taken away from them, and after another ten minutes or so it looked as if they had given up hope. At this point Simon began applying the mixers once again, but this time outside the snag where a rod could be used. Quite uncharacteristically the fish dropped their guard and started taking baits boldly and at random from around this area. Up came one, followed by another and another. It didn't matter where the baits were placed, the fish just couldn't get enough. *Now* was the time for the hookbait, and after three hours of hard work, Simon

was ready to try his luck. He attached a piece of flavoured cork to the hook, which would be draped over the end of one of the outside twigs on the edge of the snag. He scattered a few mixers in the vicinity of the branch and dangled his bait over the end without allowing it to touch the surface – he would only lower it when one, or both, of the two larger fish were in the area.

The two bigger fish were just to the left of the swim taking mixers close to a nearby bush, but as soon as they had finished these, they moved slowly closer to the snag. Here there were approximately ten fish taking with caution as they made their way out of the snag. The smaller of the two larger fish came close to the bank; at only 2ft away it looked a certain 35lb. It was a long, lean mirror with some lovely brownish-gold colourings along both flanks. It appeared red in the gin-clear water and as it approached the baits underneath the hookbait, Simon lowered the piece of cork into the water. Up it came for the first sample, and Simon's nerves were on edge at this point as it was heading straight for his hookbait.

The big lips cleared the water, then down it went with a big gulp to follow. Whack went the rod as Simon struck hard: an almighty vortex ensued and the fish looked disorientated. If Simon had been quick enough, he could have scooped it out of the water there and then;

Mission accomplished: Simon with one of the big mirrors.

but he was too late and it began to peel line rapidly off the reel. Such was its power that Matt Dent, standing behind Simon at the time, had to grab him to stop him falling in. The fish just kept its head below the surface as it powered off. At about 20 yards it turned on the surface and its whole body came clear of the water, and we could confirm its size at about 30lb. It turned once again, but thanks to Matt's assistance Simon was able to get the better of the fish and it was soon in the margins and ready for netting. After one last burst of energy, it thankfully decided to give up and the net was passed to Simon who stretched out the mesh and then gently closed it around the fish. It looked a beauty, and was well above his previous best surface-caught mirror of 21lb.

Matt took the fish to the weighing post: on the scales, the big mirror went to 34lb 8oz – and the capture of it proved beyond any doubt that a carp angler should *never* give up and take matters for granted. Simon knew what he wanted to achieve, and he devised a plan of action to suit the situation he was confronted with.

Scenario 2: Unknown Territory

Both of us authors make regular visits to new waters around the country as part of a series of day-ticket features. Most of the visits are at the weekend, and we will usually spend about thirty-six hours at each site from late Friday evening until Sunday lunch time. We find it is quite stimulating fishing like this, as we are always experiencing new situations as well as discovering exciting new waters.

One such water which we discovered towards the end of 1996, was Borwick Lake in the Lake District. It is very picturesque, situated in beautiful surroundings of woodland and open fields. Our first experience there was on a late Friday evening during October. We arrived at the lake at roughly 9pm; it was pitch black and raining hard. At the gate we were greeted by the owner, Terry Coates, who informed us that the lake had been fishing quite well over the last week. These were very warm words, as most of the time it is quite the opposite during our day-ticket visits! Borwick was a new day-ticket water, and until our visit had been run for an exclusive syndicate only. Upon arrival, this was all we knew about the venue.

Terry quickly showed us around the lake and pointed out some of the main features. There wasn't a great deal that we could see; it was far too dark, and basically we were just trying to set-up our tackle before the rain became even worse. The forecast was not looking good for the weekend: strong gale-force winds were expected,

together with driving rain. Nevertheless, after a single lap of the lake we were particularly interested in an area known as The Meadow, as here we could spread six rods along and between two island features and we could cover a lot of water from this area.

On unknown waters where we need to catch in a short period we aim to fish the area of the lake that offers the highest probability of a pick-up; we would rather concentrate on an area that offered us a 99 per cent chance of one fish than an area that offered a 75 per cent chance of half a dozen. We fish as a team, and our objective is always to catch one fish at the new water regardless of who is the lucky one; we work together well and help each other to achieve our goal of catching a fish. At Borwick, The Meadow offered a great deal of variety, as well as some excellent features that would almost certainly have fish patrolling up and down. Also, because there were no anglers on this side of the lake we could quite easily set-up without disturbance at both ends of the bank. This had to be the place, and we quickly tossed a coin to see who would choose which end of the grass bank.

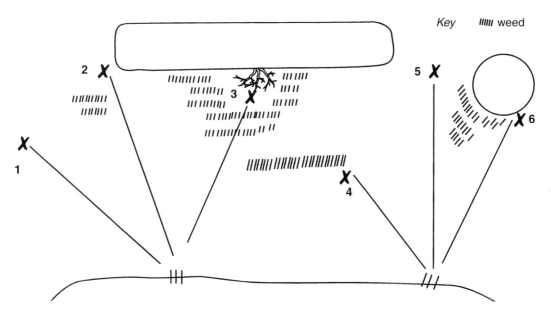

Fig 3 Unknown territory at Borwick Lake.

Rob won the toss and immediately elected for the right-hand area of the bank, as this offered the chance to fish to both of the islands instead of just one. Terry had briefly informed us of the areas at this side of the lake, but as usual we still wanted to drag a lead and plumb the depth upon our arrival, a very difficult task in the dark. We began by casting a lead as close to the island as possible. We used the line clip on the spool of the reel to help here, and just kept letting off line from the spool until we reached the island itself. When the lead landed on the island, it was only a foot or so on and was pulled off the branches and greenery very easily. We then clipped the line in place to ensure that we did not over-cast the distance in the future, and then dragged the swim in the normal way, marking all the features on a map.

So that we could plumb in the dark, we attached the float to the line in the usual way and let the line out through our fingers. By keeping the line fairly tight and measuring the distance let off the spool it was possible to identify when the float had reached the surface, as no more line could be pulled by its buoyancy when there. Obviously, both methods could be performed more accurately in daylight, but it was possible to map out the swim sufficiently well to identify any prominent features in the dark.

After an hour we had completed the plumbing and feature-finding process along the breadth of the two islands, and were relatively pleased with the areas where our baits were positioned (*see* Fig 3). Simon had found some lovely clear sandy stretches between some weedbeds and had strategically spaced his rods into three different areas: the right-hander was tight to the island in a 10ft square clear area at 50 yards, the middle one was placed on the corner of the island (which could just be seen as a silhouette on the horizon), while the left-hander was fished on a siltbed in open water at approximately 40 yards. All the rods were spaced out so that three completely different areas could be used to search out fish. Rob was also satisfied with his bait positioning, his left-hander being fished to a clear area at 20 yards, the middle rod between the two islands in a 15ft wide shallow gully at 70

The island gap swim. Teamwork allowed us to make the most of this area.

yards, and the right hander at the front of the second island on a small shelf at 60 yards.

We had discussed the positioning of the baits after analysing the features, and we wanted to cover as many options as we could between us. Rigs were also strategically chosen and we had decided on intermediate lengths of 8, 12 and 15in. This is one of our usual practices at unknown venues, and we will always fish in this way until we receive sufficient evidence that one length is more productive than another. If this occurs, then we will change all rods to that length. If it does not, then we are no worse off.

Because of the weed, we decided on buoyant links made from Kryston silkworm and strong hooks of the Nash Pattern One variety in a size 6. All rigs were accompanied with single 18mm bottom baits and three bait stringers. Bait for the session was Nashbaits Scopex and Peach S

Mix ready-mades. We had full confidence in these baits as we had used them extensively in the past; this is an essential requirement of a bait when fishing a water for the first and only time. Neither of us would introduce any free bait into the swim as we could not see what we were doing, and the last thing we wanted to do was spread a great deal of bait in the near vicinity of the traps. In this sort of situation, when time is limited, we prefer hunting down the fish rather than waiting for them to find us, and a spread of bait would only have complicated matters.

We were both settled into our swims before midnight, unsure of the outcome but confident of our approach. It was still raining hard, the wind howling through the trees: a thoroughly wet and miserable night. Our preparations were now complete, and any further work on the swim would be left until the morning when we would have a better chance to get to know the lake and its surroundings. Fishing on a day ticket is difficult because you never get the chance to learn about a water and to use the knowledge to its maximum. Anglers who live on a water can put the information gleaned from a session into practice during their next visit, but those who fish day-ticket waters on a single visit have no such advantage. Nevertheless, we are lucky enough to catch one or two fish every now and again.

Our tactics at Borwick were proving to be correct as Simon leant into the first fish of the session just before half-past midnight, a slow one that did not start to take line until it was close to the margins; here it grubbed around for almost thirty minutes, within which time Rob hooked and landed a fish from the gully between the islands. Finally, Simon's fish decided to give up and he drew the net around it and brought it towards the bank, a plump-looking mirror. Terry Coates had informed us that the lake had produced fish of up to 26lb in the past and this one certainly looked close to that weight; in fact it took the scales to 25lb 4oz.

Two fish in almost thirty minutes of fishing had us both looking forward to the next thirty-five hours. Our strategy was certainly working, and we both fired out the hookbaits back into the

area where they had only moments before been selected by the carp. By the morning we had landed a further four fish between us: a common and three mirrors, all in the upper double region. As is usual during our day-ticket visits, we settled down after breakfast to discuss tactics for the rest of our stay. Strangely enough all the fish had come to 15in hooklinks, a pattern of identical behaviour that does not always happen during these trips. Maybe we just happened to cast where they were the previous night, or perhaps there was something in this. We could not take the chance of waiting to find out, so we changed all the rods to 15in links. We also decided that we would not pursue the plumbing and feature-finding process any further, as we did not want to spook any fish that might have been present. We decided to keep to three bait stringers only, as we were reluctant to try something different when we knew the tactic had worked for us the previous night. The fact that it was daytime did not mean that we should start working harder for the fish; we were catching well, and we just needed to tidy up the loose ends.

Shortly before midday, Rob's right-hand rod bent hard into a fish – it had picked up a bait that had only just been recast to the island ledge, and had also come on a rod that had only moments before been changed to a 15in link. It put up a scrappy fight, but was a very welcome fish at slightly short of 20lb. Simon was the next into action only a few minutes later – the fish certainly seemed to come in batches. This one was from open water at the left of the swim where a couple of fish had been showing throughout the morning period. It put up a terrific battle, and even when it was in the net it continued to fight hard for its freedom. It was another fine-looking mirror, which on the scales crept to over 16lb.

Borwick was certainly beginning to show its quality. By now the rain had eased off completely and there was only a slight breeze in the air; conditions were therefore looking favourable and we hoped for another few fish before our planned departure time of noon the following day. We did not have to wait long, however, as just before dark on the Saturday evening, Simon's centre rod line

A typical Borwick lake twenty for Simon.

The following night Rob caught another.

was taken at a tremendous rate. The fish kited round the back of the island and had to be persuaded back into open water where it could be played more easily. In a matter of minutes it was in the net and ready to be photographed.

By departure time the following morning a further eight fish had come our way, including a 24lb mirror for Rob and a 20lb mirror for Simon. We were very pleased with the outcome and the way our strategy had worked for us. From the start we had worked hard, and all the tactical decisions we made were backed by solid reasoning. All the rods had received pick-ups, and we had made maximum use of the short period at the lakeside by linking our tactics to the goal we had set ourselves, as well as the available time which we had to complete the task. We had caught seventeen fish, including three of 20lb or more, in less than thirty-six hours from a water we knew nothing about and had never seen before. This result was obtained through some careful but simple calculations.

Scenario 3: Big Carp Selection

The Fishabil centre in northern France is renowned for its huge head of carp. Some anglers estimate the stock at being well over 2,000 in total, but it is just too difficult to make accurate judgements of the number there, owing to its regular habit of throwing up surprise fish that have never been seen before. From our own experience the average weight of the carp is around 22lb, and out of approximately twenty fish you should be lucky enough to catch at least one of 30lb.

To our knowledge, the biggest carp from Fishabil is a 43lb mirror caught by Ian Starmer, but there are several fish near this weight, and in particular there were two bigger fish that we both wanted to catch from the water. We have visited Fishabil on numerous occasions since 1995 and Rob has always wanted to catch a fish known as 'Bill's fish', its weight in the region of 35lb. Simon also has an attraction for one particular fish, a common known as 'Spike', with a weight varying between 27lb and 34lb.

Out of some 500 carp caught between us from the water, both of the desired fish had avoided our rods. We knew they liked bait as they had fallen for anglers' tactics on quite a few occasions beforehand, and we also knew that particular spots on the lake would produce bigger fish time and time again. Swim 36 on the dam wall is one such area, and during most trips to the water we would see it produce very few captures but a high ratio of bigger fish when it *did* decide to come to life. You could almost guarantee that out of every three caught, one would be over 30lb.

Peg 36: a big fish area, but how would you know?

We believe this may be due to the fact that a lot of catfish patrol and feed along the dam wall during the night, and the smaller fish tend to avoid this area, thus giving the bigger fish a chance to get to the bait. It may also have something to do with the shoals of fish present in the water, as results had shown in the past that the majority of fish caught in a session at Fishabil could well be of a similar weight. Out of twenty fish, the majority may be 17lb on one occasion, 22lb on another, or even 26lb on another. It was a strange pattern, but one which seemed to be very regular at the water. Perhaps the bigger fish preferred to stay away from the majority of the fish, or to hang around together near the dam wall, their preferred area – we had no conclusive proof. We just knew that Swim 36 was the big fish swim at Fishabil.

In the summer of 1996 we decided to visit Fishabil for a week and try for the bigger fish. Before that we had been happy enough to go to the water and attempt to catch as many fish as possible in a single visit, but on this occasion we decided to concentrate our efforts on the bigger fish only. When we got there we were pleased to see that Swim 36 was vacant. Following the flip of a coin, Rob elected to settle into it for the first three days, with Simon following suit in the latter half of the week.

Our tactic was to sit in the swim for a whole week and fish to the area that we knew the bigger fish always came from, at a distance of 70 yards – there is a slight undulation in the lake bed here, caused, we think, by the path of the old stream going to the mill, but otherwise the bottom is just flat and covered in muddy clay. An overcast of the spot would result in either lots of smaller fish or no fish at all, and past results told us that hookbaits had to be exactly on this spot if we wanted the chance of a bigger fish.

We had both decided on a specific baiting strategy for the swim and it was Rob who put this into practice first. He would bait a circular area of two yards' radius with two distinct concentrations of bait (*see* Fig 4). The circular area would be organized into an inner and an outer

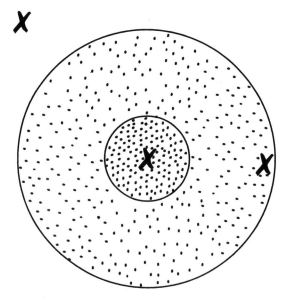

Inner circle: 3ft (1m) radius
400 baits
single hookbait (as free offerings)

Outer circle: 6ft (2m) radius
200 baits
hookbait (as free offerings)

Third rod 4 bait stringer
6ft (2m) past outer ring

Fig 4 An intense baiting method.

section, with the former being more concentrated with bait than the latter. This strategy was based on the idea of a natural feeding area where food would be highly concentrated in a very small space, as in a bloodworm bed, for example. As we have said, we knew that Swim 36 would not contain a lot of fish, and that out of those that *were* present, according to past captures, the majority were the bigger fish in the lake; we therefore did not want to risk drawing in other fish by using a larger baited area. Hopefully the tighter area would be found by just one or two bigger fish swimming past, whereas a larger area might draw in shoal fish and increase competition. The light scattering of boiled baits in the outer circle would hopefully attract fish to the larger central area. Within these circles two hookbaits would be fished, one in the inner circle and one in the outer.

Just beyond the baited area a third location would be fished, in the hope of intercepting any bigger fish that might be hanging back and feeding rather cautiously. Baiting would be absolutely precise, because at Fishabil visitors are allowed the use of boats from which free bait can be introduced. Hookbaits have to be cast, but this was not a problem as the use of two marker float rods helped us to accurately identify the edges of both the inner and outer circles.

Bait was 20mm Nashbaits S Mix flavoured with peach, which we knew had never been used on the water prior to our visit. The fish at Fishabil had seen almost everything, so we wanted a bait that would be a new experience for them and so arouse their curiosity and draw them into the swim; at Fishabil new baits have a habit of fishing better than those used time and time again. Added to this, the wind was blowing gently towards the dam wall – and the wind can be significant in determining where fish are located at Fishabil. The rigs we selected were the type with which we had previously been successful here: a 15in Kryston Super Nova hooklink which would lie flat on the snag-free bottom; and a single ⅘in (20mm) bottom bait attached to a size 6 Nash Pattern two line aligner.

So the traps were set, and it was just a matter of sitting back and hoping that our strategy would work. At the end of the first night nothing had come to Rob's rods apart from a single 20lb mirror from the edge of the baited area. As day came he went to replenish the baited area with fresh stocks, but decided that only a small amount of bait had been taken by the fish during the night. He therefore applied to the inner and the outer circles approximately half the level of bait as had originally been introduced, and sat back waiting for the moment to arrive. This was usual in Swim 36, and it was quite common to have to endure a long waiting period before getting the pick-up you wanted.

As the day turned into night, a light drizzle started and the wind began to increase very slightly. There was now a constant ripple on the surface and at approximately 11pm Rob decided to call it a night. But just as he was laying his head down on the pillow, the centre rod in the middle of the baited area shot off and the alarm sounded at a constant high tone as the reel screeched out a screaming run. He leapt from his sleeping bag and latched onto a hard-fighting fish, which he immediately knew was big. Most of the average size Fishabil carp go crazy in open water, and if you did not know otherwise you would think that you had latched onto a monster. The bigger fish in the water have a habit of swimming towards the bank and then crossing all the other lines in the swim, and this fish was doing exactly that; Rob was already weaving the rod in between the other lines in an attempt to avoid a large tangle.

The fish continued to battle strongly under the tip, and with the help of the lights in the hotel behind us we could make out that it was indeed a good fish as it surfaced then sank towards the lake bed in a vain attempt to shed the hook from its mouth. For a further ten minutes it pursued this same procedure – it just did not want to give up. However, after another two brave attempts, it was exhausted and ready for netting. Rob slipped the net underneath it and brought his prize gently towards the bank; it was difficult to lift the fish up the steeply sloped dam wall. Rob handed the net to Simon at the top of the wall, who lifted the fish onto the mat. As soon as Rob saw the fish, he immediately recognized it as 'Bill's fish'. It looked slightly down in weight compared with when it was last weighed at 36lb 8oz, but it was nevertheless the fish he was after and he was delighted with the catch. The big mirror in fact went to 33lb 8oz.

In the morning Rob moved out of the swim as he had achieved his goal, so that Simon could try his luck with the same strategy. Without wishing to go into great detail, the following night proved to be a spooky occurrence for us both because Simon landed 'Spike' at 30lb 4oz. Never before have we been so surprised by carp fishing. Like Rob's fish, this big common fell to a hookbait fished in the centre of the baited area;

Correct strategy selection by Rob led to the downfall of Bill's fish. Only its second capture in two years.

and apart from a 26lb mirror, this was Simon's only pick-up of the evening.

Swim 36 is indeed a special area at Fishabil, and with the correct strategy and preparation we proved to ourselves that it *is* possible to select the bigger fish from a water. We have used the same tactic on a couple of occasions there since and it has again proved to be the downfall of some of the bigger fish in the water.

Who would have thought it possible? From approximately 2,000 carp we were able to catch two particular fish from a single spot in two nights of fishing. Was it luck, was it due to the strategy, or was it a combination of the two? We will never know for sure, but as on so many other occasions we were convinced that strategy selection is indeed a major component of successful carp fishing.

The next night, Simon banked Spike the common, at 30lb+. What a coincidence.

Tactical Considerations

All carp angling strategies require tactical considerations to turn success into a reality. The matter of tactics is certainly one of the most talked-about subjects in carp fishing, which is why we wish to include within this book some of the considerations we cover every time we go fishing.

It is not possible to fit the topic of tactics into a single chapter without losing track of the foremost points; in our opinion, overlooking this fact is one of the main faults of many carp fishing books. We have therefore decided to split this important area into the four chapters that follow, and within each to concentrate on specific items of importance. They should be read in sequence, as an understanding of each chapter will lead to a greater understanding in the next. They each offer our own views, as well as those of our fellow anglers, on some of the fundamental issues connected to strategy selection. Their aim is also to provide an insight into some of the methods and techniques that we have used successfully on various waters around the world.

Remember, though, that these tactics will only be of use to you in a specific situation, and that a strategy always needs planning, principle and pursuing more than anything else. Only after completion of this process will you be able to reach your goals.

2 THE CARP AND ITS ENVIRONMENT

Anglers are inundated with information about rigs, bait and similar tactics for catching carp, but there is very little literature available within the carp world about the creature we all pursue. Certainly there are the odd references to the fish and its environment, but a great deal of information is based on nothing more than anecdotal evidence. One example is the matter of fish races: if you pick up a copy of one of the latest magazines you will usually see references to fish called Italians or Dinks, when in fact they are nothing of the sort.

This chapter aims to address the characteristics of the carp, as well as how it survives and lives within its habitat of lakes and rivers. This is a fundamental area of carp fishing, which many anglers unfortunately overlook. However knowledgeable you are regarding the latest rigs, baits and angling tactics, it can only get you so far when fishing if you know nothing about the carp itself. We will also consider the aquatic environment and how some of the different habitats change as we move from water to water. We begin by taking a look at the genetic background of the carp, and considering, why a knowledge of this is important when formulating strategies for success.

Carp Genetics and the Evolution of Different Races

The common carp, as we know it, is primarily a major food source. In 1991 approximately three million tonnes were reported to have been consumed throughout the world. Literature referring to the farming of carp dates back to 500BC, but it is widely believed among aqua-farmers that its earliest farming goes back as far as 2,500BC. The fish is said to have been of prime importance to nutrition at this time and its culture appears to be the earliest form of fish-farming practice.

The common carp is a native of the Caspian Sea, and during the Middle Ages it was shipped to several countries within Asia and Europe for culture within monastic ponds. Indeed, it is believed to be the monks who were responsible for the original stockings of carp in the UK, when a selection of wild carp were introduced into many of the monastery pools around the country. The fish soon became established throughout the world, and as the practice of carp farming became widespread, farmers came to appreciate that in view of developing competition a better quality fish was needed for the market. Consumers were demanding a fish that was easier to handle and that did not require hours of painstaking scaling, as well as one which could be filleted and prepared in a very short time.

Through the careful selection of common carp, farmers finally arrived at the now commonly known mirror, leather and linear carps. These fish were easy to handle for consumers, and were also attractive and pleasing to the eye. At the time, farmers were unsure of how they arrived at these end products, but over the years scientists have traced back the breeding following what is now known as genetic consequences.

Genetics involves the study of inherited characteristics of living organisms. As far as fish genetics are concerned, there are millions of different genes within each individual fish and each is responsible for a specific characteristic such as colour, size, growth capabilities or food preferences. Certain characteristics are passed down from generation to generation and this is the reason why, where carp spawn naturally in our lakes, we have many fish with a similar body form and scale pattern. Not all genes are hereditary, however, as some differences between relations are formed through the synchronization of the parents (cross breeding).

The genetic differences between common, mirror, leather and linear carp have been traced back to two specific alternative genes known as the S and the N alleles (*see* Fig 5). Both alleles are paired, and either may possess a major or a minor version (the minor is recessive). As you can see from the diagram, the genetic make up for each of the four varieties is different and this difference is said to be the major genetic distinction between the four varieties – aside from any personal traits.

The above information is a very simplistic way of looking at the taxonomic classifications of carp, and the cross-breeding of any two will normally result in specific batches of brood. Pure lines of commons and mirrors can be produced, but it is not possible to produce pure lines of linears and leathers. When linears are crossed together, one third of the batch will normally be commons and the other two thirds will be linears. Leathers crossed together will result in one third mirrors and two thirds leathers, while linears crossed with leathers will produce either linears and commons, or linears and mirrors. In the main fish farmers around the world use these parameters as a guide when aiming to produce carp for the market.

The genetic make-up of carp often causes deformities such as lumps, bumps or skeletal problems. Certainly there are fish around with structural damage caused by anglers, but many of the evident deformities are caused by the genetic balance of the fish rather than anything else. Such abnormalities will usually develop at around the hatching time of the eggs, though in some cases are passed down from generation to generation through inherited genes.

Hereditary body form is one of the major topics of discussion concerning carp genetics, and is

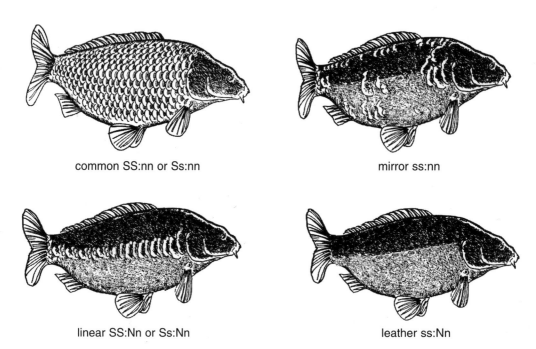

common SS:nn or Ss:nn

mirror ss:nn

linear SS:Nn or Ss:Nn

leather ss:Nn

Fig 5 The genetic differences between the common, mirror, linear and leather carp.

the main identifying factor in relation to the different races and strains of fish that have evolved over the decades. 'Race' and 'strain' are therefore terms used to identify fish from specific backgrounds where breeders have bred fish with special characteristics in body form and colour. Basically there may be several strains (or lines) within a race: to explain, a race of carp dates back to the earliest breedings of fish when farmers from different parts of the world became famous for producing carp with specific qualities (such as the Italians). These races became widely disseminated, and because of this, different strains or forms of the races evolved. At the present time, a number of original races of carp can be found within our fisheries, and from the carp angler's point of view, a knowledge of these is important so that tactical considerations can be made concerning the design and construction of end tackles. Different strains of carp feed differently, and the implications of this can be more readily appreciated through a better understanding of the various races because each has a different form of body depth, body length, head structure and mouth location.

There are seven main races of carp found around the fisheries of the world and we shall now discuss these.

The Galician Carp

The Galician race of carp is probably the most widespread variety around the world today. Galicia, where the race originates, is an area of eastern Europe north of the Carpathian mountains. Galician carp have a classic body form, very much in proportion, the most distinguishable features being a thick-set body and a tail that is pointed at both fan ends.

The Galician carp.

They have excellent growth potential and there have been some very large and famous Galicians in the UK as well as in France. Donald Leney is widely connected with this race of fish through his stocking of Redmire Pool in the early 1900s. These fish are very good-looking, easily identifiable, and there are hundreds of different strains in circulation. They are certainly the most popular sports carp existent in current times, and they can be found the world over as mirrors, linears and leathers as well as commons.

The Dinkelsbuehl Carp

This race of carp only seems to have become well known among anglers since the early 1990s. Certainly the fish was widespread around our fisheries since well before this time, but during the 1990s a fair amount was written in the press about its distribution, and this educated anglers well. One point worth mentioning is that for some strange reason this fish is rumoured to be faster growing than those of most other races. This is incorrect, however, as it grows at the same rate as Galicians; this rate is dictated by the fishes' environment and habitat.

The 'Dink', as it has become commonly known, originates from Germany and is now abundant in many lakes in the UK, the most famous being probably Frampton Court Lake in Gloucestershire and Dorchester Lagoon in Oxfordshire. The characteristics of the fish are large hooped scales across the back, and a down-turned, small-circled mouth that looks very much like a vacuum cleaner. These fish are mainly found in the mirror form, although Dink commons, linears and leathers are also sometimes seen.

The Ropsha Carp

The Ropsha originates from Hungary. However, as a sporting fish, it is most abundant in France where it is found in almost all river networks. Those who have fished the rivers in France will be aware of the large percentage of small commons that weigh in the region of 11lb to 30lb, although it *is* possible for them to reach weights in excess of 40lb; however, this capacity very much depends on the genetic formation of the fish and the nature of its environment. Ropsha commons have a very streamlined body shape, rather like a torpedo, and a strange-looking down-turned mouth similar to the Dinks, although more horizontal in appearance. Ropsha mirrors, linears and leathers do not exist as far as we are aware.

The Dinkelsbuehl carp.

The Ropsha common carp.

The Italian Carp

Of the many different races, this is our favourite. Italians are just beautiful to look at, very distinguishable owing to their high back and circle-like shoulder structure, a deep body; it is this latter characteristic that gives the fish its large potential for growth.

Among aqua-farmers, the Italian is known as the 'twenty-five-past nine' fish, because if you draw a line between the mouth and the eye of an Italian carp and point it directly towards nine o'clock on a clock face, the tail will be pointing towards five o'clock. Only true Italians are said to have this trait. A number of well

The Italian mirror.

known Italian carp are held in the UK, the most famous being within Savay and the Waveney Valley complex in Norfolk.

The Aischgrund Carp

Originating from the Upper and Middle Franken in Bavaria, the Aischgrund is named after the River Aisch, which flows into the River Main, which itself later joins the Rhine. In its original form it was quite an ugly race of fish with a strange-looking mouth, but over the years most fish of this type have faded out.

Many of the Aischgrund carp we see today are found in the large lakes of central France where they reach weights of between 25lb and 45lb after approximately ten years of growth. This carp is renowned for its high back and flat-bottomed belly; its mouth is very blunt and can sometimes look up-turned in appearance. It is found mainly in the mirror and leather varieties.

The Frame Carp

The Frame carp is not a very famous sports fish and is only lightly distributed around our fisheries (at Fishabil, for example). Its name comes from the frame-type distribution of the scales that border the upper and lower flanks of the

The Aischgrund carp.

The Frame carp.

fish. Its body shape is also more rounded than the other races, and it is bred for its looks rather than its growth capabilities.

To our knowledge there have not been many frame carp above 30lb in weight caught, but as far as we can ascertain they are not widely circulated at present. Frame carp originate from Hungary, a country that is extremely well known for its aquaculture production. Besides their distinctive body form, they are renowned for having a large gaping mouth.

The Royale Carp

This is another fine-looking specimen of a carp, and another race that has reached large proportions in some rich waters. The Royale is said to be connected with King Louis XIV of France who had a predilection for carp and decided to breed his own race of fish. Royales are now well distributed around central and southern France, and many fish above 50lb have been caught in these areas.

Their characteristics include big shoulders, long body length and very few scales, and where scales *are* present, they will usually be extremely large and either centrally located, or towards the tail end of the fish. The head of this fish is often very prolonged and the mouth vertically elongated. Probably the most famous venue for Royale carp is the big fish water at Forêt d'Orient in central France, but many are also found in France's large river networks.

The Royale carp.

Know Your Carp

A knowledge of the different races of carp as described above can help anglers to make more effective tactical decisions relating to rig length selection. The different races do vary in body shape, but very often you will come across fish from the same race and strain held within a single water (original stockings usually come from single source suppliers only); for example as at Orchid Lakes in Oxfordshire. Apart from approximately ten Dinks which were stocked in 1992, the other 150 fish in this water are all Galicians of the same strain, and knowing this helped Simon immensely when he was deciding on tactics for the water during 1995. Observation of the fish feeding in the margins, as well as studying catch-related data, and also identifying of the race of the target carp, helped him to bank almost thirty fish during eighteen nights from the notoriously temperamental day-ticket water.

Careful observation made him aware of the fact that the fish were very wary when sampling baits and that they would always close their mouths around the bait and never suck it up. Catch data proved that shorter hooklinks of less than 10in had been more successful for anglers in the past, and he knew that because of their shape and body form, the fish would slightly up-end and then level out when feeding – also that they would not move away from the feeding area. Simon therefore chose a hooklink length of 5in for his strategy at Orchid, as this would offer only slight room for movement following the picking-up of the hookbait by the fish.

Because of the way Galicians feed, 5in also meant that the hooklink would be straight before the fish had levelled out. Besides the use of a 3oz (85g) lead and a tight hair rigged bait, the length of the link would help to increase the chances of the hook pricking during the fish's natural feeding action (*see* Fig 6) rather than shortly after completion of the process. As we have said, a Galician carp usually takes the bait into the lips when it is in an up-ended position, then almost immediately adjusts to a level position as the buoyancy of the swim bladder takes over – and as it levels out, it examines the bait.

Standard rigs of 12in or so always seem to focus on catching a fish off guard when it has *completed* the examination process; however, it is more likely to be off its guard during an instinctive feeding reaction than when it is bent on examining a proffered bait. In the circumstances at Orchid, a longer hooklink would have offered too much time for the fish, as they could have achieved the levelled-out examination stage before the hook had been pulled home, and this could have led to its being ejected. Simon did not want to get to this point, as he wanted to

linear

common

Fig 6 Natural bottom-feeding instincts between specific races of carp.

Design your rigs around the size and body shape of your target fish.

that grow faster and bigger in short periods. Those that spring to mind are the Purse carp and the Big Belly carp from China: the former is reported to have certain genes that have been manipulated to achieve fast growth to a large size, while the latter is said to have big gonads that help with reproduction and the fecundity count (the number of ripe eggs). Both fish have been bred by scientists especially for fish farmers, but if the experience of the 1990s is anything to go by it will not be long before we see them at sports fisheries as well.

Physical Structure and Sensory Organs

The carp can be regarded as having a very simple body structure when compared with the salmonids (such as the trout or salmon). However, it is still an extremely well designed species with a wide range of senses that help it to survive within its natural environment. Taxonomically, the carp is classed as a cold-blooded creature because its internal temperature is always in balance with that of the surrounding environment. Its body contains a number of vital organs and these are supported and protected by a bony skeletal structure. On the outside its skin consists of two distinct layers known as the dermis (inner) and the epidermis (outer). The bony plates of material known as scales generally present on a fish grow from within the dermis.

In addition carp are covered by a layer of mucus which forms the final protection and barrier against infection. The layer acts as a major defence mechanism of the fish and anglers should always be aware of this when handling and removing carp from the water. Keep hands and weighing equipment as wet as possible and always have a bucket of water at hand to ensure that minimal damage is caused. Likewise, try to prevent any scales from coming loose, because although these will normally grow back, their openings can lead to potentially harmful consequences such as infection by *Saprolegnia* (water mould).

catch the fish off guard before they had time to know about it.

Rigs and feeding are both vitally important areas of carp fishing, and will be discussed more fully later. Suffice to say that understanding the different races and strains of fish can help anglers to be more successful: in short, get to know the fish in your water and try to recognize the potential weaknesses they possess. These will usually be related to the length of hooklink, specifically the one to which they are likely to be most vulnerable, although in many cases you may find there is a range of others as well.

As we all know, fish can adapt their feeding behaviour to suit the tactics offered by the angler, but we have always found that carp have a natural and instinctive method of feeding. To our mind this differs among races and is affected by the conditioned behaviour pattern, of the fish – namely in their recognition of danger and how they have been influenced by angling pressure. Nevertheless, all fish lower their defences every now and again, and because of this it is most important to consider the natural feeding instinct of the different races when pursuing carp for sporting purposes.

Many of the traditional races of carp will eventually decrease, as fish are continually being crossed and new varieties formed, and modern techniques have delivered specially bred varieties

Hook damage; a cause for serious concern.

The Internal Structure

The internal structure of the carp is composed of a number of important organs, and each plays a vital role towards its survival in the aquatic environment. Supported by the vertebral column which lies directly along the back the central nervous system runs from the brain, at the top of the head, along the dorsal region of the fish. Below this the kidney can be found, the most important organ of freshwater fish. The bodily fluids of carp contain large quantities of salt and the kidney is required to flush out water as it travels by osmosis from the outside environment, which contains low levels of salt, into the interior anatomy of the fish. The action of this is essential for healthy living or the fish may swell up, or it may even burst. The amount of salt contained within boiled baits is therefore a topic worth considering when using the substance as a preservative. However, at present we do not know of any research that recommends safe or unsafe levels for use.

The carp's heart lies towards the base of the fish's body just below the operculum (the gill cover), and pumps blood around the body in a single circulation. Within the gills, the blood is held in fine blood vessels known as capillaries and these draw oxygen from the water as it passes over

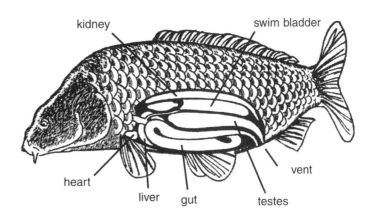

Fig 7 Major internal organs of the carp.

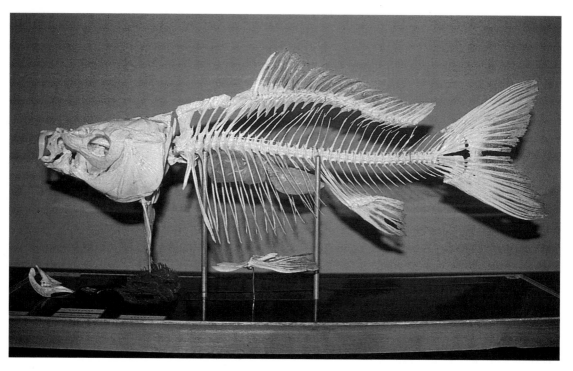

The skeletal structure of a carp.

them. Towards the centre of the fish lies the intestine, the longest organ, where the food is broken down by enzymes in the digestive juices before being passed out of the vent. The intestine is fairly long in the carp because it has a varied diet consisting of meat and vegetable matter. Consumed material such as weed requires a longer period for digestion than meat, so the intestine needs to be long enough to deal with its passage. Lying above the intestine is the swim bladder, a gas-filled sac that can be regulated to alter buoyancy and help the carp to float at a specific depth. This organ helps the fish in a number of ways, but mainly by reducing the amount of energy expended by the fish as it moves.

The External Structure
The carp has a variety of fins which help it to yaw, pitch, roll and to move backwards or forwards. There are two sets of paired fins – known as the pectoral and pelvic fins – and collectively all fins help the fish with balance as well as movement. Despite being of major importance, the carp can still survive successfully without them. One example is a fish known as 'No Pelvics' from Redmire Pool. This fish has been caught plenty of times over many years and has survived adequately without the use of its pelvic fins. Even more surprising, Rob caught a fish in France in 1990 that had no pelvic fins, no dorsal fin, no anal fin and only one pectoral fin; basically it swam on its side and used its tail as its propeller!

The Sensory Organs
Besides the internal organs and other major body components, the carp has a number of sensory organs to detect such things as food, environmental changes and the presence of danger. Most of these are located on the exterior of the fish, but are covered by thin layers of skin for protection.

The Eyes

These are the most obvious sense organ, and are paired and located at either side of the front of the head to allow for an excellent field of vision. They are well developed and sensitive to movement, but their side location does not give the fish very good binocular vision. For this reason it always pays to creep behind bankside vegetation when looking in on carp, as their eyes will focus on forward items and anything behind them will be blurred. As they are sensitive to movement, however, keep your actions slow and smooth rather than jerky and fast.

The carp's eye operates in a similar way to a camera, in that rays of light are focused onto the retina by the lens. The weight of the eye lens in carp has been connected to age determination in younger fish, but this matter is now dealt with in a number of more accurate ways such as by using weight–length ratios and otolith (ear bone) readings. Scientists studying the eyes of fish have concluded that within an angle of 97.6 degrees the fish can see in a circular window when looking outside the water (*see* Fig 8). It is no surprise, then, that carp have a habit of spotting anglers much more easily when we are stood upright at the water's edge than when we are crouching down. Outside this window, scientists believe that images can be reflected off the underneath of the water surface towards the lake bed in a very similar manner to the way that a mirror works. This is said to be one of the ways fish see items on the bottom and might explain why the windward end of a lake is often a very good area for catching carp: the water surface here will be disturbed and this may affect the carp's eyesight for examining items on the bottom, such as hookbaits. Certainly other factors may come into this reasoning, such as the location of food at the windward end, but the theory does offer anglers a conclusive explanation as to why such areas of a lake are often so productive.

Tactile and Lateral Line Sensors

The movement of water currents produced by wind – or those that occur naturally within a river network – can be sensed by a carp through its tactile and lateral line sensors. The former are stimulated by pressure changes close to the fish's skin, and they are almost certainly used by the carp to detect changes in the tension of the water created by climatic change. Although sometimes hidden, all carp possess a lateral line and this operates by detecting the movement of fluid within sensory cells known as cupula. The cupula is a jelly-like particle with fine hairs branching out from it, and as the water moves the sensors send messages to the brain regarding the direction of the water current. Besides the detection of water movement

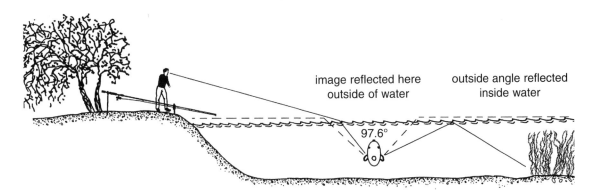

image reflected here outside of water

outside angle reflected inside water

97.6°

Fig 8 The window: within an angle of 97.6 degrees the carp sees outside the water. Outside this angle, items on the bottom are reflected. This is less precise when the surface ripples.

and underwater objects, the lateral line sensor also helps the carp to detect vibrations similar to those delivered by outboard motors or echo sounders. In this way, the sensor works alongside the ears of the fish.

The Ears

A carp's ears are buried at the side of the skull and are extremely well developed. Recent experiments show that carp are capable of detecting sound waves in a wide range of frequencies from 60Hz to 6,000Hz. Each ear – there are two – is composed of a fluid-filled sac, and helps the fish to recognize vibrations in the water as well to assisting with its balance. As the water is disturbed, the fluid is ruffled too – and as sound travels so well in water, silence is always a virtue when at a lakeside.

The Olfactory Organ

Lying just in front of the eyes is the paired nasal passage known as the olfactory organ. This well developed sense organ has an inlet and an outlet, and water can flow to and from tiny sensors located in the passage. Within the passage there are thousands of minute hairs that are capable of distinguishing between sweet, sour, saline and savoury substances. Such substances are detected by the chemical signals they give off, so a number of the flavours we use in our baits are not as special as some manufacturers would like us to believe. Many of the flavours used commercially are composed of chemical solutions that give a specific smell (such as strawberry) when in contact with air. However, when dispersed in water, such flavours have been shown to lose their individual character, so some are decidedly similar as far as their fish-attraction properties are concerned. Experiments that we have carried out have also shown that when applied to fish, certain types actually act as *repellants* rather than attractants, and it is for this reason that we are always selective about what type of flavour to use in our baits. A good flavour should send out a food message *to the fish* – regardless of what it smells like to us – and this is our only

reason for including a flavour within a bait. The chemical composition of a flavour is therefore of fundamental importance and we will normally try to match this with the natural signals given off within the aquatic environment itself. For a more detailed consideration of this subject, *see* Chapter 4.

The Mouth, Lips and Barbels

Working in association with the nasal passages or olfactory sensors, the mouth, lips and barbels of the carp carry sensors that can interpret the taste of specific objects prior to insertion into the mouth. Such sensors are vitally important for successful night feeding, as well as for directing the fish around the lake during times of poor vision. As the carp has no hands to sample objects with, it must use its mouth as a form of investigation tool. The carp is therefore a well designed creature with a number of highly efficient senses. As we have seen, each has a specific purpose and each works in conjunction with the others to help the fish to survive, moreover any deficiencies in an individual faculty will result in the increased capabilities of another. All the sensors work with the brain, which is continually helping the fish to store information for future use.

Intelligence

The carp is considered to be relatively clever compared with other fishes, its processing of data is done mainly by the memory division of the brain known as the *medulla oblongata*. Within this there are two components known as the major (long term) and the minor (interpretation) memory banks; according to scientific research, the former is the more developed of the two. Although there are plenty of contradictory examples, generally speaking all carp possess a similar memory structure.

In order to understand this, we will look at two examples involving a baiting campaign; in the first instance, if for one year we regularly introduce a suitable bait into a water prior to fishing, the fish will eventually feed extremely confidently upon it. This is an example of how the long-term memory works for the fish, as they will in time become accustomed to their own experiences. However, if we now introduce hookbaits into this scenario, the interpretation part of the brain will not be capable of informing the fish of where the danger is, due to the relative lack of development in this area. Thus a carp can have the knowledge that there is going to be a hookbait among a group of free offerings, but it can have difficulty in working out which one it is.

The subject of conditioned behaviour in carp is a lengthy topic on its own, and many of the top fisheries' scientists seem to have become enthralled with it. In short, carp can be conditioned by anglers and this can work in our favour as well as against it.

Reproduction

There is a long-held belief within carp-fishing circles that you will not catch carp when they are spawning. In some cases this may be true, but scientific experiments and fieldwork by anglers have shown that carp do occasionally feed during the spawning process. Their spawning is stimulated by water temperature: a period of approximately 200 degree days at 64–70°F (18–21°C) is required to stimulate the fish into the ritual (the number of 'degree days' is arrived at by multiplying the temperature by the number of days, so a constant water temperature of 18°C for twelve days would make 216).

When ready to spawn, female carp are capable of carrying approximately 100,000 eggs per

Hen carp like this 25lb mirror are capable of carrying in excess of one million eggs.

kilogram of body weight, and are easily recognized because of their deep swollen bodies and prominent red anal vent. Males, on the other hand, are identified by their long and lean body shape and slight discharge of milt. Carp take approximately three to four years to mature, and from this age they will shed their spawn in the upper layers of the water column anywhere close to snags, sunken branches or weed beds. The eggs are translucent and about 1mm across. Once the eggs are in contact with the water, the male fish has about thirty seconds to fertilize them, as they then start to form a hard outer shell and begin to swell. At this point,they are extremely sticky and will attach themselves to anything in their way. The milt is spread in the vicinity of the eggs by the male, but very few are fertilized successfully due to the density of the water and the way the eggs and milt disperse. At least two males are required to fertilize a single female's count of eggs. Very often when observing carp spawning you will witness two or three males swimming alongside the females.

The eggs that are fertilized successfully will take roughly five days to hatch out and the fry will be equipped with a yellow yolk sac to feed on. Once the yolk sac is empty, after seven days or so, the fry will swim up to the surface of the water and take their first gulp of air. The air will be used to fill the swim bladder and the fry can then begin to feed on the microscopic plankton and start to form the characteristics of the carp. Like the fertilized eggs, the survival rate of the fry is very poor and species such as the roach and perch – and the carp themselves – have pleasure in feeding upon them.

Given the right conditions, it is possible for carp to spawn naturally in a lake on more than one occasion within a season. This is common in warm countries such as France and Spain but rare, although possible, within the cooler climate of the UK.

Food and Feeding

Carp are renowned for having a large appetite, and have the capacity to grow to large proportions. Like all fish species, however, favourable conditions and available food are of the utmost importance to the growth of carp both captive and wild. Stocking densities, water quality and available habitat are thus of major importance if a fishery is to become proficient at producing large and healthy carp. To a lesser degree, the genetic background of a fish is also a major determinant as to whether it will achieve big carp status. As we have seen earlier, certain races of fish are capable of reaching greater weights than others; two that come to mind as having excellent growth capabilities are the Galicians and the Royales.

The growth of carp has been much discussed in angling circles for many years and well known anglers have gone to great lengths to investigate why certain fish reach high proportions ahead of

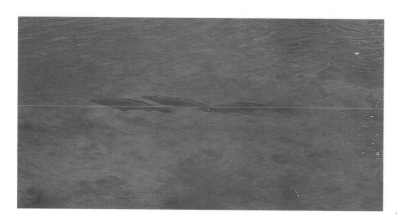

Carp can usually be seen in groups of three or more during the spawning period. This is nature's way of increasing the chances of fertilization.

others. We do not intend to investigate the growth patterns of the carp here, however; instead we shall take a look at the feeding characteristics of the fish, we will try to decipher how the food selection process is carried out, and will consider how natural food sources and cycles can be used to advantage by the angler.

Feeding Habits

A carp feeds when it wants to feed, and whichever of the latest fishing tactics are used, an angler can only sit and wait for the fish to decide when that time has arrived. As carp are cold-blooded creatures, temperature and daylight length have been identified as the fundamental feeding stimulants for the species. As we all know, though, the feeding process may be stimulated by a number of other factors, including the presence of climatic change, artificial attractants, the activity of fish or the abundance of a particular food source.

Carp possess a high level of curiosity, which they often cannot control. They need to investigate things out of interest and occasionally they

Phil Cottenier with a massive Belgium 76lb mirror.

Both water temperature and daylight length have been identified as fundamental feeding stimulants for carp.

also need to sample items, it seems, through sheer annoyance. Sampling can be done in a variety of ways – such as by creating vortexes by brushing items with the fins – but sampling by mouth is used the most. Knowing the particular action of the mouth – it varies between species – and using it to your advantage is therefore extremely important when aiming to catch carp (*see* George Sharman's book *Carp and the Carp Angler*, an in-depth study of how carp feed).

The pharyngeal teeth which lie in the throat of the carp are responsible for the eating action, while the mouth itself does the sampling, and a carp will always select an item for testing before actually eating it. In fact the carp is no different from other species of freshwater fish in that it desires to maintain an energy balance; thus when it needs a higher level of energy such as at the onset of spawning or for over-wintering, it will need more food, and perhaps of a different type. Feeding intensity is therefore governed by these energy requirements, and the procedure for food selection will inevitably be affected by this – we might call it the greed factor. When the fish is feeding greedily, its defences will be lowered to a level that may leave it open to capture – and this consideration should be the principal component of an angler's choice of bait and how it is to be applied to a situation.

Carp learn through association, and aside from the greed factor, the selection sequence in Fig 9 will more often than not be followed by all experienced carp when sampling items of food. If we take a closer look at this process, we can identify how the different levels may be related to the angling situation, and why it is important to itemize the tactical approach before deciding on a specific strategy.

Level 1: Detection
The first experience a fish has with a food item is when it detects it. It is therefore important that the angler's bait is attractive and gives off the right signals. In modern baits, detection would be related to the levels of attractant – these might consist of sweetener, flavour or amino acid. Consider whether or not your bait

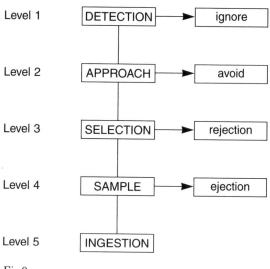

Fig 9.

is overpowered with attractants, or is not flavoured enough: thus, is the fish ignoring the bait because it cannot sense or see the food item, or is the attractant level so high as to be repulsive and the carp does not wish to advance to the bait? If the levels are found appealing, then the fish will approach.

Level 2: Approach or Avoidance
As the carp approaches a bait, it will only take avoiding action if the area does not look safe or appealing. Again, this could be connected to the levels of attractant used, or to the appearance of the bait, or the area in which it is presented. On hard-fished waters, an angler's bait needs to appear more appealing than any of the others. The abundance of a food source may also be taken into consideration at this stage. If the food item looks safe and inviting, then selection will take place.

Level 3: Selection or Rejection
Where an abundant food source is present, selection is likely to be random, and in this instance hookbait placement will be vital – it must be strategically placed. Where food is not abundant, appearance is sure to be the overriding factor and the rig design will be of fundamental concern.

Where a food source is abundant, selection is likely to be random.

Nevertheless, selection will always be cautious and rejection is likely to occur if something does not appear right.

Level 4: Sampling or Ejection

If the food source looks safe, sampling will take place and this is where the taste of the bait is of importance, as well as the efficiency of the angler's rig. If the fish have sampled a free offering, this needs to taste appealing – the tasting needs to stimulate greed, as only the desire for another piece of food will increase the chances of a fish taking a hookbait (unless you were really lucky and it picked one up first!).

Once the hookbait has been sampled, the efficiency of the rig takes over. To a certain degree, the taste of the hookbait is also important because if it is not good the fish will immediately try to eject it – and obviously, the longer the hookbait stays in the mouth, the greater are the chances of success. If ejection is successful, the rig needs alteration or fine tuning.

Level 5: Ingestion

Ingestion is connected to bait design and choice, and the process of selection will occur a further time only if the food source is attractive to the carp. The process of food selection is very much an overlooked topic and many of us fall into the trap of using baits without recording levels of attractants and rigs that have been successful during our previous trips. And if this pattern is followed from water to water the angler can expect frequently to fall short, as all waters and situations are different. As we have seen with the above process, it is essential to make the attractant properties of a bait complementary to the taste. It is also necessary to relate both these features to the abundance at which a bait is present and to the design of the rig in order for the chosen strategy to work. This relationship can change at any time on any water, and only the experience of an angler can help to predict or recognize when it has occurred.

This 26lb mirror obviously found the food source appealing, and the rig simply did the rest.

Natural Foodstocks

Food selection can be a finicky process with carp, in addition to this difficulty, baits generally have to compete with the natural foodstocks in a water. This topic also needs a great deal of understanding if anglers are to become more proficient at correct strategy selection. The natural productivity of a water is related to a wide range of factors, including the availability of nutrients, suspended solids, habitat, run-off and climate; this is why all lakes and river systems are different, and why some are well known for producing big carp and others are not. Most lakes and rivers containing carp have some form of annual cycle that produces natural foodstocks for the fish, though the proportion of the carp's diet that is made up of this natural food will depend on the biomass of the water and its productivity. Within the cycle, the various forms of natural food will bloom or diminish depending on the temperature and quality of the water and the energy demands and feeding requirements of the species present.

Within the open waters of lakes there will be an abundance of microscopic plants known as phytoplankton. These may consist of flora such as the diatoms and other algae and will be consumed by tiny animals known as zooplankton (*Daphnia*, *Bosmina* and other water fleas) upon which the carp will feed. Neither the phytoplankton or the zooplankton are evenly distributed within a water body, as both are very much influenced by the direction of the wind as well as the brightness of the light. Where a ripple is present, the majority of both will be found towards the windward end of a lake or against the side of a bank. During daylight the zooplankton will migrate downwards towards the lake bed.

Phytoplankton and zooplankton come to rest on the lake bed when they die. Here they form an essential part of the diet of the bacteria and benthic animals (such as molluscs, crayfish and larvae) which make up the largest part of a carp's diet. This can be seen very clearly if we take a look at the stomach contents of carp from three different lakes located in south-eastern France (*see* Table 1). This study was carried out in 1975 by fisheries' scientist Nicolas Gialio, and identifies the annual feeding cycles of the carp in all three lakes. The information gained from the study highlights facts that are useful to the carp angler. When related to the annual abundance cycle of specific species (*see* Figs 10–12), the

Table 1. Seasonal variation in carp diet from three lakes in south-eastern France. Figures represent percentages. From N Gialio (1975).

Food item	Jan	Feb	Mar	Apr	May	June	July	Aug	Sept	Oct	Nov	Dec
Chironomid (bloodworm etc.)	6.2	11.3	4.6	10.2	8.4	39.2	39.0	56.0	19.0	1.6	6.0	2.3
Coleoptera larvae (beetles)	2.8	2.6	–	10.8	1.2	–	1.1	–	10.6	4.2	11.0	–
Diptera (two-winged flies)	–	–	0.8	0.5	–	1.8	–	–	3.1	0.3	0.6	–
Mollusca (snails etc.)	63.0	48.3	33.6	26.5	38.3	13.0	18.0	2.3	19.0	13.6	31.0	45.0
Tubifex (worms)	–	3.3	14.2	20.3	0.9	–	–	–	6.0	14.2	24.2	10.7
Small crustacea (*Daphnia*)	–	0.3	2.9	3.4	13.2	31.4	36.0	28.6	9.0	3.4	0.1	–
Larger crustacea (water lice etc.)	13.2	9.0	6.0	3.8	0.3	1.1	2.2	1.3	18.3	16.1	13.2	11.0
Vegetable material	–	–	–	–	–	–	1.2	–	0.3	–	–	–
Leech	–	0.3	–	2.1	6.7	–	–	–	4.3	2.1	7.8	–
Terrestrial	8.5	6.0	8.0	18.1	13.0	7.2	2.5	11.3	6.1	9.5	4.0	7.0
Unidentified	6.3	19.0	19.9	4.3	18.0	6.0	–	0.5	4.3	25.0	2.1	24.0

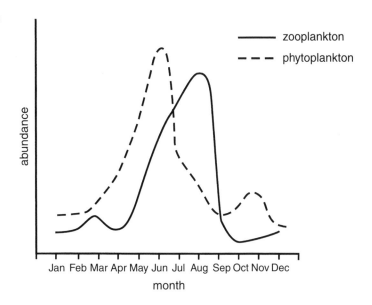

Fig 10 The annual cycle of zooplankton and phytoplankton.

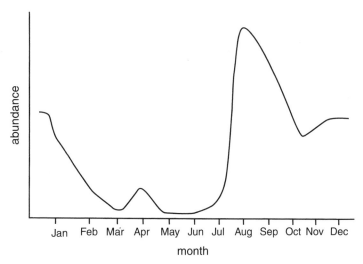

Fig 11 The abundance of Asellus *(water lice) in a typical temperate lake.*

data shows that the carp in the three lakes utilize the most available food source at a specific period of the year. Where the abundance is mainly molluscs, these will make up the main part of the diet, but where high levels of other items are present, the fish will turn to such things as *Chironomus*, *Asellus* or *Daphnia*.

Similar results were also identified in a study carried out on the selection of molluscs by carp on Lake Skadar in Yugoslavia (Stein, Kitchell and Knezevic, *The Journal of Fish Biology*, 1975, pp. 391–9). Such information is invaluable for anglers because, although site specific, it identifies the natural items a typical carp feeds upon at various times during a twelve-month period. The findings from this type of study can be used in bait design, by helping to match the attractant properties of a bait to the most abundant natural food source in a water body at a specific time of the year. This is how we approach our fishing

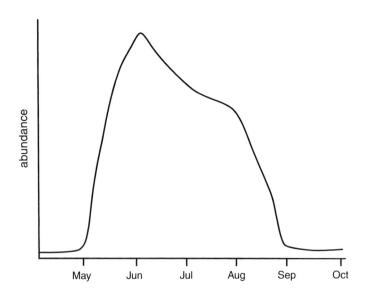

abundance

May   Jun   Jul   Aug   Sep   Oct

Fig 12 The annual cycle of the Chironomid in a typical temperate lake.

on occasions, and we will often design baits using what we know about the annual availability of certain foods in the typical lakes and rivers of the UK. You might think this is taking things too far, but if you want to start out-catching other carp anglers on a particular water it will certainly be worth the effort.

Matching Bait Attraction to Natural Food

The principle behind matching bait attraction with natural food signals is to trick the fish into taking an unnatural bait confidently because it imitates a specific natural food signal. We have both had tremendous success on plenty of waters by formulating a bait that releases such signals; one of our favourites is created with the assistance of bloodworm. First, we formulate a boilie mix with ingredients that are as plain as possible (mainly semolina, which has little taste). Second, we roll the mix in the normal way, but without adding any artificial attractants. At the boiling stage, we add liquidized bloodworm to the water. Following boiling and drying, we then apply the baits to a soak of liquidized bloodworm prior to freezing. By formulating the bait in such a way we are essentially trying to offer the fish a ball of bloodworm.

A typical mix that we have used in this way is made up of 8oz white semolina, 4oz soya flour

and 4oz egg albumin. The egg albumin certainly increases the price of the mix, but when using this approach we keep freebies (free offerings) to a minimum and allow the surrounding natural food sources to act as the attractants. When fishing in this way it is of course imperative to make sure that you are fishing near to or on a natural bloodworm bed. There are plenty of advantages with using this tactic, and the fish will more than likely never have been hooked on fake naturals of this sort before.

The same sort of approach can also be used with molluscs, or any other type of natural food that can be liquidized. Although we do not use this approach every time we go fishing, it has proved extremely effective for us on wholly natural waters where the fish mainly consume the most abundant natural food sources ahead of boilies. It also works well on waters where the fish are very shy of standard baits.

Carp's Feeding Apparatus

The carp is well equipped with feeding tools for specific items from its natural food sources. Fine gill rakers (known as bronchial apertures) are located at the back and sides of the mouth, and these help to filter out minute organisms such as zooplankton from the water. In the summer you will frequently come across carp swimming

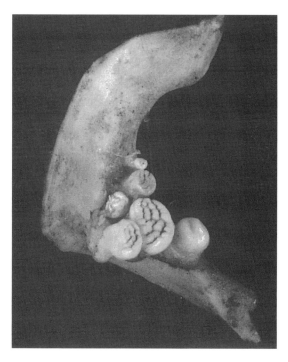

The pharyngeal teeth of a carp.

THE AQUATIC ENVIRONMENT

We will now take a brief look at some of the major characteristics of the aquatic environment. Carp are hardy creatures that can adapt to a variety of stress-related environments as well as those regarded as relaxed. Lake and river environments differ in a number of ways as habitat, but carp can survive, grow and reproduce adequately within both. Before we examine some of the different features of lakes and rivers and consider how a knowledge of these can be of use to the carp angler, it is important to look at the primary process behind the survival of fish in water bodies.

Within all aquatic environments the existence and abundance of life greatly depends upon the process of photosynthesis, which occurs on a daily basis in water bodies. Green plants containing chlorophyll convert carbon dioxide into energy and oxygen with the assistance of sunlight. All water bodies that contain fish can be regarded as ecosystems, and within each there is an abundance of living and non-living components such as animals, plants, water, substrata and incident light. The aquatic plants and their ability to convert carbon dioxide and water into energy form the basis of the various trophic levels: producers, consumers and decomposers.

Aquatic plants may be found in various forms in a lake or a river system, and of these forms the algae are the most important. They in turn exist in a variety of forms, with the most identifiable being:

- microscopic green plants that float suspended in the water (phytoplankton);
- the green slime that covers rocks in rivers;
- the large green bunches of silkweed that thrive in lakes.

Where phytoplankton are present in large numbers in suspension, they will turn the water a pea-green colour and will cling to an angler's lines, making these obvious to fish. Where present in silk-weed strands, the algae will create

around the higher levels of the water column without a care in the world as they filter out *Daphnia* with their rakers. On these occasions it is almost impossible to catch the fish, as they are completely preoccupied with the food item they are consuming.

For tougher items such as molluscs and crayfish, the carp possesses a set of throat teeth known as pharyngeal teeth. These teeth act as crushers and work against a pad in the roof of the mouth, on which the hard shells are broken up so that the contents can be ingested. After years of use the pharyngeal teeth do wear out, and this fact has been related to the reason why some carp are caught more often on waters such as Lac de St Cassien in the South of France. Here the fish depend on the molluscs as a major source of food, but if they cannot feed on them because their teeth are worn out, there is distinct evidence that they become more dependent on anglers' baits. This same principle may hold true on many other waters.

further problems for the carp angler by causing presentation difficulties, as well as weed masses within which anglers may lose fish. Nevertheless, the algae are a vitally important primary producer within ecosystems, and are found within all lakes and river networks where there are carp.

River Systems

When comparisons are made between the physical qualities of rivers and lakes, it will be found that they differ immensely. It is therefore important to have an understanding of how each functions and how specific characteristics may affect any carp that are present. As far as river systems are concerned, the habitat generally found in areas where carp are present is very similar as we move from site to site. Rivers can be split into zones for the purpose of measuring the gradient and velocity of flow; and carp lie mainly within the lowland areas (termed 'bream zones'). Here the water will be slow flowing and there will be a high amount of suspended matter present, which will cause the water to be coloured in appearance. Because the water flow will cause a regular turnover of the suspended solids, sunlight penetration will be steady all year round; when compared with lakes, the water temperature will also be at a more constant level. There may be an abundance of trees and features along the banks of the lowland river, and the nutrient content of the water will be richer than the higher sections; plants will therefore become established and there will be a wide diversity of food items.

The river bed will be flatter here than in other zones, and there will be very little sand or gravel. Mud or silt deposits will make up most of the features, and some of the natural food items found will be very similar to those in a typical lake environment, including molluscs and crustacea. Depths will be regular and often uniform, although during times of flood, snaggy features situated along each section of river may be picked up and deposited further downstream. For the carp angler, this movement of snags is a regular problem on rivers, and sections can be altered greatly following the rush of floodwater. One stretch of river in the Loire Valley that we have visited over many years changes constantly: one month it is completely snag free and then only a couple of months later it can be infested with sunken trees and driftwood. Make sure therefore that you do not fall into the habit of expecting the same features to be present time and again when you are concentrating your efforts on rivers.

Lakes

Lakes containing carp offer great diversity. Depth and size differ immensely between lakes: one may only be a couple of metres deep, nutrient rich and 2 acres (0.8 hectares) in size, whereas another may be 100ft (30m) deep, poor in nutrients and 2,000 acres (800 hectares) in size. Similarities between these two examples will be few, but the differences are likely to be very wide ranging.

Scientists classify lakes according to their productivity: those that are poor in nutrients are termed **oligotrophic**, the nutrient-rich type **eutrophic**, and those with an intermediate character are called **mesotrophic**. The natural productivity of a deep lake is generally considerably less than that of a shallow one, and this phenomenon can be related to the process of thermal stratification. Thermal stratification results in the presence of thermoclines (*see* Fig 13) – zones of rapid temperature change that lie between the layers of warm water in the upper region (epilimnion) of a lake and cold water in the lower region (hypolimnion). Thermoclines are found only in deeper lakes – deeper than 32ft (10m) or so – and they do not occur in waters that are open and subject to frequent gales. In order to understand how they are formed it is necessary to take a look at the seasonal cycle of water temperature in lakes, starting with the winter months.

Water Temperature in Lakes

Water density varies with temperature, and within a lake, water cools from the surface downwards. At a temperature of 39°F (4°C)

Cassien. The same lake but with many different features, there are oligotrophic and mesotrophic areas. The carp thrive in them both, but tactics for catching them are very different.

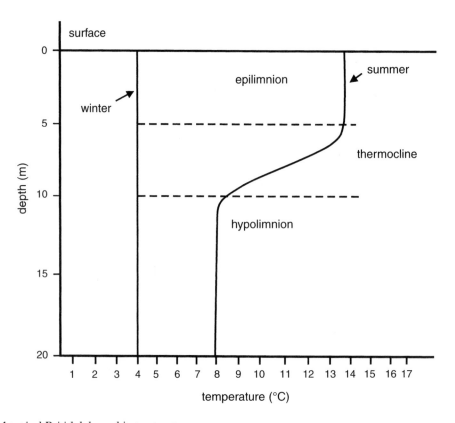

Fig 13 A typical British lake and its temperature curves.

water is at its most dense, and it will sink to the bottom of the lake when it reaches this temperature. During the onset of winter the water surface begins to cool, and a temperature of 39°F (4°C) is built up from the bottom upwards, through the various depths of the lake. When the lake is at this temperature throughout, any further cooling at the water surface results in a build-up of less dense but colder water. If the surface water continues to cool until it reaches 32°F (0°C) a layer of ice begins to form. As ice is a poor conductor of heat, its presence reduces the speed at which the water below freezes. This is why lakes in temperate regions rarely freeze from top to bottom.

Similarly, as the atmosphere begins to warm, the water heats from the surface downwards. Within shallow lakes, the water will usually become heated throughout. However, in deep-

er lakes the heat will not penetrate much below 10m so only the upper layers will become warmer. These upper layers will become separated from the lower and cooler levels by a zone of rapid temperature change known as a **thermocline**. The occurrence of this will be seasonal (*see* Fig 14), and the presence of the thermocline may cause biological difficulties within a lake. These changes are related to the penetration of sunlight within a water: below 10m sunlight energy will not penetrate enough to allow colonies of rooted plants to form on the bottom. A shortage of rooted plants will result in an abundance of phytoplankton to assist with photosynthesis, and these will be found in the upper layers of the lake. As we have already seen, when these die they come to rest on the lake bed where they are broken down by bacteria. During this process the bacteria use up a

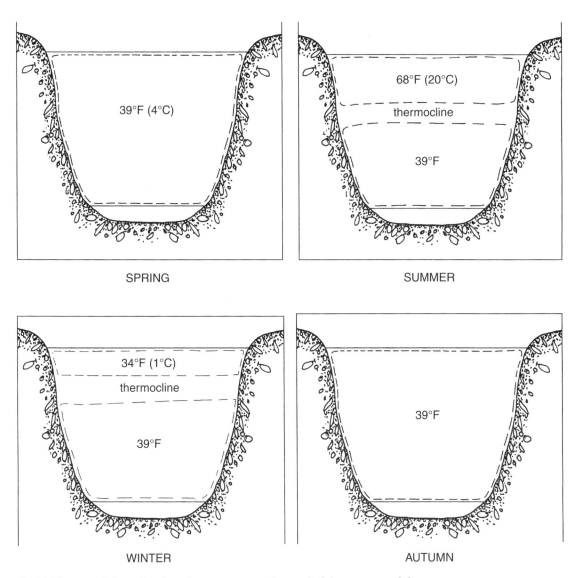

SPRING

SUMMER

WINTER

AUTUMN

Fig 14 The annual thermal cycle and turnover pattern in a typical deep temperate lake.

great deal of oxygen, and since the lake bed is far from the water surface and not capable of absorbing oxygen from the atmosphere, very little oxygen will be found in some deep waters during summer.

This leads to the formation of thick deposits of silt on the lake bed, which are black in appearance and anaerobic in form – such as those found at Jennets reservoir in Devon and the Lac

de St Cassien in Southern France. Towards the dam at Jennets the silt is very thick and black, and very few carp are caught off the bottom. At St Cassien there are plenty of deep areas that are silty and virtually lifeless. In this type of water the carp will usually only feed within the marginal areas or close to any obvious plateau regions where sufficient light penetration provides an abundance of food.

A lovely winter twenty for Rob, proving that they are still catchable at this time of the year.

The Oxygenation of Water Bodies and its Effect on Fish Habits

All water bodies, regardless of size, require oxygen to support aquatic life. This oxygen this may be obtained through absorption from the atmosphere, photosynthesis, climatic conditions, water inlet pipes and other processes. Water naturally absorbs oxygen to a level of saturation beyond which it will not absorb any more. Living creatures consume oxygen by respiration, feeding or movement. During the summer there is a high requirement for oxygen (known as biological or biochemical oxygen demand) within water bodies owing to the increased rate of activity of the living organisms.

During the winter, however, the opposite is generally found, as the cooler water temperature slows everything down considerably. Generally speaking, cooler water therefore contains greater amounts of oxygen than warmer water, and to our minds this point should lead the angler to consider carefully both the location and quantity of bait applied to a situation.

Let us explain our reasoning behind our methods of bait application as described below. The carp is a great deal more active during periods of warm water temperature, and so then requires fuel (food) at a higher rate to sustain its energy requirements. As it begins to fill itself up with food, oxygen demand is greater than when it commences feeding on an empty stomach. (we humans in fact operate in the same way – thus when we are full to the brim we are breathing at a higher rate than when we are about to start on the first course). During the summer, the lower levels of oxygen which are present in some waters result in the fish having difficulty physically with filling itself up to a maximum in one sitting (single sitting satisfaction: SSS). Leather carp are an excellent example here, being genetically different from the mirrors, commons and linears, in that they require greater levels of oxygen to feed. Where low levels of oxygen are present in a water, they cannot eat as much food in a single sitting as the other varieties, and this is the reason why many leather carp have restricted growth. Where SSS is not possible in the summer months on a water, the fish will more than likely feed regularly throughout the day in a little and often manner. Observation and getting to know your water will help you to discover if your venue fits this pattern during this period of the year and if this is the case, then a little-and-often baiting campaign may prove to be more rewarding than sitting on a pile of bait for a few days and waiting.

In the winter, however, the higher levels of oxygen present in water bodies makes it increasingly possible for fish to gain SSS and this point may be reflected in the low numbers of repeat captures which occur during the cooler months around our waters. At this time of the year the fish will be very inactive, and a single sitting of intense feeding which fills a fish up to a maximum may last it a number of weeks. With this said, however, the unpredictability of winter carping makes it difficult to judge the numbers of fish feeding at a particular time, and so also the levels of bait best used by the angler. In our opinion it is better to keep to a little-and-often baiting campaign in the winter unless you have evidence to use otherwise.

The Effects of Decaying Vegetation
The aquatic environment may be significantly affected by the process of decaying vegetation. Where waters are surrounded by trees, the autumn months will see large quantities of leaf matter fall into the water system. As the leaves come to rest, the leaf matter will begin a natural process of breaking down into silt. As it breaks down, oxygen is required, and chemicals are given off into the environment which may turn once productive fish-catching areas of a lake into completely useless areas for a period of weeks. We have found this to be a common occurrence on small, heavily wooded estate lakes where we have frequently enjoyed hot spots, which then appear to die off in the autumn; they return the following year, only to follow the same pattern.

Summary
We have indicated the fundamental variations in habitat between lakes and rivers: use this information alongside a knowledge of the carp, and always consider these factors wisely when trying to formulate strategies for success.

3 LOCATION OF FISH AND FEEDING AREAS

Find the fish before you start fishing. This has to be the best tactic that any angler can adopt, and it goes without saying that a bait presented in an area where there are no fish and are not likely to be any fish, will not get picked up. When we visit venues to research the *Carpworld* day ticket articles, more often than not we have never been there before, and usually end up arriving in the dark, not knowing what to expect. The easiest thing to do would be to jump into the nearest swim for the night and give matters a rethink in the morning. However, as we only ever have about thirty-six hours at each venue and in that time we have to extract a fish or two, we cannot waste any time.

The first thing we do, rain or shine, dark or light, is walk round the whole of the venue looking for signs of fish, or alternatively places they might visit or frequent. We would do this even if we had seen the water before and had a little knowledge of it, as there are many variants that will affect where the fish might be. Even though the Oak Tree Swim may be a renowned hotspot and the one everyone wants to occupy, for one reason or another it may be the worst place in the world to fish during the thirty-six hours that we are likely to be there. The reason we mention this, is that far too many anglers decide where they are going to fish before they even get to the venue. If you know your lake well, you may be able to judge where the fish will be at any given time or in certain weather conditions, but even if you know it like the back of your hand, there may be a full car park when you arrive and the pressure of all the lines in the water may stop the fish going to where you think they would be. In our opinion it is therefore *absolutely essential* to walk round the whole lake at least once, looking in every swim for signs of fish and angler pressure, even if the lake is 20 acres (8ha) or more and the walk will take you an hour or so. You never know whether the next swim that you walk into might be the one with a group of twenties feeding under an overhanging bush, just screaming to be caught.

What happens if you do not find any fish? You might think that you have wasted time but this is certainly not the case, as you will have surveyed the lake from every swim and may be able to hazard a guess at the holding or visiting areas. There

Always keep your eyes peeled for fish – even in periods of cold weather.

are numerous ways in which you can locate carp and their feeding areas: some of our favourite considerations are given below, and you should consider all of them within your strategy.

Visual Location of Fish

Catching a clear sight of carp is by far the best method of location, when there is no mistaking the fact that the fish you saw was a carp and not a pike or a bream, your confidence soars. You know that you are in the right place and that the fish are moving, so you are extra keen to get the rods out quickly and try to extract one. The visual location of carp can happen in a number of ways: you might see the head and shoulder of the fish, or it might throw itself completely out of the water. When this happens it gives you an indication that the fish are moving and therefore likely to feed. If you see a fish do this, especially in winter, it pays to put a bait on it. This method has been successful for us on a number of occasions, and it surprises us when we speak to anglers and they say that they have seen a fish moving, but did not cast to it. Even if it took you a while to position your rods, it is usually worth casting one of them to the moving fish: simply mark the line with a pen, or if the fish jumped closer in than you are presently fishing, put the line in the clip on the spool. As long as you line up your original spot with a mark on the horizon, you should be able to put it back in almost exactly the same place should you need to.

In addition to humping and jumping fish, you should also be on the lookout for fish cruising in the surface layers of the water column, basking in the sun, or lying in the shade of overhanging trees. Carp are also always attracted to lily pads, and with a trained eye and a little experience they are not too hard to spot as they often lie with the top inch or so with their back sticking

If you can spot them, you are also in with a chance of catching them.

Nothing like a bit of competition.

out of the water – just look for the little black lump, or alternatively the movement of the fish through the pads. A set of pads will move slightly with the action of the water, but if you look carefully every now and again one might give a more emphasized movement and this is almost certainly because there are fish there, either basking underneath or picking food items such as snails from the underside of the pad leaf. It is also quite easy to spot the activity of carp in rushes and reedbeds where they often like to lie up, especially during extremes of heat and cold.

In open water, carp can often give away their presence by topping and swirling without breaking the surface of the water: look for flat spots on the water in windy conditions, and for ripples and rings in calm conditions. In the margins, look for vortexes caused by swirling fish. And if you see a coloured area of water in an otherwise clear lake, ask yourself what could have made it: if there are no animals in the area that might have walked into the margins and you know that there are no springs in the water, then it is likely that there are carp feeding in the vicinity.

Can you see it?

Aural Location of Fish

Another way of finding out where the carp are active is by listening for sounds of disturbance. They can be quite noisy creatures on occasions, especially at spawning times and during the summer months when they will often leap and crash. Listen carefully for the sounds of moving fish and try to visualize the disturbance they might be making on the surface. This can be especially useful at night as sound carries well across water, and during the night your hearing should be more sensitive in compensation for the loss of vision. Carp are also quite noisy when they feed on the surface, and on a number of occasions we have located fish feeding in pads as a result of the 'clooping noise' they make when they are sucking snails off the underneath of the pads themselves.

Mechanical Fish-finding Methods

Binoculars and polarizing glasses should always be a part of the carp angler's kit, as it is an enormous advantage to be able to see both long distances and into the water itself when you are searching for fish. A better angle of view can be obtained by climbing up a tree, as the glare on the water will be dramatically reduced and you should be able to see both fish and the underwater features of the lake much more easily than from the bank.

Another method we use to find fish is to scatter baits in the margins in certain areas, checking at intervals to see how much, if any, has been eaten. Beware when using this method however, as coots and smaller fish may eat the bait, making you think that carp are visiting your area, when in fact they haven't.

This one popped its head out not twenty minutes before capture.

Echo sounders can be used, although they are notoriously inaccurate for fish identification purposes because they cannot differentiate between a large fish and a shoal of smaller fish. Moreover they function by sending an electronic pulse through the water which bounces off the bottom of the lake and returns to the transducer on the bottom of the boat, and this electronic pulse can be felt by the fish and in some cases will spook them out of the area. It is for this reason that we do not use our echo sounder for finding fish. As a feature finder, however, the sounder is to be recommended, as it will reflect quite accurately both the depth of water and the features on the water body bottom. It is advisable to purchase a sounder with 'greyline', a facility which indicates the character of the lake- or riverbed through the shading of the information on the screen. For example rock will bounce a stronger signal back up to the boat than silt, and the unit will interpret this and indicate silt as a grey line and rock as a black line.

Locating Frequented Areas

If you have not been able actually to locate fish before you start fishing, the next best thing is to pick out areas where you think they might feed, shelter, or travel through. The carp's existence is fairly simple in that all it has to do is breathe, eat, spawn and keep itself safe to do all these things. If we next consider what its priorities might be, we should better understand its lifestyle and the way it goes about its day-to-day tasks. In our opinion its priorities are as follows:

- Respiration
- Nutrition
- Security
- Reproduction

but can we put this knowledge to good use and relate it to the angling situation? Various external factors affect the way the carp follows its daily routine, and we will consider these further now.

The Influence of Weather Conditions on Fish Behaviour

Thermal radiation is the key to all life, as without the effects of the sun we would all die. It is an important factor for the carp too, as it governs the life cycle of the lake, the temperature of the water, how much of its oxygen is dissolved, and the light that penetrates it. Wind, rain and air pressure also have a dramatic effect on the behaviour of carp.

Wind
The wind has three main effects: first, it assists in the oxygenation of the water, thus enabling the carp to breathe, and creating a comfortable environment for it to live in. Carp can in fact survive in waters with incredibly low levels of dissolved oxygen, but in a well oxygenated lake they will be more comfortable and will eat more food and grow more quickly.

Keeping an eye on weather conditions allowed Simon Horton to bank this Cassien near forty.

The second effect of wind is to concentrate food at the windward end of the lake, and carp will generally take advantage of this accumulated food source often following the effects of a new wind. Nor is it just the items of food which have fallen onto the surface of the lake which are swept along, but also the upper layers of the water and the zooplankton and phytoplankton which live in these layers. In addition, a strong wind will create an undertow, and this will disturb the bottom of the lake, especially towards the windward end, thus unearthing other morsels for the fish to eat. In fact we have found that if there is a prevailing wind on a lake, the windward end will quite often be lower in resident natural food than the other areas, as a result of this constant disturbance.

The wind also influences the temperature of the water, and this in turn can change carp behaviour. Thus a cooling wind in the summer which drastically lowers the surface temperature of the lake often has an effect on carp, and the same can be said for a warming westerly wind in the winter. It is therefore useful to know the types of air mass prevalent in this country, as these will acquire the properties of the area over which they have just been blown (*see* Table 2).

Lastly, wind is useful from the angler's point of view in that it disrupts the water surface and clouds the water, thus affecting the ability of the fish to see out; but its major property in this respect is that it disrupts the thermoclimatic effect in deeper waters. These waters have very little natural food in depths greater than 10m, but when the wind blows, it upsets the balance of the thermocline by mixing the water at the windward end of the lake, thus allowing oxygen to penetrate into the lower water level; fresh items of food may then be located in this area. So when a new wind blows on a deep lake, consider the windward end, as that is the place the carp are likely to be.

Table 2. The types of air mass usually encountered in Britain.
The comments are generalizations, but they do reflect the nature of the wind from different directions at certain times of the year.

	Summer	Winter
Northerly	Cool and wet	Cold and wet, with snow (Polar)
Southerly	Warm and dry	Cold, sometimes with snow (European land mass)
Easterly	Cool and dry	Very cold (Siberian), often snow
Westerly	Warm, often wet as well	Cold and wet – rarely snow (Atlantic)

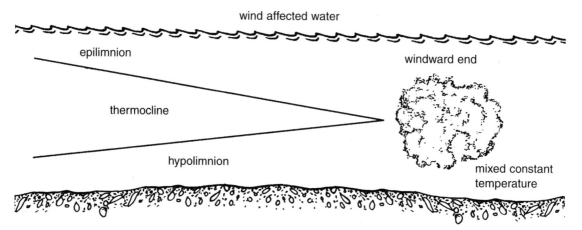

Fig 15 The effect of a strong wind on a thermoclimatic venue.

Air Pressure

Air pressure results from the sun's rays warming columns of air, making them rise and fall above the surface of the earth. These air columns are known as 'fronts' of high and low pressure, and their movement is one of the causes of wind. In the northern hemisphere, wind tends to be drawn towards lower pressure areas, and if you stand with your back to the wind, the low pressure will always be on your left. Carp feeding patterns change in times of high and low pressure, and they also change according to the season – so it is important for us to keep our eye on all these conditions and to recognize what they are in times of success. A new warm front moving in can be easily recognized as there will be a bank of cloud preceded by white fluffy clouds known as 'mackerel sky'. On the other hand strong, sudden gusts of wind and lowering cloud indicate the arrival of a cold front. Warm fronts tend to travel faster than cold fronts, but common to both is a change in wind direction.

Air pressure directly affects carp, as it regulates the amount of oxygen the water can absorb from the atmosphere through the surface of the lake: the higher the pressure, the more oxygen which can be absorbed, and vice versa. For a quick check on pressure, look where the swallows and swifts are feeding in the air: if they are high, the air pressure is high, as the flies upon which the swallows feed will be carried through the air on thermals. Pressure also affects the gases contained within the carp's swim bladder, in so far as when pressure is increased upon a gas, the gas particles are forced closer together: this acts like an internal compressor on the swim bladder, and will make the fish lethargic – it is therefore one of the reasons why, in prolonged periods of hot weather during the summer, the fish rarely move or feed. Consider in this respect the effects of a thunderstorm: just before a storm there is a massive build-up of pressure, and even to us the air feels close and devoid of oxygen. It is the same and perhaps even more uncomfortable for the fish – but once the storm has broken and the pressure in the atmosphere has been released, the fish immediately feel better and frequently feed.

There are further benefits of storms, in that the water body of the lake will be cooled down by the raindrops as they will be at a lower

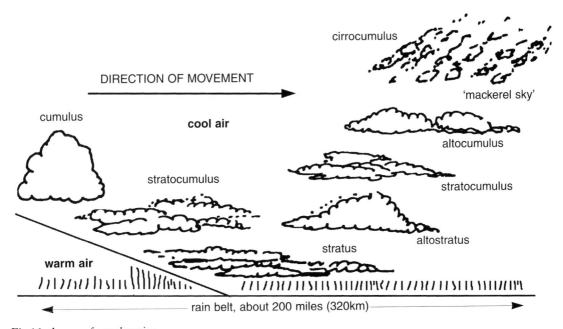

Fig 16 A warm front elevation.

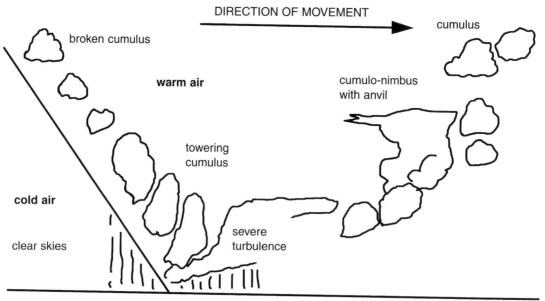

DIRECTION OF MOVEMENT

broken cumulus

cumulus

warm air

cumulo-nimbus
with anvil

towering
cumulus

cold air

clear skies

severe
turbulence

heavy rain belt, about 50 miles (80km)

Fig 17 A cold front elevation.

This Orchid Lake twenty came right in the middle of a heavy rainstorm in July.

temperature than the lake water; they also have the effect of increasing the dissolved oxygen content of the lake water as they will be saturated in oxygen. As a result of all the above, the sport after thunderstorms can be hectic, as indeed it has been for us on more than one occasion.

The Location of Feeding Spots

Carp will frequent an area where they feed, and therefore a bait presented in such an area has a good chance of being taken. The feeding area can either be a natural area, or one that you have created through the introduction of bait. Locating the latter will obviously not be a problem, but it can be difficult to establish where some of the more natural feeding areas are. Sometimes you can apply your bait to the same area for a long period of time and this should eventually become accepted by the carp as a natural food source. The best spot to place a bait is where the fish feel confident in feeding, but if they will not feed confidently on your man-made area, you will have to find a natural one where they will. In order to do this you must consider all the other points in this chapter, plus the following:

- The nature of the lake bed
- Plants in the area
- Micro- and macroscopic animals and their life cycles
- Water quality and lake size
- Features
- Other anglers

The Nature of the Lake Bed

The nature of the lake bed is important because of the animals that will live on and in it, as the carp will spend a lot of time looking for these. Carp will eat different types of crustaceans, worms and molluscs at different times of the year (*see* Table 1) and it is important for you to know when each of these are the main food, and where they live. Snails can be found all over the lake, whereas small worms and chironimids such as bloodworm will only really be found in silt and mud, because this is where their larvae are laid. Once you have identified the nature of the lake bed, you will have an idea of the type of animals found there and therefore where the carp will feed. If you can, get into the water and have a dig around in the mud at the bottom of the lake to see what you can find. If necessary taste and smell the silt.

A knowledge of the lake bed will help you to locate the all-important natural feeding spots.

Get to know the natural food sources within a lake. Acquiring an understanding of these may be considered by some as taking things too far, but for us, this is just another part of the jigsaw.

Rob with a 30lb mirror from the mosquito-ridden west arm at Cassien.

Nor is it just *in* the lake that you will be given clues, either: the plants that are growing and the flies around the immediate vicinity of the lake all tell you what the carp might feed on. A perfect example of this is at Cassien, where everyone says the carp go to the shallow end of the west arm to spawn. This is correct, but a lot of fish stay there because there is an abundance of natural food in this area in the form of all the chironimids in the silt. Those who have fished in this area during the summer will know exactly what we mean, as you get absolutely bitten to pieces by mosquitoes.

The location of areas likely to hold bloodworm and suchlike in a silty lake should not be too difficult, but what about gravel pits? There may be very little silt in the pit, but it will gather in certain areas as a result of wind action and under surface tow. To find the silt pockets you need to know the direction of the prevailing wind on the water and also the location of any bars, troughs or gullies on the bed of the lake. Once you have found these, try plumbing around at the sides of the bars and in the gullies, as the wind action often carries silt particles through the water and they will be deposited on the leeward side of the bar. A tell-tale sign of a silt pocket is the fact that weed will often grow on this side of a bar and also in troughs and gullies. All these features act as silt traps and collect the silt that is carried in the water by suspension (*see* Fig 18).

Creating Natural Feeding Areas

It is possible to create your own man-made natural feeding area – indeed we have done exactly this on a number of occasions when we have been fishing some of the crayfish-infested lakes

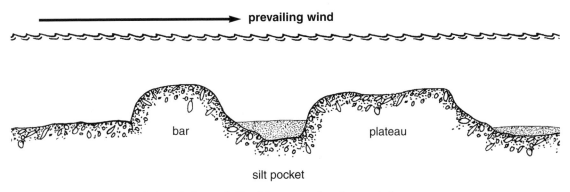

Fig 18 Silt pockets often gather on the leeward side of features such as bars and plateaux.

of France. The idea behind the strategy is that carp see crayfish as a natural food source and feed on them confidently. By attracting crays into our swim, the carp should hopefully follow on shortly behind and feed not only on the crays, but on the baits that we have introduced. In order to attract the crays, you must first find an area they feel safe in. We have found this to be a depth of 30ft (10m), where the effects of solar radiation start to decrease. The rays of the sun penetrate water up to a depth of 30ft, and

there is an abundance of food for the crays at this depth; furthermore the light is not so bright as to make them vulnerable to easy predation. We call this 'the crayfish depth', as it is here they feel comfortable during daylight hours. At night-time, however, they will venture into the shallower water, as they feel safer feeding in shallow water under the cover of darkness.

From this we can see that a bait should be fished at a depth of 30ft during the day and in the shallower water at night, if it is known that the carp are crayfish eaters. In order to enhance this effect, we have even been known to bait an area with two different baits, one soft to attract the crays, the other rock hard for the carp.

Feeding Hotspots

Sometimes the carp will make it obvious where they feed, as they keep their feeding areas clear of any debris. When you are plumbing around and you feel a clear area or a slight indentation in the lake bed, this may well be a feeding hotspot. At Orchid a few years ago we found a couple of these isolated feeding spots, and upon further inspection they turned out to be completely clear areas (Orchid is a weedy lake) which had been caused by intensive feeding by the fish. In fact you could tell when the fish were feeding in these areas as there was a milky scum formed on the lake surface. A bait fished in these areas, which were only the size of dinner plates, proved to be extremely effective.

Create your own natural feeding area. A bait boat is ideal for this.

Simon with a big Orchid Lake mirror caught tight to a set of reeds within a dinner plate-sized indentation in the silt.

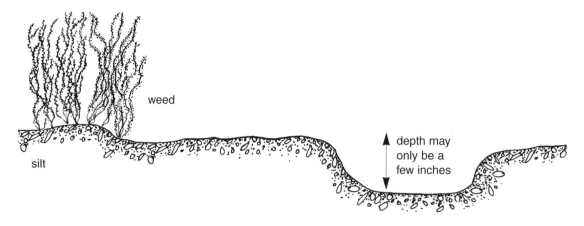

Fig 19 Dinner plate feeding indentation in silt.

The Influence of the Time of Day and Year

The carp is affected by a daily and an annual cycle, and according to the time of day or year it will follow certain patterns.

The Daily Cycle

Carp are affected by the warming effect of the sun and the cooling effect of darkness on the water and will move between shallow and deeper water at various times in this twenty-four hour period. Oxygen is one of the main factors behind this, because although site specific, warm shallow water which has been heated up by the sun in the daytime will frequently be low in oxygen, but it will also be the first part of the lake to cool down once the sun has set. The dissolved oxygen content will vary in these shallower areas, so a bait placed here in the day may not be touched, whereas the same area at night might be a hotspot.

Weed also has a direct effect on the location of carp, not just as a food source and place of security, but again, because of its oxygenating effect. Green plants release oxygen into the water by the process of photosynthesis during the day. They are what is known as autotrophic feeders, meaning that they create their own food from the nutrients and salts around them. In order to do this, they take carbon dioxide out of the water and release oxygen back into it. At night, however, the process is reversed as there is no sunlight for photosynthesis, and the plants give out carbon dioxide into the water instead of oxygen. This has the effect of lowering the oxygen content around weedbeds at night, especially in the summer months and in the early mornings, thus making them less attractive to the carp. This is often termed the 'four o'clock syndrome', because this is when the process is at its greatest.

Beware the four o'clock syndrome if your lake happens to be weedy.

The Annual Cycle

In spring, all the plants and animals in the aquatic ecosystem start to emerge from their relatively comatose state. The carp is stimulated by the increase in daylight, the warming up of the water and all the natural food that is now available. The shallows are again the first to warm up, so a bait placed in this area has a good chance of being found by the carp. As spring progresses and the water warms even more, the carp are stimulated into reproduction, and they will head for the shallows and suitable spawning areas. When they are on their way to these places they are catchable, as they will be feeding themselves up and are likely to be in groups so there will be an element of competition among them.

As the annual cycle moves on, the carp will spread themselves out around the lake, some into shoals, others to a solitary existence or in a small group. Some fish prefer to remain in certain areas, so it may be worthwhile finding out where these resident fish have taken up station, as they can often be caught from the same areas time and time again.

Bear in mind that feeding spots change as the seasons progress, and that what was a hotspot in the spring may not be a feeding spot at all in late autumn, due to the effect of rotting leaves on the lake bed. Also, as the weather cools towards the end of the year, carp will seek out the areas of more constant water temperature. These are not necessarily the deepest, and quite often through the winter you will find fish in 3ft (1m) of water in reedbeds. Even so, if your water has a decent depth to it, the carp are quite likely to lie dormant in this deeper area for much of the winter. We have found through experience that shallower lakes often fish better during the winter, as the water temperature and light penetration fluctuates more here and the fish stay on the move for longer than they would in deeper venues.

The Effect of Angler Pressure on Fish Location

A major effect on fish location is that of angler pressure. Do not discount this factor without serious consideration, as carp which are subjected to angler pressure on a daily basis are soon conditioned by it; thus areas that were once good fish-producing spots will soon fail to be as the carp are conditioned to the fact that if they eat food in a certain area there is a good chance that they will get caught. Attribute this if you will to evolution of the species, in that the carp needs to be able to identify danger to survive. To interpret this into an angling scenario, imagine you are fishing a swim that has two islands in front of it, a gravel bar to the left at 70yd (63m) and a lovely bush overhanging a 4ft (1.2m) deep margin 5yd (4.5m) down to your right. The obvious areas to place baits here would be on the bar, in the gap between the islands and next to the marginal bush – but if they are that obvious to you, it is likely they have

A winter twenty caught during a mild spell in the weather.

Only thinking anglers succeed consistently on pressured waters. Tim is a master at understanding the conditioned responses of carp.

area that you think the fish might be. If the fish are in this area, ask yourself whether they will stay there having heard the comedy show on the bank. Sometimes it pays to get as far away from everyone else as possible.

The last point on pressure, and one which we hold in high regard, is that of the effect of anglers' lines in the water. On some waters these are enough to stop the carp entering an area, or if they do enter it, they will not feed there. You could lift your tips into the air to lessen the amount of line in the water, or you could back-lead your lines to the floor, but both of these will affect the sensitivity of your set-up; moreover they may not fool the fish. A much more effective way we have found is to rest the swim, or areas of it, by fishing different spots within the vicinity. Again, we see the match tactic of feeding two different areas so as to rest the fish, and from our experience it certainly works in carp fishing also. Keep feeding a few areas in your swim and alternate your rods around these areas, but do not thrash the water to pieces by casting in every half an hour. Alternatively, take your lines out of the swim completely during quiet spells; this too is very effective.

been obvious to everyone else that fished the swim and the carp will have been conditioned to capture in these areas. Unless you know they are still hotspots, try the gully at the edge of the bar, and put one rod on the island around the corner from the gap and the other in the open water 5–10yd (4.5–9m) away from the island gap. It may be that just that little bit of variation will make all the difference to the carp.

It is not just being caught which affects carp: too much bankside noise, or the sound of leads constantly hitting the water, will also cause them to promptly vacate the area. Take a look at the other anglers around you: where are they fishing to, are they making a noise, do they constantly cast in? If they do, balance the jeopardy of fishing near them with the fact that they are in the

Predators

While carp are large enough not to be too concerned by most predators, one example of where predation *does* affect their behaviour is the catfish at Fishabil. Thus if there are large cats in the lakes that you are fishing, be aware that carp, especially the smaller ones, do not particularly like them, and that areas where cat activity is high – for instance snaggy areas and weedbeds – carp will try to avoid.

Security

Without question, carp like to have a bit of security. This can be in the form of snags, weedbeds or pads, in fact anything that will allow the fish to hide or secret themselves, especially if there is

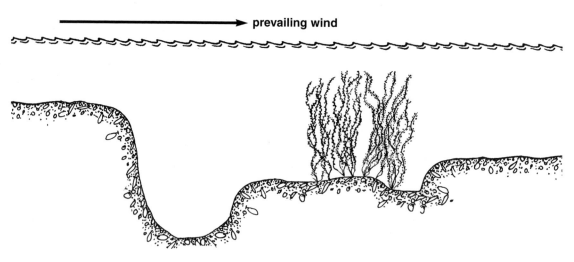

prevailing wind

Fig 20 An ideal holding area: weedbeds next to a gulley.

a food source nearby. Areas of undisturbed bank will also be ideal, as they will be provided with food from the trees and in the margins, cover from the banks and any overhanging trees, and no disturbance from passing feet. This is why most island margins are generally good areas to fish – although do remember the effect of conditioning. The majority of carp-holding areas are usually fairly obvious as they can be seen with the eye and have also been written about in almost every other angling book to date; we will therefore take a look at some of those that are less so.

If the lake is featureless and the bottom relatively flat, use a plumb to see if you can find any slight undulations or holes; even differences of 1ft (30cm) will be attractive for the carp if there is nothing else to hide in, so do not dismiss them as insignificant. We fished a river in France and rowed for miles without seeing any fish at all, until we stumbled upon an area 1ft deeper than the rest of the river – and in it were any number of fish. The river was used by boats quite heavily, and it may be that this extra 1ft was enough for the fish to feel secure from the overhead traffic. Small obstructions are also very attractive to carp if there are no other features around them; once again in a lake in France we have seen a group of fish hanging around a sunken digger

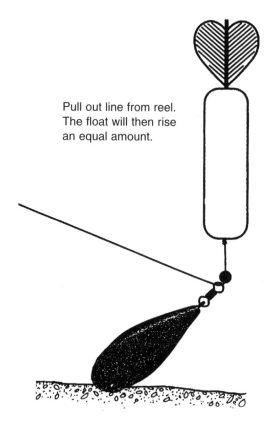

Pull out line from reel. The float will then rise an equal amount.

Fig 21 Vaned marker float.

The beauty of river carping.

bucket. Tim has experienced a similar occurrence at Fishabil where he had been using conduit piping as a marker and the fish actually swam towards it when hooked as they saw it as a safe area.

The Location of Carp in Rivers

The above section applied mainly to the location of carp and their feeding areas in stillwaters. Carp are found in rivers across Europe and while many of the methods above can be applied, there are other ways of locating the fish and their feeding areas in these water bodies. The main difference is obviously the current, as this carries food to the fish; in these circumstances the carp can be located in and around areas of slacker water, especially where an eddy current forms and food items are carried into this still area. Backwaters, eddies and slower water at the back of islands and bridge supports are all recognized fish-producing spots, and it is either here or at one of the natural areas mentioned in the section above that the river carper should start to search.

If you embark on a river carping session and find that your bait is not holding bottom, you are fishing in the wrong place: you should be looking to find a slack area where the current deposits food. If you can find such a place, the carp will not be too far away.

Many river fish are nomadic and travel long distances in their search for food. Competition for food is high and many rivers, especially those in the west of France, have a high population of hungry Ropsha common carp. These fish generally live in large shoals, and when they move into an area that you are fishing, the action can be hectic. It therefore pays to bait quite heavily to stop the fish and hold them for long enough for you to take advantage of a feeding shoal. We adopt a 'little and often' baiting strategy once they move in; to allow them just to feed on the baited area would mean that they would soon move off, having consumed all the bed of bait.

In rivers with few features it will be difficult to find holding areas, although even a small indentation in the river bed can attract fish. Carp are likely to keep moving up and down the river in search of food, and in this circumstance the best approach would be to organize your own feeding area so that it describes a large diagonal line of bait across the river. Any fish swimming up or down will come across a bed of bait applied in this manner and should, we hope, stop for a feed. Hookbaits should be positioned at varying distances across the river, and if a pattern emerges, then move the rest of the rods to that area.

That is more or less all we have to say on the location of river carp and their feeding areas. Try to apply your still-water knowledge and adapt it for flowing water. As a rough guide to possible holding and feeding areas, we have displayed below a number of scenarios, including the areas where we would place our hookbaits and free offerings.

Rob and a typical river mirror of 30lb.

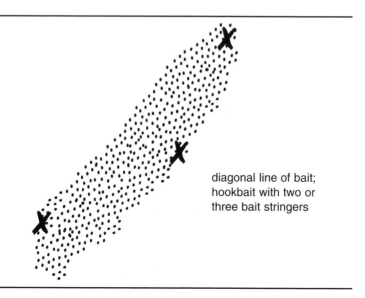

diagonal line of bait; hookbait with two or three bait stringers

Fig 22 Favoured method for rivers.

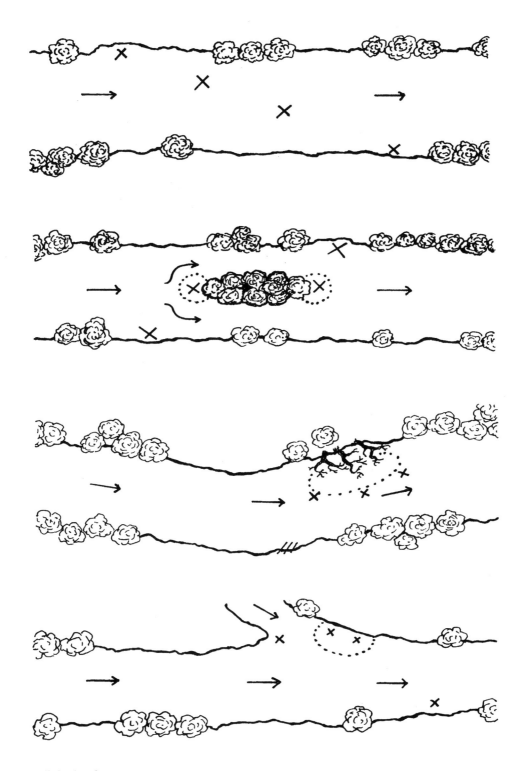

Fig 23 Likely river hotspots.

4 BAIT

A book on carp angling would be incomplete without a section on bait and its application, but what can we say that has not been said in almost every single piece that has been written on this subject already? For a start, what qualifications do we have which allow us to talk with authority on one of the most complicated, and also most confusing areas of carp fishing? We do have some credentials in that we have both been commercially involved in the making of carp bait since 1990, and used to be partners in our own small bait firm. In total we used to supply over thirty retail outlets with base mixes and flavours, and throughout the time of our involvement, and indeed for a long time before, we spent many hours playing around with base mixes and ingredients formulating baits that would prove irresistible to carp. During our time in business, and also on our own beforehand, we learned some valuable lessons.

In 1994, Kevin Nash approached us to enquire whether we would be interested in joining his company as bait and tackle consultants. This was a turning point: business had escalated so much that our own carp-fishing time was being considerably curtailed because we were required to make more and more bait in order to keep up with the demands of our retailers; moreover at about the same time, a fellow carp angler approached us to see if we would be prepared to sell the business. After some consideration we decided that we could not put the requisite time into our business, and a decision was made to sell up and move on.

In this chapter we do not intend to let you into the latest secrets of the bait world: for one, there are very few major breakthroughs at the moment; and second, we are bound by the rules

Kevin Nash and one of his three British forties.

of confidentiality not to discuss any discovery outside work circles. Instead, we hope this section will help you understand the whole concept of bait and the importance of its application, rather than just giving you answers and tactics. In addition, the main text will deal with the most common bait which is of course boilies. Whilst boiled bait is not, of course, the only bait that can be used, it is one of the most versatile, and it can be designed to do a number of things and will suit a number of occasions.

There are many writers these days who seem to speak with absolute authority on certain subjects, especially bait – but in fact most are not qualified to give the reader any answers, as they are not in the same position as the reader: if they were, their advice would be much more valid. As writers ourselves who are often asked to give advice to anglers for certain situations, we appreciate fully the difficulties. A writer can only give an opinion on what is, to him, a hypothetical situation. If it came to a practical situation however, the advice tendered might be completely different due to any of a number of given factors, which might only become apparent upon visiting the venue under the same circumstances. What we are trying to get across, is that all the advice you see written in angling publications is only applicable to precisely the situation it was written about, *not to yours*. It may lend itself to your scenario, but your situation, even if it appears to be very similar, will be different. The important thing to learn from any writing on bait is not what and how to do, but when and why.

There is no such thing as a wonder bait, and the sooner the carp angler realizes this the better. Certainly a number of commercially available baits are excellent carp catchers, but after they have been used for a prolonged period on a water, even their effectiveness will slow. You need to be ahead of both the carp and the other anglers when it comes to your bait choice and application.

The General Concept of Bait

Clearly bait is there to induce a carp into taking the hookbait into its mouth. However, it is more than just the bait on the hook: it can be an 'attract only' bait that will attract fish into the swim without feeding them; it can be a 'feed bait' to induce feeding competition between the carp; or it can be an 'attracta-bait' which will bring other fish or food sources into the swim in

the hope that the carp will follow along afterwards, either through their inquisitive nature, or because they want to feed on the smaller animals, for instance crayfish.

There are, of course, a number of methods of persuading a carp to take the bait, and the way you go about it will depend upon the specific carp that you are trying to catch and also the venue that you are fishing. As with the other aspects of the carp fishing equation, bait is very site specific, and you should never be content to use the same bait or baiting principle in the same way on every water that you visit. When considering the make-up of a bait, it is useful to consider first the stages of consumption of that bait by the fish. As we see it, they are as follows:

- Attraction
- Palatability
- Digestibility.

By understanding the effect that the bait will have on the carp, the angler is halfway to understanding when, how and why it will be effective. All three of these aspects are important, although the order of priority changes according to factors such as angler pressure, annual cycle and carp stocks. For example in the summer when the carp are on the lookout for food almost all the time, the requirement for a high attract bait will be lower than during the winter months.

Attraction

A bait should be able to attract a carp and then induce it to take it into its mouth. Carp are strange, inquisitive creatures however, and will often sample nonfood items just to see if they are edible, for instance, we have seen fish taste cigarette butts floating on the surface. Nevertheless, the primary aim of the angler is to induce the fish to take the bait, and to achieve this, it is necessary first of all to make it attractive to the carp. It must give the impression of being food, because if it does not, it will generally be left where it is.

Gary Bayes, without doubt one of the leading authorities on bait in the world today.

Flavour

Initial attraction can be provoked in a number of ways, and the main one is by the inclusion of a label or flavour to the bait. A multitude of flavours are available to the angler, and these can often be the source of a great deal of confusion. First and foremost it is important to realize that what *we* recognize as a certain flavour, the carp may not. Carp have exceedingly good chemo-receptors which can detect minute amounts of flavour, but it will not sense the same smell that we do. Take, for example, a strawberry flavour and a mango flavour both made up on the same base (for example alcohol). It would be fairly easy for us to notice the difference between the two, but the carp's chemo-receptors may read that the two flavours are almost identical, other than perhaps one or two extra molecules of a certain chemical contained within the flavour. It

doesn't know what a mango or a strawberry is – it can only read the chemical message given off by the flavour. In a practical situation, this means that what may be two completely different flavours to us, could be two very similar flavours to the carp. Accordingly, if you are considering the inclusion of a flavour to your bait, you should look to see what the other anglers on your lake are using, and then decide whether you would like to use a similar flavour, or something completely different.

Standard flavours are by no means the only method of attraction, and a carp might be attracted because of the change in pH of the water surrounding the baits – it will sense the chemical change in the water, and will look for the food source as a result. However, if a bait is overloaded with flavour, or alternatively too much bait is put into the swim, the excessive release of flavour may repel the carp – it may not want to approach any further because the level of attraction is presumably overwhelming to the extent that the carp no longer actually finds the bait attractive. It sounds perverse, but a fish can be repelled by too much attractor. (*See* Chapter 2).

Generally, liquid attractors are the better choice, as they are more soluble than powders and are thus easier to detect. In our opinion, the best liquid attractors available are the ranges of pre-digested liquid amino acids available from chemists, and most of the larger bait companies. The original concept of liquid amino acids was used by athletes who required an extra source of protein, and also persons recovering from operations where they could not digest food. It is literally a food source, and being in liquid form is easily digestible. There is very little waste product, and the advantage from the angler's point of view is that it is very high in nutritional value, soluble in water, and therefore very easily noticed by the carp.

Colour

Flavours are by no means the only way of attracting carp into your swim: colours are also very important, and whilst many people consider that colour makes no difference to catch rates, we are firmly of the opinion that it does. No one actually knows through which spectrum of light the carp sees. We use the standard visible light spectrum, but there is some evidence to suggest that fish see either through the infra-red spectrum, or at least towards the lower end of the standard visible light spectrum. This means that they can utilize much lower light sources than us and still be able to see, but what they cannot distinguish are different colours. What we see as different colours will be different shades of red to them, and whilst you may say that this in fact means that colours can not be relevant, they are, because the carp can still differentiate between shades of colours. In the infra-red spectrum, colours towards the red end of the scale – for instance red, brown, dark orange and so on –

Simon and a French river thirty-pounder caught on a new flavour and mix.

will be much less visible than colours such as blue or bright green. In addition, black and white will be at opposite ends of the scale, with white being the most visible, and black being invisible as it reflects no light at all. However, as with any rule there are exceptions, and just because a black bait reflects no light, it doesn't mean that it will be unnoticeable; it will always stand out if placed over a lighter surface, for instance a sand-bar.

The application of colours to your angling situation is important because you can disguise your bait by matching it to the surrounding lake bed, or alternatively make it more obvious by utilizing a colour that might be easier in the circumstances to find. The choice of colour should be dictated mainly by pressure and annual cycle, and we felt this was a major consideration when it came to our choice of bait colour for the World Cup. We were almost certainly the only team using a black bait, and indeed there are no companies at the time of writing other than Nashbait that provide one. For some reason the concept of black baits has not yet caught on. We are 100 per cent confident in a black bait, and the success of the World Cup should help to lift its popularity.

Bait as a Food Message
As mentioned earlier, carp may be attracted into the feeding area by other smaller fish eating the free baits. If there is a large population of 'nuisance species' in the lake, it may well be worth baiting up with a small particle bait such as hemp to attract them in, thus enticing the carp. This will also work in the case of crayfish, and a bait such as a soft boilie should be introduced into the swim, and a larger hard bait fished on the hook for the carp. Floating and buoyant free baits are also an excellent way of inducing the carp to feed once they have entered the vicinity of the bait. This can be done by using a dissolving bait such as a ball pellet. As the pellet breaks down, some of the particles stay on the lake bed whilst others float up to the surface of the water, thus leaving a food message at all levels of the water column. This has the advantage that if a carp is swimming on or near to the surface, it

will still come into contact with a food message from the bed below, and will hopefully follow the message down to your hookbait. The same principle can be followed if you are making up a bait soak or glug. Instead of using just one oil or flavour, mix a few together, but ensure that you use one which is dense and that will remain on or around the hookbait, another which has a neutral buoyancy that will stay suspended in mid-water, and one that will float to the surface and leave a food message in the upper levels of the water. By following this method you will leave a food message throughout the whole depth of the lake.

Bait as a Food Source
This has been said many times before but is worth repeating again, that if you are attempting to establish a bait as a food source through a long-term baiting campaign, it is foolish to have a high flavour level within that bait. It does not matter that the carp are not immediately attracted to the bait; in fact it is better for your long-term food bait if it doesn't scream 'boilie' as soon as it is introduced into the water. The fish will find it themselves if it is introduced correctly, and the higher the attractor level, the more likely they are to connect your bait with danger. Most good quality base mixes will not require an attractor at all, though if you want to include one for your own peace of mind, ensure that the levels are as low as possible. You will see later on when we discuss pressure, that one of the main reasons for a bait 'blowing' is that the flavour can be recognized by the carp and they will associate that bait with danger. So if in doubt, leave it out.

Palatability
Once you have persuaded the fish to pick up the bait in the first place, it must want to eat it. It may sound ridiculous that a fish that has just picked up a bait would then refuse to eat it, but if it does not like the taste, it will soon spit it out. Remember that the initial attraction is only a promise of what is on offer, and the bait must follow through on that promise not just with the taste, but also the food message.

One of six twenties from Orchid in three visits, all caught on the S mix.

It may be that the taste of the bait has been diluted by the surrounding water so as to have become attractive to the carp, but that once in the mouth, the taste is so strong as to be actually off-putting. It is therefore vitally important that the free offerings you put out in your swim taste good to the carp. Consider a large baited area that gives the message of an attractive food source, and the disastrous effect of the fish deciding they don't like it once they have tasted it. The chances of your hookbait being the first to be sampled are of course fairly remote, and the ultimate likelihood is that you will not get a pick-up at all because the fish does not want to eat any more bait than the one it has already picked up.

But what exactly will make a bait unattractive to the carp? As we have seen, the first thing is an excess of flavour. Not only is a high flavour level likely to make the carp suspicious of the bait through recognition or the realization that something is unnatural, it is also possible that it will make a bait actually taste unattractive. The same for sweeteners, especially synthetic intense sweeteners, as too much flavour or sweetener can make a bait taste hot.

Bait manufacturers we approached had very definite ideas on the subject of palatability: without question they felt that a fish must like the bait if it is going to eat it in any large quantity, and that this aspect is one of the most important areas of bait-making. Certain ingredients are more attractive to carp than others, but this is site specific in that certain lakes will respond better to certain mixes, ingredients or flavours. They must want to eat the bait, and the primary objective is then to create a bait that tastes good, is easy to eat, and does the carp some good in the process. The introduction of an appetite stimulator or enhancer such as m.s.g. or one of the sense appeals, is ideal for stimulating taste as it will hopefully induce that 'just one more' sensation which is the downfall of many a carp. In short, once that carp has picked up one bait, it is vital that its taste receptors are stimulated enough into wanting to pick up another one – if you can induce a greed element, the easier the carp will be to catch.

However, it is not just the flavour and attractors within the bait that make it attractive to the carp: the design of the mix, and also the amount of time that the boilie is boiled are also vitally important factors. Certain ingredients lock flavours in more than others, so be selective when you choose a mix for your campaign. It is indisputable that silty-bottomed lakes *do* affect the flavour leakage properties of a bait, so it is important that you choose your mix wisely, and apply it to the type of water that you are fishing. If you are new to a venue, find out as much about the water as you can, including what the popular bait is, as there are venues where certain baits will be very much more successful than others. What you use does not necessarily have to be exactly the same as the others, but a little knowledge about what they are using and how successful it is, will assist you in your choice of both concept and content.

The definitive test is that you should sample the bait yourself for taste. Give a boilie to any thinking angler and the first thing that he will do is have a sniff, then a taste; this is to check the levels of the attractors within the bait, as one which is overloaded will taste unattractive. Our senses of taste and smell are nowhere near as sensitive as those of a carp, so if a bait tastes strong to us, there is no wonder it will be unattractive to the carp.

Digestibility
This is a subject that has been more in the public eye of late, with the attitude being that the sooner a fish can digest the bait, the sooner it will want to eat more. Most people relate digestibility to the way that it will pass through the carp, and also how it will obtain the goodness from the food source, but it is more than just that. The carp must actually be able to eat the bait with a minimum of effort, and the choice of your bait can have a dramatic effect on this.

Take, for example, the difference between a hard and soft bait. It may be the case that the lake you are fishing has a large proportion of nuisance fish, or that you want to create a feeding area at long distance and require a bait that will not break up on its way out of the stick. The natural choice here would be a rock hard bait, but we have already seen that a bait of this sort

will affect the attraction of the boilie as it will lock in the flavour. In addition, the carp may find the harder food source less attractive than a softer bait, as it is more difficult to both masticate and digest. A working example of this can be seen with some of the larger Cassien fish that now get caught on boilies more often than their smaller brethren. The general theory as to why this occurs, is that the older carp have fed for most of their lives on hard food sources such as crayfish. In time, their pharyngeal teeth wear down so that they are not as effective as they once where, and as a result the carp has to be more selective about the type of food that it eats. A rock hard bait may be refused purely because the fish cannot actually chew the thing! Be aware of the age and feeding patterns of the carp in your lake, and choose your bait wisely.

Just to confuse the issue somewhat here, cooking times should vary not just according to the required hardness of the bait, but also by the ingredients contained within the mix. Some of the coarser ingredients (for example, egg biscuit in Red Factor and Necterblend, and coarse fish-meals), will cause a bait to become brittle when cooked for a long time, and far from being a disadvantage, this can often be advantageous to the angling situation. A bait that has a high content of coarse ingredients will break down quickly once inside the mouth, and also on the lake bed if it is not eaten quickly by the carp. This has the advantage of not leaving a large quantity of uneaten bait in the swim, and also assists with the speedy utilization of the bait as a food source.

If we now consider the benefit of the bait to the carp, the HNV theory is still one of the most vital considerations when it comes to your choice of bait. A carp must be able to utilize the food it eats in the most economical way possible in order to get the best from it. Consider the fundamentals of nutrition. Animals need to vary their diet just as we do, to obtain all the essential elements of nutrition in order to survive. A balanced bait which offers the carp the correct mix of vitamins, proteins and fats will be the best food source for the carp, but do not think that this is always the best bait in an angling environment. The application of a high protein bait by the majority of anglers on a lake may mean that the carp will suffer a shortfall in the fat stakes. Accordingly, an angler providing the carp with a fat source will be using a bait that the carp will find highly attractive, as they cannot find that essential element in the other baits that they are used to. In addition there may also be an element of competition for the fatty bait, as there is only one source of the shortfall. This can often be seen where there are a number of anglers on a venue using a quality high protein bait, and someone turns up with a cheap soya- or semolina-based mix, and has a good result.

Some anglers might argue that this complete-ly disproves the HNV theory altogether, and that it is possible to catch using any bait. They would be totally wrong in this assumption, and in fact the opposite would be the case! A result

of this nature would in fact reinforce the HNV theory, in that the previous baits were not pro-viding for all the necessary nutritional require-ments of the carp, and they were forced to go elsewhere to find them. The point can be reiter-ated further if you consider our own nutritional requirements and the scenario where you suffer a craving for a certain food item, for instance chocolate or orange juice. Your craving for that item is the way your body tells your brain that you have a deficiency in something – sugar car-bohydrates or vitamin C. The brain does not recognize that the orange juice is an immediate source of vitamin C, but the body generally will relate the consumption of orange juice with the provision of this essential vitamin. Accordingly, when you need a top-up of vitamin C, your body will tell your mind that you are thirsty, and that orange juice is the thing you need. It is nature's

This one must have thought that the bait was doing it some good: it was Rob's third capture of the fish on the same bait in three months.

way of applying the HNV theory to our lives, and although not as efficient it certainly applies to the cyprinid world as well.

Watch what others are doing, and if there is a shortfall, provide it. At the end of the day the fundamentals of business apply: spot a gap in the market and fill it!

Specific Strategies

As well as attracting carp, a bait can also be specific not just for carp generally, but for individual or groups of carp too. The following four different strategies will cover the angling requirements of most anglers:

• Catching carp in a pressurized scenario
• Catching large numbers of carp
• Consistent carping on a time limit
• Fishing for virgin carp.

Bait choice is vitally important, and the type we would apply in any of these given situations would be different according to the carp that we were chasing. For the purposes of the scenarios we will assume that the angler does not have anything particular already in mind, and that a new bait has to be designed. Each scenario would require one with different properties, and these will become apparent as we consider the strategies in turn.

Pressurized Carping

Pressure is a very difficult thing to define, and is once again site specific; what is heavy pressure on one water might be considered light pressure on another. For example at Birch Grove there is a limit of four anglers on a little over 4 acres (1.6ha). Any more than four and the lake feels overcrowded. This may not seem like pressure to some, but the fact is that there are almost always four anglers on the water, fishing up to four rods each, nearly every week of the year. In fact the only time there is less pressure than this is during the self-imposed six-week close season. You may encounter a different sort of pressure where

there are twenty anglers on your 4 acre lake at weekends, but only the odd angler throughout the whole of the week. Whatever the type of pressure, carp will still react to it, and so must you if you want to get the best out of your time on the bank. Don't forget that bait is only one part of the equation, and that location, application and timing are also important, but on a par with these aspects is confidence. You must be confident with your bait, not just in a pressurized situation, but anywhere you fish. If you are moving to a pressurized water for the first time, pick a bait that has a proven track record. We never consider going to a water without a bait that we know is going to catch wherever we take it, and it should be the same for you. It does not matter too much whether the track record is your own on another water, or someone else's that you have confidence and trust in – the fact is that you must not let your bait worry you in any way, shape or form.

As far as the actual bait is concerned, the fish in a pressurized water will be used to a great deal of bait going in, so you won't need to spend time educating them to eat boilies. They will, however, know that boilies are a source of danger, and therefore you do have a hurdle to overcome in this respect. In addition, you will be competing with the other anglers on the lake when it comes to the provision of the best and most available food source. This is where the quality of your bait is important, in that it should provide the carp with everything they need so they don't have to go elsewhere for their nutritional requirements to be fulfilled. Our choice in this circumstance would be a high quality HNV mix with a flavour that is very subtle, but at the same time strong enough to differentiate our bait from that of the other anglers on the venue.

The make-up of the mix should be complex, and by this we mean that it should have a large number of different ingredients, as opposed to a simple mix with just four or five. The reason for this is two-fold: first, you want to fish for yourself (or your group of friends if you have decided to team up), and if you have a complicated mix, the chances of someone else having exactly the same bait are much reduced. In addition, the more complicated in construction that a mix is, the longer it will take for the fish to recognize it as a danger source. Take for example a bait that has a high content of Robin Red: after the fish have been caught a number of times on the same bait, they will start to associate that bait with danger; but drop the Robin Red and the bait may have a new lease of life, as the main recognizable danger element is no longer there. In short, we feel that the effectiveness of a base mix will start to decline as a result of one recognizable ingredient which stands out more than any other; but if a number of ingredients are used that are subtle and complementary to each other, the chances are that the life of the bait will be considerably longer because there is no obvious danger trigger, and the carp will have to get its mind around a dozen possibly dangerous ingredients as opposed to just six. In this circumstance, the only thing that will be easily recognizable as the danger source will be the flavour, and this can be easily changed as and when necessary.

On the subject of the life of a bait, we feel that a normal successful life should be three years (as long as not everyone is using it). The reason for this is that during the first year the bait is becoming established as a food source, and the carp are not yet feeding heavily on it. During the second year the results should be at their best, because the fish will be used to the bait and should be happy to eat it whenever they find it; but by the third year they will be starting to recognize the bait as a danger source either through their own capture, or that of their companions (*see* the next section). It is therefore during this third year that we would look to change our bait slightly, to keep the fish interested and to remove the danger element. To do this we would almost always just change the flavour. If you are using a quality complicated base, it is highly unlikely that the carp will recognize that as the danger; it is more likely to be the case that they have been caught on a certain flavour too many times, and are now getting sick of it.

When you do feel the need to change your flavour, avoid making this too drastic straight-away, as you will waste time having to re-establish your bait again. Drop the original flavour almost totally, though keeping just a little bit of it for recognition purposes, for example 1ml. Add a new flavour that is slightly different, keep the levels subtle, and hopefully the carp should take the bait with renewed gusto, but without any fear. When the fish are well on the bait again, you can drop the original flavour altogether, the transition to the new bait having been successfully completed.

Sadly, far too many anglers throw away a lot of the good work that they have done by changing their baits too soon. It seems to be the case on many waters that anglers want to change their bait each season, and more often than not this can be counter-productive. It is generally better to persevere with it, apply the correct baiting strategy and above all plan your future angling strategically.

Catching Large Numbers of Carp

For some people, the attraction of carp fishing is that they like to go out and catch a lot of carp; this may be the whole population of a lake over a long period of time, or a multiple catch each time they go out. If we were to attempt to catch a high proportion of a lake's population which we regularly fish, we would apply the strategy that we use for pressurized fish (i.e. baiting campaign). If, however, we were on a one-off trip or an infrequent visit to a water and wanted to catch a few fish, we would choose a different bait altogether: in this situation our choice would be a bait that is easily recognizable as a food source, attractive, and also cheap to apply in bulk. This would normally mean a cheap fishmeal-based mix, or alternatively a carrier mix bulked out with fish-meals to add flavour and increase attractability and palatability. To this we would add a palatant and a flavour at a medium to high level in order to persuade the fish to take it straightaway.

Our policy would be first to locate the bulk of the fish, then to apply the bait in quantity to persuade them onto it and hopefully to feed confidently. Large catches can generally only be achieved on a water with a high stock of carp, and if the lake you have in mind has only a small population, we would suggest that you lower or amend your target somewhat. The main approach is that you should locate the fish and attempt to induce them to feed confidently on the large area. The quality of the bait is not as important if you intend to visit the water on only a few occasions, and your money is better spent on quantity rather than quality. Of course other matters will affect the measure of your success, such as how often the policy of extensive baiting has been used on the water before, and also whether the fish are in a feeding mood. If they are, you might anticipate a huge catch; if they are not, your job is harder in that you will have to induce them to feed heavily enough to get the results you are after.

Attraction and palatability are the main qualities you should be looking for in your bait in these circumstances, although again you should keep an eye on the other anglers on your venue to see exactly what they are doing, and whether their results or strategies will help you in any way. At the end of the day, we have found that the best way to achieve large catches is first, to choose a water where such an achievement can become a reality; second, to apply a lot of bait either in bulk or by a little-and-often strategy; and finally, to make the bait so attractive to the carp through the use of stimulants and palatants that they want to eat huge amounts of it. Stimulate the greed, and the fact that some carp are feeding will induce others to feed, thus increasing competition and in turn catch rates.

Whilst on this subject, it is interesting to speculate how many carp within a population is it possible to catch on a bait before the effectiveness of that bait starts to slow down, and we discussed this with Kevin Nash and Gary Bayes. There are carp in some lakes that never, or very rarely get caught, and there are others that are caught all the time because they are boilie-eating machines. Our conclusion was that the probable percentage of carp that you are likely to catch on a certain bait is between 30 and 50 per cent of a lake's population; this is because the carp can recognize them as a danger source relatively easily, especially those that have a straightforward constitution, such as, for instance, simple fishmeal baits. If you catch 30 per cent of the population on a bait, the next time that those fish come round to eat that bait, they may be on edge because they remember a danger. If those 30 per cent go round in groups, the other members will be put off feeding by the nervous attitude of their companions. Finally there are some fish that might never touch boilies, or alternatively not like the flavours or combinations that you are offering them. This is where the more complex base mixes are more effective in the long term than simpler ones; but for occasional hits or infrequent visits, we would suggest a simpler mix.

Carping on a Time Limit

Probably this method will be practised by most of our readers, and it is the one we practise most frequently when researching for our day-ticket reviews in *Carpworld*. We have only a limited time to get to the water and account for a fish or two, so we want a bait that we know will be instantly attractive to the carp. On short sessions, the most important aspects are location and bait application, but you can amend your bait slightly to suit the precise circumstances that you are fishing.

The primary factor regarding the constitution of the bait itself is of course attractability. We want the carp to notice the bait straightaway, either by its sense of smell or its sight, and we want it to be attractive to taste, so that if we are using any free baits the carp will want to eat them all. The choice of colour is important as you will see from the application section, but in the main we always carry with us a number of colours, sizes and also flavours of bait. If you were a matchman you wouldn't dare go to a venue with just one bait, and we apply this to our day ticket reviews. Normally we would take two different flavours and colours of 18mm boilie, a 10mm substitute, some ball pellet, micro-mass, and also perhaps some maggots and groundbait just in case things became really tough. At the end of the day the fish might not be feeding on one bait but can be tempted on another, and if you have taken just the one bait with you and they won't eat it, then you're in trouble!

The bait we would use would normally have quite a high flavour level, and would be of a high leakage variety, for example birdfood. We want it to give off a food message as easily as possible, and we would fish it either on its own, with a stringer, or in a small clump, the idea being to create an area of immense attraction without too much food to eat, so that when it is found, it will be taken quickly.

We would always use a high quality base mix irrespective of whether we wanted a long term food bait or an instant attract bait. The constitution of the mix most certainly has a bearing on the catch rate as our result in the World Carp Cup showed.

Fishing for Virgin Carp

Those anglers who have virgin carp to play with are very lucky. Gone are the days when there were plenty of waters that had not yet seen any angler pressure, and when one of the main problems was to get the carp to recognize boilies as a food source. Many anglers used to start off with sweetcorn as this was seen to be instant, although we feel that it was the mass bed of bait that was the main attraction. If, however, you venture across the Channel to do a bit of pioneering, then you may be in this fortunate position. We have been on a number of occasions, especially when fishing some of the rivers in the west of France, and it is a myth that carp will not take boilies straight-away. Once again it is rather the application of the bait which is important, in that you should create such a large area of bait, that the fish have no option but to investigate it. If you were to fish with just a handful of bait, it might be years before a carp picked one up, but if you positively inundate the water then they will have to take notice.

A large bed of bait is no good unless it screams 'food' at the carp. Accordingly you should use a bait that lets out the flavour very easily, and also has an attraction in its own right. For this we would use a cheap, high leakage, birdfood base mix, to which we would add Robin Red, the latter having proved itself over the years as an incredibly successful attractor of carp, and apparently instant in most cases. The carp also seem to like the taste, so as well as having attraction qualities, it acts as a taste enhancer and appetite stimulator too. We would add an appropriate palatant as well, and used in a large area, those fish should be persuaded onto the bait.

Birdfood would be used as the base because generally it tends to allow a quicker release of flavour than other mixes, owing to the nature of the ingredients. In addition it is easier for the carp to break down in the mouth and digest, once again because of the coarser ingredients – all of which may increase the likelihood of the carp wanting to eat more.

Bait is all about establishing an advantage, over the carp that you are fishing for, and over the other anglers on the lake, and you should always think about the situation you will be in before choosing a bait. Most baits will catch fish at most waters, but some are far superior to the rest, and like anything else, you should tailor your bait to a specific situation. You need to do everything within your power to make *your* bait the one that the carp want to eat, and that takes a great deal of thought.

If you are not getting the results that you had hoped for, analyse exactly what you have done so far, and why it has gone wrong. Even so, conclusive answers are very difficult to come up with, and only experience will be able to guide you in the correct direction. If you know that your bait is a good one and that the flavour is about right, persevere with it: a good bait applied in the correct way will be successful, it may just be a matter of time before your labours are rewarded.

Bait Application

The way in which bait is offered is probably just as important as its make-up and location. If you were to ask any matchman what his priorities were, he would tell you that the first thing is a lucky draw, and after that, how he presents his bait into the swim. Arriving at the lake and throwing in a load of boilies is not effective any more: the carp have seen that all too often, and it is important that you work the area of the water in front of you if you want to get the best from your carping.

We have described a number of different ways to apply bait already, and you may want to use those in your own situation; our purpose in this section however, is not to give you set methods to follow: rather, we hope that it will encourage you to use your mind when you apply a method to your own fishing, instead of carrying on with the same tactics regardless of the individual situation. Try to be autonomous, not automatic in your decisions. Take stock of each situation, and apply yourself and your baiting strategies to it accordingly. In order to do this, thought should be given to the contingencies described below.

The Number of Carp Present

What exactly are you trying to achieve? If you want to catch many fish and the lake is well stocked, then the best method may be to apply a large amount of bait according to the numbers and size of carp present. However, if that has been done by a lot of people before, you will need to look at an alternative strategy. Our choice in these circumstances would be to bait little and often in an attempt to build up a go-faster version of the baiting pyramid: get the small fish interested, and the bigger ones will come in sooner or later. Keep the bait going in even when the fish aren't feeding, but only put a little in at a time; the fresh bait, the noise of the bait hitting the water, and the fact that there are a lot of fish in the lake means that there should always be fish in the vicinity of the baited area.

Theoretically, all you have to do is draw them in to feed. The ball pellet lends itself perfectly to this scenario, and twenty or so pellets an hour, with a light scattering of boiled baits to give them something to find would be ideal. A strong food message in a competitive swim, with very little to eat except for the hookbait, is a recipe for success,

The ball pellet.

as the fish will be hungry and looking for food, but will only be able to find the hookbait.

You will need to apply a different strategy if you are fishing an understocked lake for just a handful of fish, because in this situation you are effectively stalking. You need to know the features of your lakes, and the habits and feeding patterns of the carp very well. Only once you have established these will you be able to apply your bait effectively. In this situation, we would try to pre-bait a good quality bait to the fish, then to lay a trap along one of their known patrol routes in the hope that they find the hookbait both safe and irresistible.

Feeding Requirements and Patterns

Some lakes have definite feeding patterns, and it pays to know these so that you can establish your bait in the swim *before* the fish arrive to feed, and not as they arrive. Dawn and dusk are hot times on many waters, but the number of anglers who reel in and bait up about half an hour before dusk, or as soon as they get up, amazes us. Get the baits in place well in advance of the feeding periods, so that the swim has had a chance to settle down by the time the fish come on the feed. In the morning when you get up, don't reel the bait in: leave it where it is until mid-morning, as you may be upsetting the swim in the middle of a feeding period. Timing is an essential part of successful carp fishing, and recording information such as capture times is certainly one of the best ways to ensure success time and time again.

Nuisance Species

The nuisance species in your lake should be considered, as these will affect your strategy in a number of ways. For a start they will come in and eat the bait you have laid down for the carp, although in some circumstances this may be considered a tactical advantage as they may draw the carp in. This can happen in two ways: small fish such as bream and roach may move in to mop up the free offerings, and carp, being inquisitive creatures might saunter along to see what all the fuss is about, and then stumble upon a free meal. Also, crayfish might be drawn into the swim by the bait – this applies to France more than to England and the carp will move in as they hunt for the crayfish which for them is a safe natural food source. In both circumstances it is the 'nuisance' species that have brought the carp into the swim for you.

If there are a lot of nuisance fish in your lake and contact with them is unavoidable – or even preferable, as is the case with crayfish – take advantage of this by actually feeding them with something they like, such as particles or hemp in the case of small fish, or soft boilies in the case of crays. This will keep them away from your hookbaits, although do make sure that these are adequately protected against their advances, either by making them so big that they cannot get them into their mouths, or so hard that they cannot crush them. Use a flavour they don't like, and if necessary, sheath the baits in a stocking-type mesh.

What Anglers Around You are Doing

Make note of what the others are doing, where they are doing it, and at what time. Analyse their results, and if they seem to be having success, follow suit, but try to improve on them. If no one on your lake seems to be having many more fish than the others, and most of them are using similar tactics, try something completely different.

The fish in a lake will soon wise up to a tactic that has been used day in, day out for a long period.

One of our main considerations is how much bait other anglers are putting in, and where they are putting it. Some love to pile in the boilies regardless of the situation, whereas others are too mean to put in more than a handful each time they go fishing. It pays to know the characters on your lake and also their preferences when it comes to baiting strategy, as you may have to follow them into a swim one day, and if you don't know how much bait they are likely to have used you may come unstuck. There is nothing worse than finding that a swim was occupied until just before you arrived, and that the previous occupant used enough bait to feed a small army of carp but didn't catch anything. What to do? Should you stay and fish over his bait, not knowing whether he has left a large food source which might bring in the carp, whether they actually like it, or even if it is something unpalatable that will put them off. If it worries you too much, move, because it is pointless sitting there in a pickle over something you can do little about.

Loads of bait isn't always the answer: think strategy.

Generally, don't just arrive and pile in the bait: wait until you see some positive signs that fish are in the area, or are likely to arrive there soon.

It is best to fish with some friends if you can, as a team of four anglers is a very good way to dominate a lake. Confer together, devise a game plan that involves you all using the same bait, and keep introducing it into the water so that the fish will come to accept it as a safe food source. Formulate a strategy of both application and angling method, and follow it through, making only slight changes where and when necessary, and your tactics should pay off handsomely.

Conditioned Behaviour

You should also consider whether the fish in your lake have been conditioned by the actions of other anglers. Carp are quite intelligent, and they can soon learn from both their own and their companions' experiences. Quite often they will be conditioned through angler pressure to do, or

not to do certain things – for example, they will often avoid picking up boiled baits or feeding in the daytime. It is important therefore to be aware of what the fish have been subjected to in the past, and also what they might have learned from it; application will be affected by a number of things such as areas where they have continually been caught, bait quantities, and bait size.

Type of Bait

Always think about the type of bait that you are using, and don't just limit yourself to standard boilies all the time. Most of the fishing we do involves using a boilie on the hair, but we will often feed another bait into the swim and fish the boilie over the top of it. This might be ball pellet, micro mass, chopped boilies of the same type as we are using on the hair, or alternatives such as maggots. The humble maggot is ignored by so many carp anglers, even though these same anglers spend ages trying to create a natural

Resting the swim resulted in this lump of a mirror for Rob.

feeding area in their swim. There is nothing as natural as a bed of bloodworm, and a large scattering of pinkies with one or two mini boilies thrown in is an excellent method. A couple of mini boilies on the hair in the middle of such a presentation has proved to be very effective for us in the past – although one of the problems with maggots is that they do tend to make themselves scarce rather quickly. They can be scalded with boiling water to stop this, and are equally effective scalded as they are alive. Generally we do not scald them however, as the carp will find them even if they bury themselves in the silt.

Bait colour and size are other important factors, as we have mentioned briefly already. Decide whether you want the carp to find the bait by sight or by its olfactory senses. Your choice should be governed by the way the fish feed, what

(Left) *The World Cup. Was the black bait strategy a reason behind our success?*

Is it possible to select specific fish from our waters through bait choice? The Sting certainly seems to be a favourite of the grass carp.

Bill's fish in its full glory.

(Below) *Simon with a near thirty mirror from a typical French lake.*

A truly awesome scene at a truly awesome place: Lac de St Cassien.

Simon with a near forty from Cassien. One day we will return.

The one they call the Scud: thirty-five pounds of muscle. Did it fight? Did it ever!

(Above) *Rob with the much sought after Queen of Old Bury Hill.*

(Right) *'Faraggi Island'.*

(Above) *Heavily scaled mirrors are Rob's favourite kind of fish as this upper twenty shows.*

(Left) *One half of the first-ever brace of thirties from Shropshire mere Birch Grove, and* (right) *the other half.*

A 30lb mirror looking glorious in the morning sun.

Sunrise over the River Loire in north-west France. The home of some monster river carp.

An upper thirty from the River Loire, one of our regular haunts.

(Below) *Performing for the cameras during the video shoot of 1996.*

(Above) *Crowies koi. What a peach!*

(Below) *This fish was one of a dozen twenties caught over three nights.*

Giving it the big one at Cassien.

(Above) *'Bit of a lump'.*

(Left) *Cath.*

(Right) *Winter success for Rob in the form of this beautiful Birch Grove mirror.*

Nashy, a good friend and one of the best thinking anglers around.

(Above) *The Godfather.*

Le Coupe du Monde 1996: the biggest fish of the match, but it didn't count.

others are using, the nature of the lake bed, the time of year and the weather conditions, and so on. We have found that a bright white bait over the top of a bed of darker baits is effective, but not particularly so the other way round. From our experience, angler pressure and the light factor certainly govern the carps' preference, so consider the conditions that prevail, and the water clarity, each and every time you apply bait.

Where Should You Put the Bait?

Bait application isn't just about how much, when and how, it is also about where, and putting the freebies in the right place is as important as all the other factors. It always pays therefore to investigate the bed of the lake before applying bait. What looks to you like a good spot might only be a foot deep with stinking mouldy leaves on the bottom; or if you put the bait in a gully when the fish are following the top of the bars, you might as well have not bothered to have put it in at all.

The same can be said for fishing snags. Always study the situation, and try not to apply your bait into the snags themselves unless there is a particularly good reason for doing so – for instance, baiting to establish a food source throughout the close season. Basically, get to know your lake, its features and its habits, then apply your bait accordingly. Likewise consider the placement of your hookbaits: if your time on a water is limited, then don't put all your baits in one place, but try to cover as many different areas and situations as you can, placing them in both shallow and deep areas, on top of and by the side of bars, and so on.

Your strategy will need to be different on a pressured water where the fish have become used to encountering a single hookbait within a scattering of free offerings; in these circumstances you might try fishing more than one hookbait into the baited area. We have seen that the carp has both a short- and a long-term memory. Relative to angling, a carp will recognize, through conditioning, that a bed of boilies is a potentially dangerous area. Also through conditioning it may think that there is only one hookbait within that area, as that is the tactic that most people use, and

that once it has located the dangerous bait, the rest are safe to eat; this could well be the explanation for the common occurrence of a bed of bait being eaten except for the hookbait. If it is conditioned in this way, the carp will be wary and will sample each of the baits until it finds the dangerous one, and once it has done so it should then take the rest without as much caution. Departing from normal practice and placing more than one hookbait on an area of bait may therefore lead to more takes, as when the carp have found one rogue bait, they will not be on the lookout for another. You can actually take this strategy one step further by making one of the baits very obvious to the carp: for example, have one of the baits exactly the same as the free offerings, and make the other a pop-up positioned a couple of inches above the bed. The carp will see the rogue pop-up, then hopefully get its head down on the rest of the bait. Even if this theory is totally incorrect, at the very worst you have doubled your chances of a pick-up off the baited area.

The Time of Year

As a cold-blooded creature, the carp's metabolism slows down considerably in the winter period and so intense feeding in winter is very sporadic and not as frequent as during the warmer months. Piling a load of bait into a swim without a second thought is therefore possibly one of the biggest mistakes an angler can make. Adopt the habit of considering whether or not the fish are feeding, and if so, in what numbers, and at what intensity. It is vital to take into account water temperature and weather conditions in this respect, and there seems to be a general rule of thumb that winter means a minimum of freebies. This may be the right approach more often than not; however, as we have seen previously, carp *can* feed intensively in the winter due to SSS (*see* Chapter 2) so always be aware of this when choosing your strategy for winter.

The Size of the Carp

The amount of bait that the fish need should be another contributing factor to your application. A group of smaller fish might need as much bait as one larger fish, so you need to know the type of fish that you are after, and also their grouping habits, that is, whether they swim around in shoals or groups, or if they are in the main solitary. Basically, if you are targeting an individual fish, consider how much bait will be required to stimulate it into feeding and achieving satisfaction – a larger fish generally requires more food than a smaller one. A ratio of 1 to 20 in weight is about the amount we would use in a normal situation, so if you are fishing for carp that normally swim around in groups of two or three, and the average size of the fish within this group is 20lb, we would introduce between 2lb and 3lb (0.9kg and 1.3kg) of bait, topping it up once we received some action. The same ratio can be applied to larger shoals of smaller fish, although if the water is quite a hungry one, we would increase the ratio slightly.

Always remember that everything is site specific, and that you should read the situation as accurately as you can before making any decisions. There is nothing worse than sitting there thinking that you are fishing over too much bait and not being able to get it back. Remember you can always put in a bit more if you need to.

At What Distance are you Fishing?
There is no use in using a bait which you can only catapult or stick out to 20yd (18m), if you are casting twice this distance. Bait spread in the wrong areas can be detrimental to your fishing situation, and if you know it won't go 40yd (36m) then don't spread it at all. Make sure it goes where you want it to, and ensure that you stick to this. And if you are hopeless with a throwing stick, then practise! Over 40yd they can be incredibly accurate, and it is up to you to keep practising!

If you make your own boilies, be sure they are perfectly round so that they work efficiently with a throwing stick or catapult. If they break up as they leave the stick, add a little egg albumin or whey protein concentrate at a rate of 1oz (28g) to the pound (454g). This will solve the problem of splitting, although it will also lock in the flavour of your bait thus slowing down its release

into the water, so you may have to increase your attractor levels slightly to combat this.

If you know that you want a bait to go out a certain distance, then design it to be able to get just that far. This can be achieved by varying the binding ingredients, by the inclusion of the protein concentrate mentioned above, or alternatively by varying the boiling and drying times. A bait that will not reach the distance that you want it to is next to useless, and a bait that is rock hard and will fly out miles will be less effective than a softer, fast-release bait that is fished at short range. Similarly, if you are planning to fish on the side of a sloped feature such as a gravel bar, use a bait shape which holds the bottom well. As with every aspect of your carping, amend your strategy to the situation you are fishing.

The Pre-baiting Campaign
The practice of pre-baiting is probably one of the most important when applying a bait as a food source, and one which is overlooked by many anglers. It can be a crucial component behind success on so many occasions, and conditioning the carp into taking your freebies has to be the ultimate method for enhancing catch rates. It is a time-consuming practice however, and one which needs to be carried out in an efficient method following some sort of strategic planning. In order to maximize the chances of catching, freebies should be introduced as regularly as possible when not fishing. One of our favourite approaches is to pre-bait as often as possible with large quantities when not fishing, and then to use very few when we actually do decide to fish.

Pre-baiting campaigns can, however, follow a number of routes – for instance, bait concentrated in a few areas, or spread around many areas, lots at irregular periods, or little and often – but whatever you decide, it is essential to maintain the correct levels of flavourings and attractors in a bait at all times. This is fine if you are using naturals, but with boiled baits and many others it is difficult because ingredients and attractors are not always readily available. This is where planning comes in, since all the above information needs to be considered alongside your projected strategies. If you are going to be using the same bait for the whole of the season on a certain water, make up enough before you start your campaign, and make it exactly the same every time. If you do not have sufficient space to store large amounts then be sure that you have enough ingredients to last the season, as there is nothing worse than the bait really taking off in late autumn, and finding that you have run out of it, and the flavour has sold out or is discontinued.

One point we would like to raise here is that of consistency within your bait. When you make up your own bait, it is normal to follow the directions on the packaging regarding eggs. However, as the size of eggs varies, and you may not use the same size every time, you may be making a bait that is not exactly the same. We therefore use a liquid measure of eggs as opposed to a specific number; thus if you always use 2fl oz (50ml) as one egg, then your mix will always be the same irrespective of the size of egg that you use (for instance six eggs = 10fl oz (300ml) liquid egg).

Don't skimp on bait quality.

Cost is important for many anglers, and you must always follow what your pocket will allow. It's all very well starting off with an expensive mix, but again, if you find that halfway through the season you can't afford to carry on, or the fish are on the bait so heavily that you can't put enough in, your catch rates will drop off, and all your initial hard work and expense will have been for nothing.

It is always difficult to know how much to put in, and this is dictated by the other factors we have looked at within this section. As a guide regarding frequency, when concentrating on a water within reasonable driving distance, we will apply bait as regularly as possible, preferably every other day during the spring, summer and autumn period. In winter, we have found that bait introduction can certainly enhance the fishing situation as it can help to keep the fish on the move. Waters that are regularly fished in the winter tend to be more productive than unfished waters, and we feel that a continuous introduction of bait is one of the reasons for this. In the main however, introductions in the winter need to be considerably less than during other times of the year. Obviously this sort of statement is very much site specific, but even on heavily stocked waters, we would decrease the quantity applied in the winter. For the spring and autumn period we would steadily taper the amount applied, exactly how much depending on angler catch rates and overall fish movement – thus in early spring we would steadily increase the amounts applied, and would decrease them for the autumn; but even if there was little or no fish activity or captures, we would still put a bit in.

For a water which is not within regular driving distance, but is one that we are likely to fish on a regular basis, we would make up a large batch of bait – 22lb (10kg) perhaps – prior to visiting; following the fishing session we would apply all of it to specific areas. Baiting campaigns basically set out to compete with natural food levels in a water, and educate the fish into overlooking the danger aspect present when feeding on anglers' baits. It is possible to do this, but as we have emphasized throughout this book, forward planning and good strategy play an all-important role.

'You must be joking!'

5 RIGS

Rigs! Everyone wants the latest top-of-the-range rig, but are they really necessary? Some of the rigs we see these days are so complicated and finicky that by the time you have tied one, set it up, and cast and then recast it because the trap was sprung in the air and not in the water, you are either so frustrated with it that you immediately take it off, or you don't have much time left as you have been messing about for so long. Furthermore, any fish that may have been within a reasonable distance of your swim when you arrived, will have disappeared to a safe two mile radius as a result of all the disturbance. However, sometimes complicated rigs *are* required, as carp can be so cunning that only the latest rig – the one they cannot possibly have seen – will be the one to outwit them. It is therefore vital that you do not close your mind to the subject of complicated rigs – just take care, not to overcomplicate the issue and tie your own mind and probably the rig you are using, in to knots.

This book is about strategic carp fishing, and the idea behind any strategy is that you come up with a plan, put it into action, and watch it come to successful fruition. In order to do this you must be constantly thinking about what you are doing, and be prepared to change or modify your tactics accordingly. The easiest way to failure is to stagnate and do the same old thing time and time again. Just look at the anglers around you: how many anglers do you know that use the same rig every time they go fishing and at almost all the venues that they visit? Most anglers do it, some out of laziness, others because they only like to use one rig, as it is the one they are confident with. However, when you look at it through the eyes of the carp, it does not take too long to associate a link of 8in to 12in (20cm to 30cm) with danger. Carp are only simple creatures, but they do learn by association through their own experiences and those of their peers. If a carp has been caught a couple of times on a particular method it may associate that method with danger, but it will also sense the fear in another fish within its group, and that will, in turn, affect how confidently it will take a bait. Imagine a group of carp feeding on a small baited area: some of the fish may sample the bait but reject it because they feel the rig, and eventually all the fish in that group might reject that baited hook even if they did not sample it themselves, because they can sense fear in the other carp who will also not touch the trap.

Now this may be obvious to most of you, but you should be aware of the fact that carp can wise up very quickly with regard to rigs. As with any associated learning, the more an animal is subjected to a certain source of danger, the more wary it will become – indeed without this ability to identify danger, the species would soon become extinct. This concept is discussed at more length in the chapter on bait, but with rigs, the importance to the angler is that probably 75 per cent of the anglers fishing on any given lake will be using a similar method of presentation. The bait and the application of the bait may be different, but the constitution of the rig will be similar and from the fishes' point of view, very easy to detect.

All of this could make the subject of rigs very depressing; however, do not panic: just remember that the rig is only one part of the equation, and that location, bait, other anglers and weather conditions all play a part. As you will see from the bait section, the greed factor almost negates the effect of most rigs if you get it right – but rigs are still a very important aspect to bear in mind.

Major Rig Considerations

Before deciding on a rig to use for the particular situation you are fishing in, a number of points should be considered. The idea is to take into account all parts of the equation, and only then will you be able to come up with the appropriate rig. The following contingencies should therefore be considered:

- The size and strain of the target fish;
- The casting and tangling properties and requirements;
- The nature of the lake bed over which you will present a bait;
- The shock effect – bolt and running requirements;
- Other external factors such as pressure and feeding patterns.

Why is each of these important? For example, many of you might wonder what the size and strain of the fish has to do with the type of rig you should choose. The fact is that every factor should be considered if you are to be successful

and make the most of your time on the bank. Try to organize everything you can in your favour, because even a small hiccup can make the difference between a good and a bad day.

The Size and Strain of Target Fish

First we must consider the way in which the fish in our lake might feed, and this comes down to the build of the fish, as different carp feed in different ways. For example a larger fish, or a carp of the Italian race, will have to up-end to feed, whereas a long lean common may be able to pick food items off the bottom of the lake without having to up-end at all. The relevance of this is that the turning and hooking ability of a rig is greatest if it comes into effect after a fish has picked up the bait, or just before it levels out fully. If the rig is too short and the fish moves off and straightens the hooklength out fully before it has levelled out, the hook may not have had a chance to take a good hold as it may not have gone far enough into the mouth.

The mouth of the carp will also vary depending on its race and strain: thus some have a down-turned mouth more suited to bottom feeding,

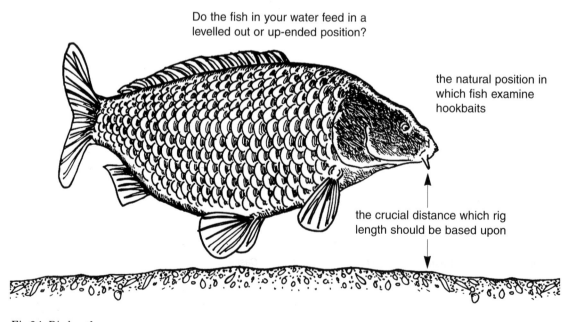

Do the fish in your water feed in a levelled out or up-ended position?

the natural position in which fish examine hookbaits

the crucial distance which rig length should be based upon

Fig 24 Rig length.

whereas others have neither a down- nor an up-turned mouth, and this will affect the area into which the hook will take hold. Due consideration should be given to the length of the hooklink, as it is vital that the hook has a chance of finding a hold before the fish can eject it, and also that it will provide you with the best possible chance of a hook-up before the fish moves off. The type of carp you are fishing for and its conditioned behaviour will also affect the choice of hook you should make; this will be considered later on in the hook section.

Casting and Tangling Properties

It is obviously no use at all to have a rig that tangles in flight, as its fish-hooking capabilities will be severely affected. Even the slightest tangle such as the line wrapping once around the swivel, will have a dramatic effect on the performance of the rig. Furthermore if you have a rig which *is* susceptible to tangles, you will spend most of the day worrying about whether it is lying on the lake bed in a big knot. Always ensure that the rig you choose is virtually tangle free: there is no excuse these days for blaming a tangled rig for a fish loss because there are plenty of products and methods around to prevent such occurrences – so make good use of them. Many people use tubing to solve the problem, but we prefer to stay away from it as much as possible. We strongly subscribe to the opinion that the end tackle should be as unobtrusive as possible, and the addition of tubing will not serve this end – on the contrary, it will make the rig very obvious indeed. Some people might disagree with us on this point, and in turn we cannot dispute that many carp are caught on rigs with tubing on them; but for us, the only use for tubing is to protect the line against wear, and also because it can sometimes be of conservation benefit, in that it does not damage the flanks of the fish as much as might a sharp leader material such as Quicksilver during a long battle.

In addition to anti-tangle properties, the distance you need to cast is another major factor in rig choice. Wind resistance on a baited rig is incredible even on the calmest of days, and the longer the rig, the more the wind will prevent the bait from getting to where you want it to go. We have been to venues where we have seen people struggling to cast 400ft (120m), but when they changed their choice of rig, both in design and length of hooklink, they were able to reach their target area. As a result of what we witnessed, we decided to conduct an experiment to see just how much further we might be able to cast with the correct rig choice. We therefore took a rod to a field and measured out a casting area. Using a bomb of 3oz (85g) and a hooklink of 6in, we then made half-a-dozen casts and noted the distances they reached. We then took off the rig and replaced it with one of 12in long; the same sized lead and bait were used, and a further six casts were made and measured. The results are detailed in Table 3. As you can see, it is quite surprising how much distance you can add to your cast with the correct choice of rig.

Although not necessarily rig related, one of our favourite methods of fishing for carp is at long range and it is vital that you master the method of long distance, casting. Many traditionalists complain that too many people these days throw to the horizon when the fish are under the rod tips, and it is quite right that you should always fish where the fish are; but if they *are* out at long range and all you have with you is your centre pin and split cane rod with which you can only cast 30ft (10m), you may as well not be there. Have the option to fish at long range in your armoury and use it when you need to.

Table 3. The effects of rig length on distance.

Rig length	Cast 1	Cast 2	Cast 3	Cast 4	Cast 5	Cast 6	Average
Long rig (12in)	97.6m	100m	100.9m	98.6m	103.8m	97.8m	99.7m
Short rig (6in)	106.4m	110.7m	105.1m	107.9m	108.6m	107.4m	107.7m

Birch Grove, a silty and pressured water where rig choice is absolutely vital. Rob certainly got it right for this winter caught 25lb common.

Table 4. Rig choice in different situations.

Situation	Material	Length	Reason
open water	Super Nova 12	med 8–10in (20–25cm)	sinking link to disguise rig
weedbed	Merlin 25	med 8–10in (20–25cm)	neutral but strong to cope with weed
silt	Merlin/Magma	long 12in (30cm) plus	neutral but weighted to land on (not in) silt
firm bottom	Amnesia/Super Nova	med 8–10in (20–25cm)	lie flat on bottom
wary fish	Snakeskin/Combi	med 8in (20cm)	difficult to detect
pop up	Silkworm 15	long 12in (30cm) plus	long and buoyant to sit on weed

The Nature of the Lake Bed

This is one of the most important aspects of rig choice, as it affects the ultimate presentation of your bait. It is vital to tune the hooklink and its length to the nature of the bottom over which you are fishing. The type of hooklink material should be your first point of concern, and you should decide whether you want a sinking, a neutral, or a buoyant link to combat the lake bed and any problems it may cause you. For instance if you are fishing over heavy silt then a neutral link may be the best choice: you want it to be as unobtrusive as possible, but not one that might sink into the silt if this is of the heavy soup variety. Conversely, a clean bottom will require a sinking link so that it will lie flat on the bottom out of harm's way. The link should be camouflaged so that it blends in with the lake bed, and this can be done either by using an already coloured link, or by colouring the link with a permanent marker pen (we prefer not to use this method in case the carp can smell the ink), or by rubbing some of the lake's mud into the braid – give it a good going over so that it takes the newness out of the braid (this is the more favoured method). In addition to the colour advantage, it will also add a bit of weight to the link, helping it to sink, and will reduce the number of air bubbles that become trapped in the braid as it flies through the air on the cast, thus again helping its sinking properties.

If you are not familiar with the nature of the lake bed, you should make a few exploratory casts to ascertain what it is that you are fishing over. It never ceases to amaze us the number of people who go to a new lake and do not have a plumb around before casting in – in fact the only time that it would be excusable *not* to do so, would be if you had found some fish and did not want to spook them by casting around on top of them.

Once the bottom has been established, you can then make an evaluation as to what the most appropriate hooklink material should be. Table 4 details a number of angling situations and the type of rig we would start off with in certain given situations. However, please do not think that this is a golden rule for rig choice; it is merely a starting guide, and you should always be on the lookout to change or modify any of the components where necessary. For example, if you were in a swim with a large amount of fairly open water in front of you and the bottom of the lake was relatively firm silt, your choice might be to use a medium-length link of Kryston Super Nova 12lb b.s. There are no snags in the area and therefore nothing to worry you with regard to the abrasion resistance of the link. You start to get one or two indications of fish arriving in the area, and eventually you get a pick-up: the take is a screamer, but when you attempt to connect with the fish you feel a couple of kicks and then the line goes slack. What went wrong? The carp obviously like the bait, the presentation couldn't have been that bad or the fish would not have picked the bait up in the first place, and you have checked the hook and it is as sharp as if you had just got it out of the packet.

The likely problem was that the fish were feeding, but not that confidently, so the link was not long enough to allow the carp to pick up the bait and take it properly before it felt the hook. A change to a longer link may well solve this problem, so instead of the standard 8in to 10in hooklink, you should replace it with a 15in to 18in link. The extra 6in (15cm) may be just enough to fool the wary fish into thinking that the bait is safe to eat.

Shock Effect

This subject will be covered in more detail later in this chapter (the section on component parts discussing leads) and also in the next, but the main choice you should make now is whether you want a running, fixed, or bolt rig. The difference between a fixed rig and a bolt rig in this context purely relates to the weight of the lead. It is quite possible to have a fixed lead which is so light that its effectiveness as a bolt rig is minimal, so the two have to be classed separately. The whole point of a bolt rig is to shock the carp into bolting off with the bait, thus registering a screaming take on the

indicator. However, to achieve this a large weight must be used, as a lighter weight is unlikely to bring the hook home sufficiently hard to prick the fish and therefore make it bolt off. Conversely there are situations when the last thing you want the fish to do is head for the horizon, in which case a lighter, free-running lead may be a better choice. (More on leads later.)

Pressure and Feeding Patterns

Another factor that cannot be ignored is pressure and feeding patterns. It is as well to be aware of what everyone else on your lake is using by way of rigs: there may be a new rig which is catching them, or perhaps most of the anglers are still using the rig which used to catch them, but whose effectiveness is now slowing down. If the latter is the case, it is best to get onto something else and be completely different from the others. We both subscribe to the view that if it works, why change it; but to stick to this rule in all circumstances is to start on the slippery slope to stagnation. In order to progress you must change, so be aware of the pressure and the type of rigs that the other anglers are using, and keep ahead of them all. The feeding patterns of the carp will also affect the type of rig you should choose. If you are trying to establish a tight, baited area with particles, or a blanket feed such as pellets, you should adjust the length of your hooklink to take into account the fact that the carp will not have to move very far before it finds the next morsel of food. If the carp have really got their heads down and are feeding confidently over a bed of hemp, then a link of, say, 6in would be about right, as you want to get an indication as soon as possible after the fish has picked up the bait. A longer link might allow the fish time to move, to realize that something is wrong, and to reject the hook before you have had any indication at your end that a fish has picked up the bait.

Rig Components

Here we take a look at the components which make up the rig itself, and the considerations we should give to each before making a choice as to the rig we should use for the given situation:

- Hooklink material and length
- Swivels and hooks
- Knots
- Tubing
- Leads
- Fine tuning.

All are equally important, and you can ruin a brilliant set-up if just one of these points is wrong – even the slightest change can drastically effect what you are trying to achieve (*see* next chapter). We have spent a lot of time over the years playing around with rigs and different set-ups to see just how effective they are, and we can categorically state that there is no 'wonder' rig. Some rigs we have used have been very effective in certain situations, and next to useless in others. What you must always remember, is that most of the modern-day complicated rigs were designed for a certain purpose, and if they are used outside that certain purpose, they may actually hinder rather than help you.

Hooklink Material and Length

As we have already seen, it is most important that this aspect of a rig is correct; let us simply reiterate here that you should always ensure that the material you use, be it a braid or a stiff link, is suited to the bottom over which you are fishing. Even more important is the length of the link: if you have a rig in which you are confident and with which you have caught a few fish, but your results are now starting to tail off a little, do not immediately assume that its effectiveness, or worse still that of the bait, is exhausted. Play around a little before making any drastic changes – in particular try lengthening the hooklink a little, or increasing the length of the hair to allow the bait to behave a little more naturally. This is often all that is required to re-establish the rig's success rate.

Swivels and Hooks

We are spoilt these days with the quality of the swivels available; even as recently as the mid-

1980s, some of the twisted wire swivels we had to use left a lot to be desired. In fact modern swivels are of such good quality that most people pay very little attention to them, although they are a very important part of the whole rig. Nevertheless, a weak swivel can result in a fish loss, so they should always be checked to ensure that the eyes are not damaged in any way. Such damage can occur as a result of a defect in the manufacturing process, or if you have had to cut the line or braid off a swivel. Always check to ensure that there are no sharp edges where your scissors or blade may have nicked the eye, and make sure that the eyes do in fact swivel. We would choose American Bear swivels in either 40lb or 60lb test depending on where we are fishing. The size is important because the barrel of the swivel of the 40lb test will fit snugly into the tubing through the middle of most in-line leads, therefore giving a very neat set-up which should help to avoid tangles. If you use a larger barrelled swivel and want to use a semi-fixed lead set-up, we would advise using a short length of Gardner catapult elastic (black, of course, not the day-glo yellow variety) because it is just the right bore to grip both the barrel of the swivel and the tubing of the lead.

Hooks are probably just as important as hooklink length and knots in a rig. They are also a very personal thing and the hook which one angler may have absolute confidence in, another may hate. Do not, however, just rely on one hook for all your fishing situations. A fine wire pattern hook may be satisfactory for open water carping, but will be next to useless for hook-and-hold snag fishing, and vice versa. For 99 per cent of our fishing situations we would select the KN pattern 1 and 2 varieties in sizes between 2 and 8. More often than not we will use a size 8, because we want the hook to be as unobtrusive as possible and these are quite light but very strong. If you are using a pop-up, you should match it with a lighter hook that will not stand out as much as a heavier gauge model. Consider also your hook attachment and whether you use a line aligner or not. Again our choice

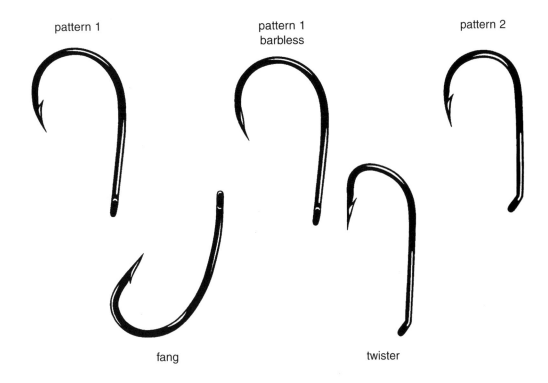

pattern 1

pattern 1
barbless

pattern 2

fang

twister

Fig 25 Hook choice is critical.

depends on the situation that we are in: thus if we are fishing over silt and the hook is disguised against the lake bed so as to be fairly well hidden, we would always use a line aligner, whereas if the hookbait was being presented on a clean sandy or gravel patch, we would either dispense with the line aligner altogether and use a knotless knot set-up, or alternatively match the colour of the tubing used for the aligner with the lake bed and use as small a piece of tube as we could get away with. It may seem as if we are being extraordinarily particular, but in our opinion it is vitally important that the fish should not be able to detect the hook, and a large chunk of black tubing sitting on a clear area does nothing for our confidence. If you do not use a line aligner set-up, we would strongly advise you to do so; and if you are not yet sure of its effectiveness, take a look at the section on hookholds in Chapter 6 and reconsider.

The hook should of course always be incredibly sharp, and the chemically sharpened hooks that we use today are infinitely better than the old forged hooks that we used to use. However, a disadvantage of these hooks is that they are so sharp, they only have to touch a stone on the retrieve, or connect with a tough area of gristle or bone in a fish's mouth, and they will turn over at the point. It is important therefore to check the point of the hook not just after every fish, but after every cast. If the point is even slightly blunted or burred, it will affect the ability of the hook to prick the fish, and as you will see from the next chapter (Experiments), we need as much in our favour as possible. Finally, if you leave your rods set-up in the holdall between sessions, as we do, always check the hook before you next cast it out again; the normal method for packing away the rods is to hook the hook onto one of the eyes of the rod, but this too can damage the point.

When making your choice of hook, always consider the following:

- The carp itself must be the first consideration, and both its size and its race are significant. Some carp have tougher mouths than others owing to their genetic make-up, and also the food on which they have been brought up, and a sharper or heavier gauge hook may be required.
- Similarly, it is important to know what the carp usually eats, as this too will affect your hook choice. If it spends most of its time rooting around in silt eating bloodworm, then a very sharp hook might tear the flesh of the mouth and pull out easily. Alternatively if the carp is a big French crayfish-eating monster, the flesh of its mouth will be tough, and a very strong, sharp hook will be required to penetrate it.
- The nature of the lake bed can help you on this point if you are unsure as to what the carp normally feeds on. Generally, carp in lakes with a soft bottom will often have a soft mouth – although this is only the case if the fish have been bred in the lake, or have been in there for a very long time. Moreover carp will quite often have been stocked into a lake from fish farms, and many of these will have been pellet fed in their early years; as a result these too will have very soft mouths as they have never needed to eat anything tough. Nature will soon rectify this however, and after a few years their mouths will toughen up. Do bear this in mind if your lake has had a recent stocking of fish.
- Lake features also play an important part regarding the hook you choose: it must be strong enough to hold a fighting carp away from snags in a hook-and-hold situation; and always bear in mind the fact that very sharp hooks blunt easily, especially on the retrieve in a gravel pit where contact with stones might turn the points over. Check them constantly.

Knots

We have all experienced the pick-up which comes after what seems like an eternity, and then eventually the fish is lost. In acute disappointment we examine the remnants of the limp line to discover that the mainline has broken near to the swivel. Was it the knot, or a weak spot on the line? The likelihood is that it was both, because when the knot was being tied, it weakened the line.

In a rush to get the rods out, you perhaps do not pay as much attention to the tying of your knot as you should. Modern coated lines are very susceptible to line breakage if you use the wrong knot with them, and if the knot is a strangulation knot such as a blood knot, or even a more appropriate knot such as a palomar or grinner which has not been bedded down properly, they will fail. That is not the fault of the line: you can only blame yourself when the line breaks, either for not checking it properly, or for tying the wrong knot in the first place. When it comes to tying knots, we have spoken at great length with specialist manufacturers on this subject and their tips for success are that you should, where possible, use a knot lube or some spit to lubricate the knot and to help keep the line cool when the knot is tightened up.

Also, when you bed the knot down, always tighten it by pushing the knot into the eye of the hook or swivel with the nails of your thumb and forefinger, as opposed to pulling the line and the hook. The latter method is guaranteed to burn the line, and is the cause of many anglers lines snapping about an inch away from the swivel. If you have encountered this problem, it would almost certainly be for this reason.

When you have tied the knot, check that the line next to it is not kinked or damaged in any way. If it is, the line has been burned and will be significantly reduced in strength and will need changing.

When you have a satisfactory knot, add a drop of rig glue to stop it from slipping. This will safeguard the knot from any slippage which may occur during the fight with a fish if it has not been bedded down properly. After it has had time to dry, give it a good tug or two to check that it holds. If you follow all these guidelines, there should be no reason why your knot should fail you.

Tubing

Although we see tubing as a hindrance more than a help, there are occasions when it can be useful. Its main use is for its anti-tangle properties, although if your rig is well constructed and neat, and with no jagged edges, there should be no need for a long length of tubing to stop it from tangling.

In our opinion tubing only serves to reduce distance and to bring your end tackle to the attention of the carp, so it should be avoided at all costs. Our ethos is that you should ask yourself 'Why?' whenever you put something into operation.

Question: Why is the tubing there?
Answer: To stop the rig from tangling.
Question: Will it tangle without the tubing?
Answer: If you make the correct choice of rig for the situation you are fishing, it will not usually tangle and therefore the tubing can be removed.

We both use rigs without tubing at ranges in excess of 460ft (140m) and do not have problems with tangles. In fact until we set to writing this book, neither of us had really given much thought to tangles because we are so confident that our set-ups will not fail us in this way. If you are one of those anglers who thinks you need tubing to cast out 200ft (60m) safely, then you are wrong: give your rig choice some more thought, and you will soon be able to dispense with the tubing!

Sometimes, however, the fact that tubing will make your end tackle more conspicuous to the fish has to be balanced with the fact that you need some extra protection on your line because you are fishing over gravel bars and suchlike. In that circumstance we would suggest that you take a look at Kryston's amazing Granite Juice, a liquid coating which you apply to your line and allow to dry; once dried, it will increase the

Simon with an early morning Patshull common of 20lb.

abrasion resistance of your line dramatically, often to twice its previous capacity. If you are still not convinced and insist on using tubing, try to use something inconspicuous such as Mussel Cracker or No Spook, which will at least blend in a little better than most tubes.

While we do not use long lengths of tubing, we do employ very short lengths within our rigs to assist their anti-tangle properties. Normally these are as follows:

• A 5cm length of 2mm No Spook tubing which we place on the hooklink itself, pushing the end over the swivel. This is just enough to hold the link away from the lead in flight, thus stopping it from tangling around the swivel.

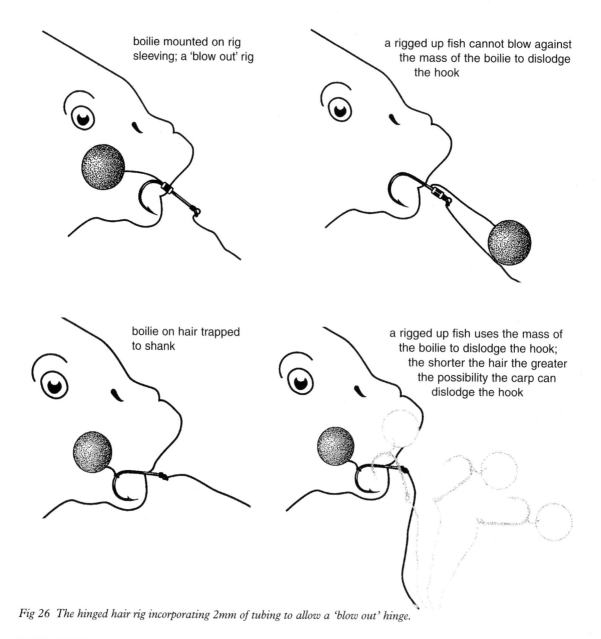

Fig 26 The hinged hair rig incorporating 2mm of tubing to allow a 'blow out' hinge.

- A tapered rubber sleeve which we would place on the rear of an in-line lead to prevent the link catching on the plastic tubing at the rear of the lead.
- A 1cm length of silicon tubing out of which we make a line aligner.
- A 2mm piece of tubing which we slide onto the shank of the hook when we are using a long, hinged hair rig (*see* previous page).

As far as we are concerned, anything more than this is surplus to requirements and should be avoided unless there are extenuating circumstances.

Lead Choice

A lead is an integral and important part of rig design and can serve many purposes:

- To enable the rig to be cast out;
- To act as a mechanism for hooking fish;
- To assist in ascertaining the nature of the lake bed;
- To assist the angling situation generally.

The first consideration must, of course be how far you want to cast your baited rig, as the lead can make a huge difference to the distance you can reach. Some leads are very aerodynamic and will fly easily; others are not aerodynamic at all, but are very good from a bolt rig point of view. As an experiment, we took six different leads down to a field and measured out a casting area; we then made a number of casts with each lead and noted down the performance of each as regards distance. The results and full details of the experiments are described in the next chapter; but it was clear to see that the correct choice of lead is vital if you want to reach the horizon.

After casting properties, the main use of the lead is to assist with the hooking of the fish, and another experiment was carried out to see the difference in effect between various types of lead. The results were significant and as with casting leads, the differences are quite dramatic. Take a look at the next chapter, the experiments section, and think carefully about your lead choice.

Leads have a number of less obvious uses, too, one of these being to assist in identifying the nature of the lake bed in a swim. We have seen in earlier chapters that a knowledge of the character of the lake bed is useful, as it will help you to decide which rig to use, how long the hook-link should be, how tough the mouth of the fish is likely to be, and also what the fish might feed on in the area that you are fishing. The best way to use a lead in this situation is to cast out an old battered bomb lead and drag it back so that you can feel the vibration of the lake bed through the line and the rod. As the lead is drawn back through the mud on the lake bed, it will pick up particles, especially if you have cut a few silt-collecting grooves in it. Once it is back on the bank, you can smell and feel the silt to see whether it is sweet or foul smelling. If your swim has weed in it, the lead will also drag back pieces so you can analyse these as well. In a gravel pit, the lead may come back with new score marks along it, thus indicating the fact that there may be rocks or sharp objects on the lake bottom;. you should therefore either use a snag leader or protect your line with Granite Juice.

Leads can also help you when you are fishing over weed. A heavy lead will dive straight into weed, especially if it is aerodynamic, whereas a flatter, lighter lead will sit on top of weed allowing you to present a bait on top of a weedbed instead of in the middle of it. An extra tip here is to feather the line just as the lead hits the water: that is, hold onto the line until you feel the lead hit the weed, as this will slow its descent through the water.

Whether it is best to use in-line or swivel-fixed leads depends on the situation you are fishing in. It should never be the case that you use the same lead every time you fish, so the factors which affect your choice are those we discussed earlier, and also whether or not there are any snags or weed in the vicinity. If there are, it is generally better to use an in-line lead, as this is less likely to become stuck should the fish reach the obstruction. The other alternative is to use a breakaway lead, where the lead will fall off the line if it gets stuck. This can be a useful tactic, because once the carp is free of the lead you have a more direct pull on the fish and so it should be easier to extract. It is also the case that the fish will sometimes rise to the surface of the water once the lead has come free. This is quite an expensive method, as you lose the lead every time, but if it results in a fish being safely landed, most would say it is worth the expense.

The way to set-up a breakaway rig is to use a Nash safety clip and to cut out the retaining lug. The rig should be fished without the use of the retaining rubber that pushes over the end of the clip; like this, the lead will easily pull off the clip if it gets stuck.

Fine Tuning

Once you have organized the major construction of your rig, you need only fine tune it. By this we mean attending to the subtle edges and differences that you can add to it to make it slightly more effective. Examples of this might be the choice of a line aligner or a knotless knot attachment, the addition of some 'Drop Em' to ensure that the link sinks properly, or the use of some rig glue to stiffen the link. There are occasions when

any, or all of these fine-tuning tactics might make your rig much more effective, so keep them clearly in mind when putting your rig together.

By using some glue to stiffen the last inch of your hooklink, you will assist the hook to turn if you are using a fine braid, and at the same time will make the bait harder to eject once it has been taken into the mouth.

The addition of a short piece of tubing on a rig may help its anti-tangle properties, so if the one you have is efficient, but is prone to tangling, instead of using a long length of tubing up the line, use a short piece on the hooklink and push it over the swivel. This will help to keep the braid out of the way of the lead and swivel during the cast, and also when the rig is falling through the water.

Finally, always consider the length of your hair and also the material it is made of, as either a more subtle, or even a stiffer hair, might make a difference to the effectiveness of the rig. The length of the hair is important, because a long hair used correctly will act as a hinge and will help in the hooking of the fish. (More on this subject later!)

Rigs: no time for experimenting.

A Few Good Rigs

We will now take a look at some of the rigs we use and the situations we would use them in. For most of our carp angling, we like to keep the rig as simple as possible, leaving the really complicated ones for when we visit exceptionally hard waters. Having said that, if the tuning of your rig is right first time, even the simplest of rigs is deadly effective – in fact, many people are surprised when they see how straightforward ours are. The fact is, we have been caught in the rig trap, and have found that all it does is lower your catch rates because you are forever trying out the latest rig, or changing your rig to one that your mate is using. Most of the top anglers in the country use very simple rigs. However, in spite of the advice of most sensible writers, we have seen some amazing contraptions, especially when we have helped out on the *Carpworld* Fishabil trips.

In short, before you put your rig on, always ask yourself exactly what you want it to do, and then consider whether there is any simpler way that you could achieve that aim. Generally all that you will need to do is change the size of the hook, the length of the link or hair, and the material that the link is made from – and you should have an effective rig every time. A line aligner should be fitted on almost all occasions; and that's about it!

A simple but effective rig led to the downfall of this 25lb mirror for Rob.

Standard Rig

This is the rig that both of us use for the majority of our carp fishing, and it is in fact the one that we used to win the World Carp Cup in 1996. We normally use 15lb Super Nova, as it is superbly supple and it lies flat on the bottom of the lake. We do change the material according to the situation, however, and the most usual reason would be when we are fishing over weed. In that circumstance we would change the material to a bouyant link such as Silkworm, and increase the length of the link. As far as the length of the link is concerned, that would depend on the factors we considered earlier, but

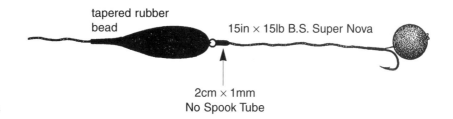

tapered rubber bead

15in × 15lb B.S. Super Nova

2cm × 1mm
No Spook Tube

Fig 27 Standard Rig.

we would have no problem fishing links between 6in and 24in long with this set-up. The hair should be long enough to allow the bait to sit just off the bend of the hook, and the hook itself would always be attached with either a line aligner, or a knotless knot attachment, with the hair coming off the shank opposite the point of the hook. Finally, a short length of No Spook tubing would be placed over the link and pushed over the barrel of the swivel to help reduce tangles. It is equally happy fished with a straight- or in-line lead (*see* Fig 27).

Hinged Hair Rig

The only difference between this rig and the one above, is the length of the hair and the method of hook attachment. We usually tie this rig with a five-turn knotless knot and bed the knot down to the eye as far it will go. This is to allow the hair to hinge right back to the eye upon ejection by the fish. The reason for this is that when a bait on a tight hair is blown out of the carp's mouth, the bait can sometimes force the hook out, as opposed to helping it find a hold. Try this test yourself by pricking the skin on your hand with a rig that has the hair coming off the shank opposite the point and the bait tight to the hook. Simulate a fish blowing out the bait and you will see that the point of the hook will often just scratch along the surface of your hand. Now repeat the exercise with the longer hair that comes off the hook just above the eye; the bait hinges all the way round and will exert a downward force on the hook, pushing it into the bottom lip.

The one disadvantage of this rig is that the hair can sometimes twist around in flight, causing the bait to catch on the point of the hook. To stop this happening, take a 2mm long piece of 2mm bore tubing and push it over the hair on the shank of the hook so that the hair exits the shank opposite the point. The tubing *must* be loose enough to slide down the hook upon ejection, or the effect of the hinge will be lost (*see* Fig 28).

Snowman Rig

This is another favourite of ours and one which we have found is particularly effective during the winter months – Rob had considerable success with this rig method in 1989. It is yet another version of the standard rig, and this time the only difference is the length of the hair. It leaves the

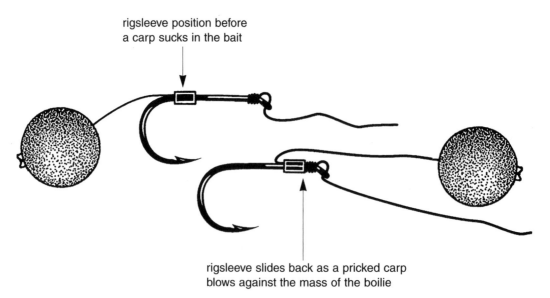

rigsleeve position before
a carp sucks in the bait

rigsleeve slides back as a pricked carp
blows against the mass of the boilie

Fig 28 Hinged Hair Rig.

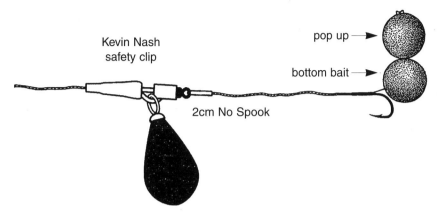

Fig 29 Snowman Rig.

Kevin Nash
safety clip

pop up →

bottom bait →

2cm No Spook

shank opposite the point and is long enough to take two baits that will sit just off the bend of the hook. It can be fished with a longer hair, but is a bit bulky if the hair is *too* long. As the name suggests, the rig lies on the bottom of the lake like a snowman with one bait sitting on top of the other, an effect which is obtained by threading first a standard bottom bait and then a pop-up onto the hair. The baits should balance each other, and the rig will be critically balanced, but you can play around with the buoyancy by using a heavier bottom bait or a more buoyant pop-up.

This rig can also be used as a pig rig by using just two standard bottom baits, or three or four 8mm baits – the latter we have found to be very effective. You can play around with the colour of the baits, too: try using two different colours on the same hair. We have had a lot of success on what we call the Minstrel Rig, one black one white bait. Furthermore in the winter we have found that an over-flavoured bottom bait and a bright white pop-up can be deadly (*see* Fig 29).

Debris Dodge and Weed Rig
Weed seems to cause many anglers problems, in that the hook may easily become snagged up in it, thus affecting the anglers' confidence. Very often this problem can be solved by lengthening the link and using a lighter lead and a critically balanced pop up. Apart from during the winter when we want our hookbait to stand out, we would not normally use pop ups that often, as

we prefer a more natural presentation of the bait (that is, on the lake bed). However, when presenting a bait over a weedbed, or in fact any other form of debris, it is important that the point of the hook does *not* get caught up, and the most effective way of achieving this is to pop the hook up above the weed. By using a long link you can afford to let the lead sink a little way into the weed, and if a critically balanced pop-up is used, the bait should slowly sink down until it comes to rest on top of the feature, well after the lead has landed.

If you want to be extra safe, you could adopt the debris dodge rig alongside the critically balanced hookbait. To use this method, all you need to do is PVA a second pop-up to your already critically balanced bait. This will be enough to hold the hook above the lead until the PVA melts, and the bait will then sink slowly down until it comes to rest on top of the weed. The height the bait is popped up off the weed should depend on the type and depth of the weed (*see* Fig 30).

More Complicated Rigs

The rigs above cover 95 per cent of our fishing, but occasionally a more complicated set-up is required to overcome conditioned behaviour of carp. In this circumstance we would adopt one of the methods of presentation as described below.

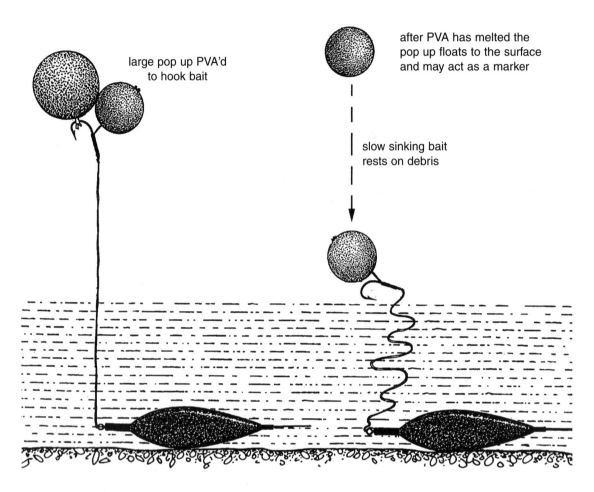

large pop up PVA'd
to hook bait

after PVA has melted the
pop up floats to the surface
and may act as a marker

slow sinking bait
rests on debris

Fig 30 Debris Dodge Rig.

NOTE: Before anyone starts to complain, this chapter is not meant to be an advertisement for Kryston products. However, we can only comment on the tackle we use, and we have never had cause to look further than Kryston for all our needs.

Snakebite/Snakeskin Variations
One of the latest successful rigs is the combi link, but it used to be difficult to tie, as the two materials were not always compatible with each other and often parted company. When Snakeskin was brought out, however, a whole new range of rig connotations was made available.

A standard combi link is now child's play, as all you need to do is peel back the plastic coating – not only can a standard combi link be made, but all manner of variations. Here are some of the ones that we have used to good effect:

- *Combi link with stiff hair* Simply peel back a couple of inches of coating but leave the plastic coating on the hair, and you have a stiff hair which gives a different presentation effect as the hook moves exactly where the bait is blown (*see* Fig 31).
- *Bristle rig* When you peel the plastic coating back to create the combi effect, start about an

1in (2.5cm) from the hook and peel back 2in (5cm) of plastic coating towards the swivel. If you attach the hook by way of a knotless knot, and tuck the link back through the eye, you will leave a stiff bristle 1in long next to the eye of the hook that will help prevent ejection of the rig.

- *Stiff link variations* Do not peel any of the coating off and you have a straightforward stiff link. Alternatively, peel back ⅜in (1cm) or so at either, or even at each end, and you have a hinged stiff link that will give you the anti-eject properties of a stiff link, with the presentation properties of a supple link.
- *Broken back rig* We have found this rig to have excellent anti-eject properties. To set it up you

simply peel back and break off ⅛in (2mm) of coating near to the hook, then about ⅜in (10mm) further along, break the coating again but this time do not peel anything off. This should allow the link to move freely at two points, and ejection will therefore be difficult for the fish.

Helicopter Hook Rig

This one should raise a few eyebrows, because to set-up the helicopter hook rig you do not tie the hook on. The whole idea is that the hook is free to spin around on the hooklink, and this enables it to take hold in the mouth of the fish when the line is tightened on a strike. The way the hook is

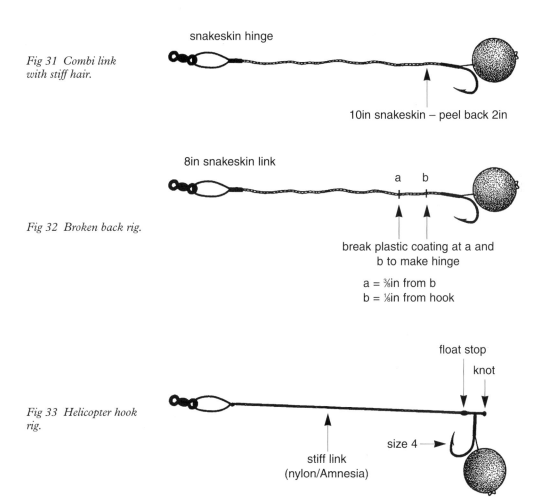

Fig 31 Combi link with stiff hair.

snakeskin hinge

10in snakeskin – peel back 2in

Fig 32 Broken back rig.

8in snakeskin link

a   b

break plastic coating at a and b to make hinge

a = ⅜in from b
b = ⅛in from hook

Fig 33 Helicopter hook rig.

float stop

knot

stiff link
(nylon/Amnesia)

size 4

attached acts as a line aligner, and the hook bites home every time. It only really works in conjunction with a stiff link of either Amnesia, Snakeskin or stiff nylon, and the larger the hook, the better it works. We feel that a size 4 is the most effective, as the eye is big enough to allow the hook to spin round freely, but the hook is not so big as to be glaringly obvious. This rig should only be used with a bottom bait; a critically balanced or buoyant bottom bait is best, as it counters the weight of the hook and the hooklink. Most of our fishing with this rig has been done in France where we could keep it secret, and fish to over 30lb have been landed on it. First place a float stop on the link, then thread the hook on. Tie a secure knot in the end of the link, then glue it to make sure it holds. Obviously the knot should be larger than the diameter of the eye of the hook, and as long as it is, the hook will not fall off. At the other end, tie the swivel on with a loop knot so that the link is free to move at that end, thus increasing movement. We would use this rig as another alternative when things are getting hard (*see* Fig 33).

Trigger Rig

We only use this rig if the carp we are trying to catch are known to back off with the bait in their mouths, testing for the pressure of the lead. We invented it in 1990, but have kept it a closely guarded secret, telling only two other people about it. It is quite a simple idea, but complicated to tie and set-up, as you must get everything absolutely right or it will not work correctly. It does not cast very well and can only be used for short to medium range fishing, but it is deadly. However, *if you cannot master it, do not use it.*

We began to think about such a rig when we were fishing a lake and noticed fish picking up baits, then backing off with them before they would confidently take them. We tried lengthening the links and using confidence rigs, but as soon as the fish felt the whole pressure of the lead, they would drop the bait. We felt that if we could come up with a rig that delivered an even pressure as the fish was backing off, perhaps it would not drop the bait. Originally the idea came from the old tactic of putting sponge in the rod rings to keep an even

pressure on the hook, and after much playing around, we came up with this rig which we christened the 'Trigger Rig' (*see* Fig 34).

As its name implies, it works on a trigger principle: when the fish backs off with the link, it stretches a section of pole elastic within the rig, which is in turn released from a clip; this results in the elastic contracting rapidly, hooking the fish in the process. Here is one example of how to set-up the rig: tie up a normal line aligned hooklink of just over 10in (25cm) long, but about 3in (8cm) in from the hook, tie a Drennan or Nashy ring. Take a 7in (18cm) length of stiff plastic tubing (the sort that you get with in-line zipp leads is ideal) and a short length of pole elastic. Experiment with the length of the pole elastic until you have got a piece that, when tied to the swivel and the ring, will stretch to about three quarter capacity when pulled the length of the tubing.

When you attach the hooklink to its swivel, use a diamond-eye swivel, or alternately, very lightly squeeze the eye of the swivel so that it will fit firmly into the end of the tubing. Be very careful not to damage the swivel at this point – it only needs a very light squeeze to make it fit. The fit must be tight, however, as if it is too loose, the swivel will pop out of the tubing and the rig will trigger in flight or when it makes contact with the water; obviously the effect will then be lost. Make a small nick into the end of the tubing closest to the ring, and pull out a little flap that the ring can hook onto. Slide the hooklink knot round to the side of the swivel, and then push the tubing onto the swivel so that it is firm and will only pull off with a good tug. *Do not* glue the swivel into the tubing, as this must be able to come off in the event of a crack-off, or the fish will have to tow the tube around with it. *This is very important.*

Once the swivel is securely fixed, pull the rig tight so that the elastic stretches to allow the ring to hook up on the flap of tube that you cut earlier. Push the swivel and the end of the tube into a rubber gripper. Now place this over a Nash safety clip or an in-line lead – and you are ready to go! The rig cannot tangle in flight as the tubing holds it clear, and if it triggers in flight it will still be effective as a rig, albeit a somewhat

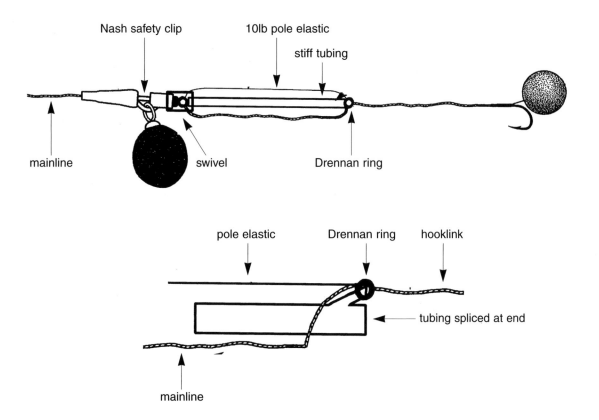

Fig 34 Trigger rig – for shy feeding fish.

conspicuous one with all its plastic tubing and elastic. In reality it hardly ever triggers in flight, as the hook itself has first to be pulled to unclip the ring from the plastic.

The lead is a vital part of the rig, and it must be as heavy as possible so that it is not dragged along, preventing the elastic from triggering. We normally use at least a 5oz (140g) lead, and it must be semi-fixed as a safety factor. As an extra safeguard against tangles, and also one which will help prevent the rig springing in flight, PVA the loose hooklink and the elastic to the stiff tubing.

Where conditions and situations allow, this rig can be very effective, but you must take the time to get the tuning of it right. Too stiff an elastic will mean that the rig will never trigger and the fish will just pull against a heavy lead; too light, and the rig will trigger too often.

Bait Application Through the Rig

While the main object of the rig is to present a bait to a feeding carp, it can also be used as a means of bait application. For most people this would mean by way of PVA dissolving string, bags or tape, but the possibilities are not just limited to PVA; there are numerous methods of putting bait into the swim using the rig, and as they affect the way your rig works, we will discuss them within this chapter.

First let us consider some of the methods that we have used to good effect on both easy and pressured waters. It is also important to consider the effect of putting bait into your swim; this subject has been covered in more detail in the bait application section, but do give it appropriate thought, because if you do it wrong it is one way to spoil what might otherwise have been a good result.

In the context of this chapter, bait does not mean just boilies: it encompasses liquid feeds, attractants and flavours, as well as mass particles and dissolving baits such as the ball pellet. One of the best ways to induce a carp to feed is to fill the swim with a food message that will stimulate its taste and smell receptors; but then give it only a limited food source so as to provoke competition between it and its rivals. This is best achieved by way of a dissolving bait such as ball pellet, or one of the liquid flavours and stimulants available, although with the latter there is the logistical problem of getting it into the water. We have found the following to be very effective ways of combating this problem:

- Attracta-lead-capsules are an excellent way of getting a flavour message into the swim, but for some reason not that many people use them. Nevertheless, they are easy to use, cheap to buy, and very effective in the winter months. Liquid flavour is injected into the capsule, and as the latter dissolves, the flavour slowly leaks out into the area around the lead. Use a blend of stimulants of a different density, as they will disperse to different depths of the water; one flavour alone may be dense and just lie on the bottom of the lake. Ideally you want to fill the whole area with the food message. Do tank tests to recognize at what level of the water column your attractants will sit.
- Another way of filling the swim with flavour is to use a swimfeeder instead of a lead and fill the feeder with sponge or a piece of foam. All you need to do is to submerge the foam in an attractant and squeeze out the air. As it expands again, it will suck in the attractant (minamino and carpmino is ideal) and release it once it is cast out into the swim. As well as liquid attractants, you can use all manner of other things in a feeder: 'The Method' is one example, ideally suited to lakes with a large population of hungry carp; and don't forget the matchman's tactic of filling a feeder with maggots – an absolute winner in the right situation.

Whilst on the subject of foam, another strategy is to use an earplug on the hair instead of a boilie. The method is exactly the same as with the swimfeeder, and is best fished as a single bait in the winter months, brightly coloured and highly flavoured.

- Ball pellets can be incorporated into your rig in a number of ways. Firstly they can be fished on the hair instead of a boiled bait, as their flavour leakage properties are excellent; they do need to be tied into a piece of stocking, however, as they will obviously break down and dissolve if they do not have something to keep them together. Make sure that the stocking is very tight around the pellet, or you will be left with a sloppy mulch. As the ball pellet takes in water, it swells and continually gives out tiny food particles through the mesh of the stocking. When tying the rig, use the same method as you would to combat the problem of crayfish.
- You can use your rig as a vehicle for transporting pellet out to your feeding area. This can be done by way of a stringer, but it will affect the distance you can cast. Our preference is to drill out the pellets, then thread them onto the hooklink or the mainline just above the lead; this way they are in line and will cast a lot further than a normal stringer. You must ensure that if you thread the baits onto the mainline above the lead, a float stop or something similar is used to prevent the baits sliding up the line on the cast. Beware not to create a death rig, though, as this may stop the lead pulling off the line, for example, if you are using a shock leader. Finally, this rig should only be used in conjunction with fast dissolve pellets, because if they do not dissolve and clear the line as quickly as possible, you may find that the carp are attacking the wrong bait.

PVA and its Uses

The uses of PVA are endless, and there are many varieties around now in comparison with a year or two ago. Gone are the days when the only sorts available were Gardner string that you had to stretch before using, or the old Redmire string

Fig 35 Quick dissolve pellet threaded onto stiff link/Snakeskin. Dissolve times can be varied by drilling extra holes into the pellets.

Fig 36 Try to use alternative stringer methods of circles/clumps etc.

that didn't stretch at all and more often than not broke when you pulled it through the boilie.

PVA now comes in all manner of applications, and it opens up a whole set of options to the angler who is prepared to spend a bit of time setting up a rig. Everyone will have seen the effectiveness of the PVA bag of trout pellets method that took many waters apart in 1995–6 and if you have not yet experimented with the application of PVA, now is the time.

No Strings Attached

For most people, using PVA just means stringers, but carp are not fools and as this method has been around a long time now, they may have conditioned themselves to the fact that a line of five or six baits is dangerous to them. Thus even a slight change to the set-up might be useful, and may help to outwit the fish. For example, a dozen baits on a stringer can be very effective, because you are creating a small clump of bait that the carp may not associate with danger. Alternatively, instead of attaching the stringer to the hook at one end only, try attaching it at both ends thus making a circle of bait, or in the middle thereby creating two lines of bait. There are numerous permutations that can be adopted, and all will help to fool a carp that is used to seeing lines of bait.

One of the more effective stringer methods that we have adopted involves the use of mini baits of 8mm in size. Use a long hair with three baits on it, and then use a couple of stringers

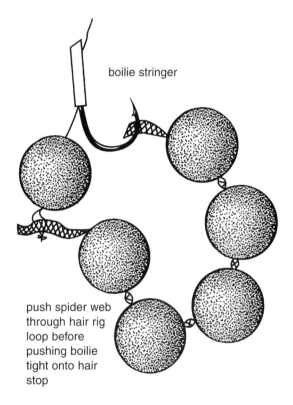

boilie stringer

push spider web through hair rig loop before pushing boilie tight onto hair stop

with the baits grouped in threes and fours on the PVA. This provides the fish with a small clump of bait that they will not recognize as dangerous, and it also makes it hard for them to differentiate between the hookbait and the freebies.

Another useful stringer method can be adopted when you fish the hinging hair rig. As previously mentioned, the hinging hair has a habit of swinging round the front of the hook in flight and the bait can snag on the point. The use of a ring or a small piece of tubing alleviates the problem, but you can also get over it by using an exploding stringer. Thread four baits onto a piece of stretchy PVA tape or string, then wrap them around the hair. Tie a knot in the tape so that the four baits are held tight to each other and also so that they hold the hair away from the shank. If you look at the rig from the bend of the hook, it should look like four baits in a square, with the hookbait sitting in the middle on top of them all. The stringer will stop the hair turning in flight, and when the tape dissolves and the tension is taken out of it, the baits will spring unevenly around the hookbait.

As far as types of PVA are concerned, your choice should be governed by your requirements. By that we mean that a stringer which has to be cast a long way will have to be strong enough to withstand the force of the cast. Alternatively, a stringer that is used in very cold water, will need PVA that dissolves easily in low temperature, as the rate at which PVA dissolves is affected by the temperature of the water around it. It is thus important that you make the correct choice of PVA – we have heard of occasions where anglers have reeled their rigs in after a winter's night, only to find that the stringer is still attached. It is useful therefore to have more than one type of PVA in your tackle box to cope with different situations as they arise. Our choice is for Kryston Meltdown for our distance fishing, and Nashy's tape for the other occasions. Meltdown is strong enough to be used at over 110yd (100m) with two bait stringers, and Nashy tape dissolves almost immediately upon contact with the water. The latter is also strong enough to be used for all but the farthest of casts and comes in a very convenient dispenser.

Clearly it is vital to keep PVA dry. Put it in a separate snap-seal plastic bag if possible, and always dry your hands properly when using it. We have wrecked whole spools by not drying our hands after catching a fish and then tying up a stringer.

It is interesting to consider the attraction properties of PVA: many flavours are alcohol based, and string is also made of an alcohol base, so when it dissolves, it will release a flavour into the surrounding area. This could work in the angler's favour, as the carp may recognize the smell of the PVA and remember that it only experiences that smell when there is food around. Alternatively it may work against the angler in that it may also remember that the food is a danger source, and the smell will then act as a repellant.

Finally, PVA tape can be put to good use when you are fishing over weed, in that you can wrap a couple of loops of tape around the point and the shank of the hook, thus masking the point and making it less likely to pick up debris and weed. Shortly after the lead has reached the lake bed, the tape will have melted and you should have a perfectly presented hookbait.

Bagging Up

As well as string and tape, PVA comes in stocking or bag form. These bags come in various sizes, from hookbait bags that will deposit a small clump of bait, to longer more aerodynamic rig bags that will take a lot more and into which you tuck the whole rig, including the lead.

The success of bags has been well documented in the press over the last few years, with the

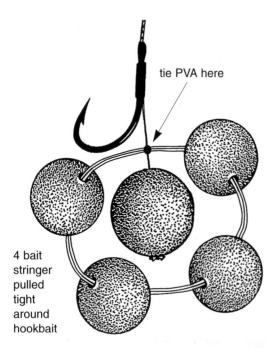

tie PVA here

4 bait stringer pulled tight around hookbait

ensure that PVA is pulled tight. Upon dissolving the four baits will shoot away from the hookbait in an explosive manner

Fig 37 Exploding stringer set up.

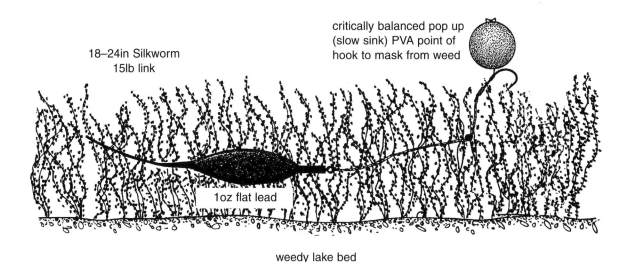

critically balanced pop up
(slow sink) PVA point of
hook to mask from weed

18–24in Silkworm
15lb link

1oz flat lead

weedy lake bed

Fig 38 Preferred presentation over weed.

pop-up and pellet method being the most popular, but this is certainly not the only one which is effective. All manner of baits can be put into bags and the only thing that you have to ensure is that the bait is dry. Bags lend themselves well to standard trout pellets, ball pellets, chopped boilies, micromass, mini baits, maggots and in fact anything else that is awkward to bait up with at any distance.

It is essential to take care how you attach bags, as they may leave a residue of semi-dissolved PVA round the rig, especially in winter when the water is colder. Do not knot the top of the bag or it will never melt. The best method is to wrap a bit of PVA tape round the top of the bag, as this will dissolve easily and let the water through to the bag itself.

Most people use a bag as a way of presenting a small tight clump of bait on the lake bed, but with a little bit of thought they can be used for much more than that. Think about the application factor and exactly how you want the presentation to look on the lake bed: to give you some ideas, we use bags in the following ways:

• In order to achieve the standard tactic of a tight clump of bait on the bottom of the lake, we would use stocking instead of a bag, primarily because the stocking will melt away much faster than a normal bag, and there is also less chance of it leaving any residue on the link. In addition, a bag will trap air inside, making it bulkier to cast thus reducing distance and also

Fig 39 Bagging up?

more prone to floating. If you do use a bag on the bottom, make sure to prick holes in it to let out the air – although in some situations it can be an advantage that the bag floats or just sinks slowly.

- Slow-sinking bags are excellent to use over weed. You should experiment with the size of lead that you need to use, just so there is enough weight in the bag to make it sink slowly down to the weed below. As your rig is completely contained within the bag, it cannot pick up any debris and tangle; also the speed with which it sinks can be adjusted by the number of holes that you punch into the bag.
- When it comes to using bags, the exploding sort are one of our favourites and there are two types which we use. If we want to spread bait

over a slightly wider area than we could achieve with a bag on the bottom of the lake, we will allow the bag to float after it has been cast out. Do not puncture the bag in any way, because when it melts slightly, the air pressure inside will cause it to pop, thus trickling the bait in from the surface of the water. The effect on the bottom of the lake is a scattering of bait, instead of a little pile. It is important to remember that the bale arm should be left open after you have cast out, to allow the lead to sink directly down on top of the free bait; if you tighten up, the lead will kite on the line as it sinks, thus moving it away from the baited area. This strategy is excellent if you are using irregularly shaped baits, because they will spread out a little as they sink.

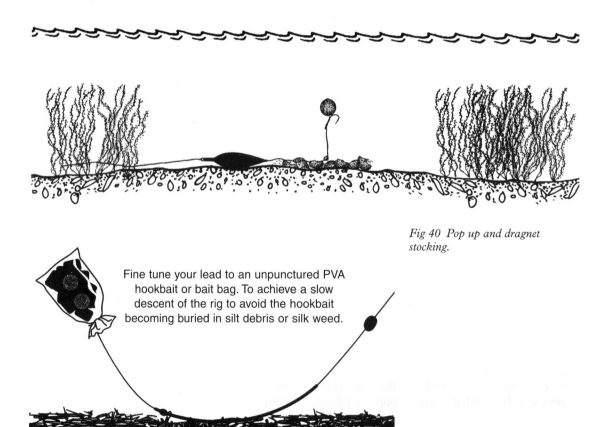

Fig 40 *Pop up and dragnet stocking.*

Fine tune your lead to an unpunctured PVA hookbait or bait bag. To achieve a slow descent of the rig to avoid the hookbait becoming buried in silt debris or silk weed.

Fig 41 *Critically balanced PVA bag.*

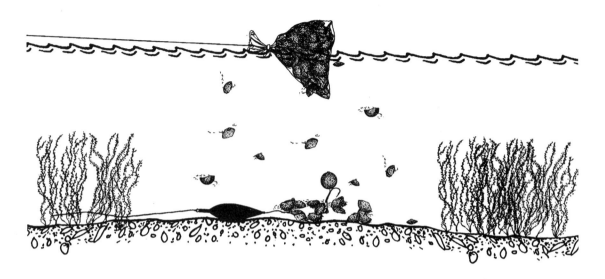

Fig 42 Exploding bag (floating).

(Right) *Waveney, a water which has seen it all over the last twenty years. An exploding PVA bag assisted with this capture for Simon.*

The other method is where a small hookbait bag is used and filled with very light baits; we have found that micro-mass, hemp and more particularly maggots, are deadly when fished in this way. The lead is not tucked into the bag, and is heavy enough to sink it so that it pops up off the lead on the bottom of the lake. If you are struggling to get the bag to sink, use a larger lead, or attach a stringer to the lead, but do not punch holes in the bag, for this reason: when an air-filled PVA bag melts, it explodes, a bubble of air being expelled as soon as the bag develops a weak spot. The advantage behind this, is that the bubble will suck up some of the maggots or hemp and expel them in a similar way to a fall-out cloud after a nuclear explosion. You will then be left with a scattering of freebies around a more concentrated area of bait.

6 EXPERIMENTS

In our opinion, if you want to put something into successful use, you need to know how and why it works. We have all had experience on the banks, and can learn a lot from that – indeed, there is no substitute for time spent on the lakeside, putting theories into practice – but if you have an understanding of how things work in the circumstances that you are going to be using them, you will be able to adapt and modify your tactics accordingly to make the most of a situation should things require it. For example, consider what you would do if you were fishing a lake at a range of 200ft (60m) with a bolt rig and you had taken a couple of fish already. Then the runs dry up and you find that you have now got to follow the fish out into the centre of the lake. You know from past experience at the fishery that the carp are quite wary, and tend to back off with the hookbaits to see if there is anything wrong with them, so you need to use an effective bolt rig that will come into play as soon as the fish tightens the line. The rig you are using does the job very well, but you are unable to get it out to the distance that the fish are now feeding at. You need to change your lead, so which one will you put on? You have got to balance the bolt effect requirements with the ability to get out to the required distance, but the wrong choice of lead might be more trouble than it is worth, as it may allow the fish to feel that something is wrong, before the lead has had a chance to do its job.

This chapter takes a look at a number of different angling scenarios and the options that you could choose to make the best of a given situation. Obviously the results are not conclusive, as most of the tests are bench tests and a natural situation may be slightly different and give a different conclusion. However, the results we have found do give you the general idea, and this should be enough either to start you thinking about the position a little more, or to prompt you into carrying out your own experiments to see just how effective your own fishing style is. Some of the results could have been predicted, but others are quite surprising and have certainly made us change our approach in a number of ways.

The main areas that we have looked at are as follows:

The importance of lead choice
- Casting effectiveness
- Effectiveness in bolt rigs

The hooking arrangement
- The pressure required for the hook to penetrate into a carp's mouth
- The effects of the line aligner
- The effect of the strike and baitrunner

The sensitivity of your set-up
- The effect of the angle of your rods
- Sensitivity generally
- The importance of using the correct indicator
- The effect of backleads on sensitivity.

All these topics have a major bearing on catch rates as they affect a number of points. If you think about the order of priorities, the fish needs first to be attracted to the bait, then to pick it up; and once it has picked it up, you need to be sure that it will get hooked. This is where the correct choice of lead and hooking arrangement is important – it is also one of the areas that many anglers fail to organize successfully. Sadly we see this time and again, where the angler has taken the trouble to get his bait and rig exactly right, but his bite indication is inadequate, and either he doesn't know that there *is* a pick-up, or by the time it is indicated on the bank the fish has found the sanctuary of some snags or weeds and will inevitably be lost.

All the component parts have to synchronize with each other and complement the set-up. For example, it is no good using a heavy drop-back indicator when you are margin fishing, and vice versa. This example is obvious, we know, but the number of times we are asked some very straightforward questions would indicate that a lot of anglers just don't give their strategies very much thought. Make sure that you give appropriate consideration to every part of your set-up, from the way the rods are positioned on the bank, to the manner in which the hook is attached to the hooklink.

Some anglers maintain that the way the set-up looks on the bank is of no particular concern, and that you should put your energy into making the last 12in (30cm) of it perfect; their contention is that it is only this last 12in that matters. This is absolute nonsense, and you should be concentrating on making sure that the *whole* of it is perfect – as it is no good at all getting the fish to pick up the bait if you don't know that it has done so.

We have already itemized the important points to consider: now we will examine them more fully.

The Importance of Lead Choice

How many different types of lead do you have in your tackle box, and how often do you put them to proper use? We consider that the majority of anglers' use the same lead for most of their fishing situations, and that although the lead is one of the best weapons in the carp anglers arsenal, they are rarely used to their full effect. A lead is more than just a tool for getting your hookbait out to where you want it to be: after the hook itself, it is the next major thing that a carp comes across once it has picked up the hookbait – indeed, in some situations it comes to the visual attention of the carp before it picks up the hookbait, and can be the factor that puts the carp on edge and stops

it from taking the bait in the first place. Some anglers use camouflaged leads in these circumstances, but is this the correct thing to do? We will see later that a coated lead slides more easily along some lake beds than an uncoated lead, and that this can affect its properties as a bolt rig. Furthermore it has been argued by one well known angler that leads do not need to be camouflaged because carp have got used to seeing old leads on the bottom of their lakes due to the ones that have been lost through all the years of angling. Our opinion on this subject is that most of the leads lost through crack-offs will have buried themselves in the mud at the bottom of the lake, and those that were lost through other means – for instance, line breakage as a result of snags or weed – may be accepted by the fish, but they will know exactly where they are and will have accepted them through conditioning and the passage of time. Therefore a new lead on the lake bed, even if it is a battered old thing that might look as if it has been there for ages, will not fool the fish. If the lead does not sink into the silt, disguise it – though consider how you will do this, as it may affect its other properties.

We will now take a look at the two main requirements of the lead, namely for casting and for the bolt rig effect.

The Casting Properties of Leads

The primary use of a lead weight is to get the hook and bait to the place that you want it to be. In addition to this and of about equal importance, is that it must be able to do so without tangling the rig. The main cause of a rig tangling in flight is that it has not been set-up properly by the user, although on occasions it is because an incorrect lead for the rig being used has been selected. This is the first reason for making the correct choice of lead.

The secondary use for a lead is that it can be a means of hooking the fish by way of the bolt effect. This aspect is covered in more detail later on in this chapter, and for the time being we will concentrate purely on the casting properties of leads.

Using the correct tackle, there is no reason why most capable anglers cannot cast over

The leads used for the experiments. From left to right: Arlesey, pear, ball, flat in-line pear, in-line bomb, and in-line square bomb.

120yd (110m). Not so long ago a cast of 100yd (90m) was deemed to be a good one, but these days that is really only average. However, it is not just the lead that is the important factor with distance casting, as the rod, reel and line all come into play. Again we go back to the point of balancing everything, so that each item of tackle complements the next.

Some leads are clearly more suited to distance casting than others, but it is often the case that anglers can be seen on the banks struggling along with the incorrect tackle, when if they changed their set-up only slightly they would easily make the distances that they are trying to cast. If you are looking to add a few metres onto your cast, here is what we found from conducting a simple experiment:

Experiment 1

Problem To evaluate the casting properties of various different styles of lead, and ascertain the best to use when intending to cast long distances.

Method A field was marked out into a casting area with marks placed at 50, 75, 100 and 125m distances. Each lead was cast six times and the distance measured to the nearest 10cm. The lead and rig were then removed and the lead was replaced with the next one that was to be tested. The same rig was used throughout.

The distance of each cast was recorded and the average was then calculated to ascertain the best lead for the purpose.

Equipment used The following items were used:

- KN Pursuit 2¾lb test curve rod coupled with Daiwa PM 7,000H reel
- KN Power Plus 12lb breaking strain line
- Kryston Quicksilver 25lb Shockleader
- Hooklink with 18mm boiled bait attached
- 50m tape measure
- Six different leads in 3oz (85g) weights:
  - Arlesey bomb
  - Ball
  - Pear
  - In-line bomb
  - In-line flat pear
  - In-line square bomb.

The leads were attached to the mainline by threading the line through the eye of the swivel in the case of the bomb, ball and pear leads, and through the centre tubing in the case of the in-lines. The eye of the swivel was pushed into the tubing of the in-lines to create a fixed-lead effect, and the others were left free running with only a bead used to buffer the lead against the hooklink swivel.

Variables The weather conditions on the day of the test would have had an effect on the results. The wind was light, blowing slightly across the field with the direction of the cast, but the conditions were constant throughout the experiment and therefore would have been the same for all the leads. However, the less aerodynamic leads would have their distances enhanced

Table 5. The casting effectiveness of leads.

Lead type	Cast 1	Cast 2	Cast 3	Cast 4	Cast 5	Cast 6	Average
Bomb	97.6m	100.0m	100.9m	98.6m	103.8m	97.8m	99.7m
Ball	82.1m	83.9m	85.7m	81.7m	82.3m	78.4m	82.3m
Flat pear	86.2m	81.2m	86.6m	84.2m	85.0m	84.8m	84.7m
Pear	84.8m	86.5m	88.2m	87.0m	86.4m	85.1m	86.3m
In-line bomb	91.1m	86.6m	92.3m	92.6m	93.2m	87.4m	90.5m
In-line square	89.6m	93.7m	91.4m	87.2m	92.6m	94.7m	91.5m

The average was obtained by adding together the distance from the six casts for each type of lead then dividing the sum by six. The experiment was conducted on 28 March 1997; weather conditions were dry and sunny with a light wind blowing from behind and across the casting field.

slightly more in calm conditions than the other leads as they would catch the wind slightly more.

When casting out, Rob tried to keep the pressure of the casts as consistent as possible (approximately 75 per cent of full strength) with all the leads. He did not attempt to cast as far as possible with each lead, as we felt that to do so would result in a greater margin for error than to use a constant pressure. Had more strength been used in the cast, the distances reached would have been greater on a pro rata basis for each of the leads.

Results The results are shown in Table 5.

Findings The main finding – and one which was not all that surprising – was that the aerodynamic leads flew further than the others. The ball lead, as expected was the worst out of all the leads, but what surprised us was the effectiveness of the in-line leads to cast reasonable distances. We thought that the in-lines would be a long way behind the others, as the pressure of the rig pulling on the nose of the lead should, in theory, have slowed the lead down a little. It may be the case that it did, albeit by a negligible amount.

The results of the test were as follows, and the average distance the leads were cast is also given:

- Arlesey bomb, 99.7m
- In-line square, 91.5m
- In-line bomb, 90.5m
- Pear, 86.3m
- In-line pear, 84.7m
- Ball, 82.3m

All of the leads were fairly accurate and stable in flight, although the in-line flattened pear was the worst in this regard. The Arlesey bomb out-performed all the others and is clearly the best choice for distance fishing.

Conclusion Lead choice is a vital aspect of distance fishing, and even over 100m the correct choice of lead can add up to a massive 17m to your cast. If you couple that with the correct line, an appropriate rig and a good technique, there is no reason why you should not be reaching those enormous distances that you see other anglers attaining.

We mentioned earlier that the rig makes quite a difference to the distances that you can reach. As a reminder, the difference between long and short rigs can be seen in Fig 43, and this is just more evidence that you should match the rig to the situation you are fishing. A 12in link may be suitable for a cast to the near island, but if you have to wind up to get it out to that open water

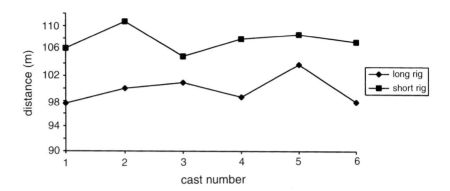

Fig 43 The casting effectiveness of long or short rigs.

mark, change the rig put the correct lead on, fix on a smaller bait and sling it to the horizon. It will pay dividends. (*See* the rig section for further information on this experiment.)

The Effectiveness of Leads in Bolt Rigs

Bolt rigs in the form of fixed or semi-fixed leads are used by the majority of anglers in a number of different situations. It seems that the current trend in rig design is towards fixed-lead set-ups, but just how effective are they? Having conducted a previous experiment into the amount of pressure it takes to hook a fish, we thought that we would look into the effectiveness of leads when they are used in a bolt rig situation. We have seen the rigs of many anglers when they are attempting to use a bolt rig set-up, and their choice of lead has in fact severely compromised the effectiveness of the rig, and has sometimes even hindered it by the use of a lead which is incorrect.

It is imperative that every aspect of your rig accords with the reason it is being used. For example, a 1oz (28g) lead is next to useless as a bolt rig, because it does not have sufficient bulk to prick a fish. We have found through practical experience that a lead of at least 3oz (85g) is needed in a bolt rig, and its shape is also vitally important. Different leads behave in different ways, and again, your choice should be governed by applying thought to the situation and the effect that you are trying to achieve, as opposed to a quick delve into the lead box using the first lead that you pick out. Sometimes there will be

more than one factor that will cause you to make to your choice. For example, while you may want a bolt rig effect, you may also need to cast a long distance, so you will have to sacrifice some of the effectiveness of the bolt rig in favour of being able to cast the lead the distance required.

Experiment 2

Problem To test the effectiveness and efficiency of different lead weights when used in a bolt rig situation.

Method A tank of water was set-up with a simulated lake bed (firm silt). The effectiveness of different leads in an aquatic environment was tested by simulating a carp picking up the bait and moving off in four different directions. The amount of pressure required to move the lead positively along or off the lake bed was recorded. Movement is defined as follows:

- *Along the lake bed*: the lead moves its whole length along the lake bed, the hooklink having been pulled parallel to the bed of the lake.
- *Turning the lead*: the pressure that is required to turn the lead through 90 degrees while not moving its position.
- *Pulling at an angle*: the pressure taken either to lift the lead through 45 degrees, or to move its position on the lake bed when the link is pulled at an angle of 45 degrees.
- *Lifting the lead*: to simulate the fish picking up the hookbait, and the hooklink straightening vertically.

Fig 44 Bolt rig test.

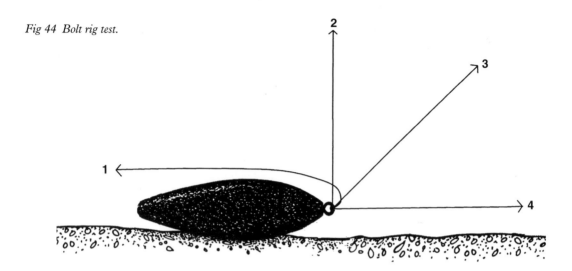

Each exercise was carried out four times, and the mean average of the tests was calculated.

Equipment used The following equipment was used:

- Tank and water
- Salter scientific spring balance
- Silkworm hooklink
- 3oz (85g) lead weights of the following six types: Arlesey bomb, in-line bomb, pear, flat in-line pear, ball, square in-line bomb.

Variables Allowance must be made for the fact that the tank was shallower than the environment in which the rig would be used during a normal fishing session, in so far as the pressure on the lead caused by the depth of water would very slightly increase the effectiveness of the lead.

The simulated lake bed used in the experiment attempted to duplicate a relatively firm area of silt which would not allow the lead to sink in. Allowance must also be made for the different types of lake bed over which the bolt rig might be used; thus the results would have been different had an alternative bottom been used, although the effect of each lead could be gauged fairly accurately as the same scenario was used for all types.

A certain margin for error within the equipment must be allowed, although materials and

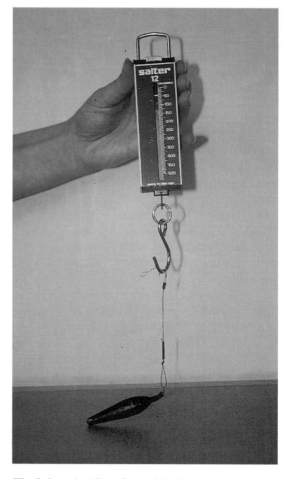

The Salter scientific scales used for the experiments.

equipment were used which were guaranteed as accurate as possible. The scales were loaned to us by the Science Department at Nottingham Trent University.

If the lead is left in the silt after it has been cast out, the bolt effect of the lead is superseded by the pressure it takes to pull the lead out of the silt. Some leads will bury themselves further than others, and when this happens, the bolt effect is caused by the pressure it takes to pull a lead out, not the lead itself. Leaving the lead in the silt will of course increase the bolt effect dramatically, but if you choose to use this tactic, be careful that you can get an indication that there is a fish on. A carp could quite realistically hook up on the rig and then eject it, or pull itself off the hook as it cannot pull the lead out of the silt.

Results The results are shown in Table 6.

Findings The effectiveness of each of the leads would depend very much upon the way the fish took the bait and moved off with it. In all experiments conducted the effect was at its greatest when the fish would pick the bait up and the hooklink straightened vertically above. This gave a direct vertical pull on each of the leads, and almost immediately its whole weight was brought into effect. However in this situation, the bomb and the pear lead would give the fish an indication that something was wrong before the lead was effective enough to prick the hook home. The reason for this is because the bulk of the weight is situated towards the rear of these leads at the end which is farthest away from the swivel, and the fish would be lifting the light end of the weight, not the heavy end. This would almost certainly allow the fish time to eject the hook. Both of these leads are less efficient for use as a bolt rig unless the fish picks up the bait and swims off with it at speed so as to reduce the time between the first time it felt the weight of the hook and the time the whole weight of the lead came into effect.

Where we have simulated the fish backing off along the lake bed causing the lead to be pulled along, all the leads should in theory have the same results as they are all the same weight. However, friction comes into play here and we found that the leads that were coated with plastic lead camouflage coating slid along the bed of the lake better as they reduced the friction factor. This was substantiated in that the three coated leads did not perform as well as their uncoated counterparts in this part of the experiment. Furthermore, this movement was also affected by the shape of the lead, in that the flat leads tended to move more easily than the rounded ones. Our thoughts behind this are that in the situation of a silty bottom, a rounded lead will sink in slightly more than a flat lead, thus increasing friction. The less the surface area of the lead, the more pressure there will be on that smaller area, thus making it harder to pull along.

Table 6. The bolt effect of leads: the force needed to complete the movement.

Type of lead	Pulling along lake bed	Turning lead through 90°	Lifting lead	Lifting at 45° angle	Total
Bomb	25g	12g	44g	39g	120g
Ball	30g	10g	75g	40g	155g
Flat in-line pear (coated)	17g	21g	55g	37g	130g
Pear (coated)	20g	14g	34g	30g	98g
In-line bomb	27g	12g	53g	46g	138g
Square in-line bomb (coated)	18g	25g	62g	35g	140g

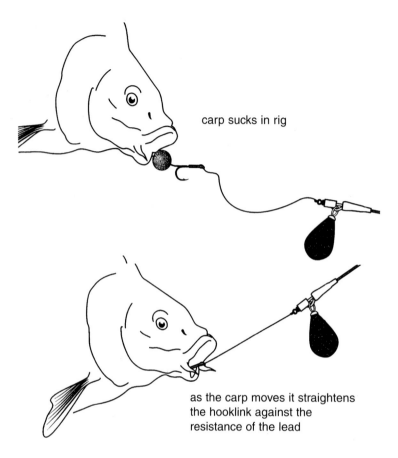

Fig 45 Think about how the fish size and strain will affect your rig.

carp sucks in rig

as the carp moves it straightens the hooklink against the resistance of the lead

The worst scenario from the angler's point of view was where the fish would have picked up the hookbait and moved through 90 degrees without lifting the lead at all. Neither the weight nor the friction factor came into effect much at all here, and the rounded leads tended just to roll around through 90 degrees without having any effect. The best leads in this situation were the flat ones.

As far as the general bolt rig effect is concerned, leads with the weight towards the end where the hooklink was attached were much more effective than those without. The others – the Arlesey bomb and the pear – were more suited to casting than to bolt rig effectiveness.

The final results were as follows, with the leads being listed in order of average all-round effectiveness as a bolt rig, taking the four situations into consideration:

- Ball
- Square in-line bomb
- In-line bomb
- Flat in-line pear
- Arlesey bomb
- Pear.

Conclusions When using a bolt rig set-up, ascertain exactly what you want the rig to do. Is it there purely as a bolt rig, or do you need to cast it a long way as well? For more information on this, refer to the experiment we did on the effectiveness of leads for casting. Generally speaking however, for maximum bolt rig effect, always use a ball lead, or where this is impractical due to the angling situation – for instance, presenting a bait on a slope – one which has the bulk of the weight towards the end where the hooklink attaches. If you want to fish a bolt rig

Fig 46 The most effective short-range bolt rig.

at a reasonable distance, we have found, both from field tests and actual angling situations, that the square in-line bomb type is the best all-rounder.

Many people think that bolt rigs are not really necessary and are hardly effective. We have conducted a number of tests into the pressure that is required to hook into the simulated mouth of a carp. The results (which can be found in the next section) make interesting reading when considered in conjunction with this section.

Overall Conclusions on Lead Choice

We have seen in the foregoing experiments that lead choice is vital in a strategy for success, the only problem being that the requirement for a bolt effect and the need to cast long distances are at odds with each other. What do you do if you need to fish a bolt rig at ultra-long distance? The answer is that if you need to get out to the fish and you cannot reach them with your normal bolt rig-set-up, you have no choice other than to put on a distance lead and compromise some of the bolt effect. You could compensate for this loss by not pulling the lead out of the silt, in which case you will have a very effective bolt set-up. The other option is to pull it out, and then fish a very tight line between the hook and the rod tip. Put the line into a clip near to the reel and this in itself will act as a bolt factor.

If you think about the situation that you are in and apply your mind to what you want to achieve, there are a number of methods to reach that goal; but do not ignore the fact that leads are a very important part of your set-up and the wrong choice may cause you to lose fish.

The Hooking Arrangement

Once you have induced a fish to pick up the hookbait, it is important that the hook takes hold. We have seen that the lead plays a vital role in hooking a fish, but a number of other factors are also crucial if your strategy is to be successful. The hook can make all the difference between a result and a failure, so bear in mind the points regarding hook choice mentioned in the rigs section: once again, we emphasize the importance of matching your equipment to the situation that you are fishing – this is the whole ethos of strategic carping.

In order to hook a fish successfully there are four stages to consider:

- The pressure needed to hook the fish in the first place;
- The effect of the method of hook attachment;
- The effect of the tension of the baitrunner;
- The effect of the strike.

Remember that these points can work against you, as well as in your favour; thus too hard a strike, or too tight a baitrunner set-up, can mean that the hook will be pulled out of the fish's mouth.

The Pressure Required to Hook a Fish

We will all have had the experience where we get a run, but when we strike we feel the fish for only a couple of seconds before the line goes slack; upon examination we see that the hook pulled for no apparent reason. This situation can occur for a number of reasons: first, the fish may not have been feeding confidently enough for the hook to have been taken far enough into the mouth; this can be rectified by a change in the rig (*see* 'Rigs' section), or the baiting strategy you operate. Alternatively the fish may have taken the bait fully into its mouth, but if the hooking set-up was not very effective the hook may have only just nicked the skin inside the mouth. This can be rectified by a change in the hook attachment (*see* the next experiment), or again the rig itself. Finally the set-up may have been correct, but the flesh in the fish's mouth was either too tough for the hook to penetrate properly, or conversely, too soft so the hook pulled out of the flesh as soon as it was put under pressure.

We wanted to conduct an investigation into these factors, but obviously it would have been improper to have conducted it on live fish. We therefore used items which we felt reasonably represented the scenarios we wanted to emulate, and ones which we hoped would give us some idea of the pressure it would take to hook into the mouth of a fish.

Experiment 3
Problem To ascertain the amount of pressure needed for a hook to penetrate the mouth of a carp, and to consider the a difference in pressure required to penetrate a firm and a soft mouth.

Method What materials to use was the first problem, but after many hours of looking at both man-made and organic possibilities, we decided upon the following:

- Soft mouth: banana skin
- Medium mouth: lemon
- Tough mouth: cabbage.

We appreciate that the materials were not perfect, but the only thing that *would* have been was the mouth of a real carp and we were not prepared to use that, even in the name of science!

We set-up a rig and, using exactly the same rig with each item, measured the amount of force it took for the hook to penetrate the object. Three measurements were recorded, namely the pressure taken for just the point to penetrate, then as far as the barb, then for the hook to bury itself

to the bend. Each experiment was repeated three times, and the average pressure was calculated and is recorded in Table 7.

Equipment used For the experiment the following items were used:

- Banana
- Lemon
- Cabbage
- KN pattern 1 size 8 micro-barb hook
- Kryston Silkworm 25lb hooklink
- Salter scientific spring balance.

Variables Of course the exercise is only a simulation, and a natural scenario may result in different findings. In addition, the categories of tough and soft mouths cannot be accurately defined, and indeed in the natural environment there would be no way of fixing these categories. Nevertheless, the items used were as near as we could get to give a situation that would provide constant pressure throughout the penetration. However, account must be taken of the fact that as the hook penetrated further into the banana and the lemon, the flesh inside was softer and therefore easier to penetrate. It is not known whether this is the case with carp.

The effect of the pressure of the water would also have to be taken into consideration, as these tests were carried out on a bench and not in an aquatic environment.

Results Table 7 shows the results of the experiment, which was carried out with only one pattern of hook. Other patterns may be easier or harder to penetrate as the gauge of the wire, its size and the sharpness of its point will have an effect.

Table 7. The pressure required to hook a fish.

Mouth type	Prick	Barb	Full hold
Banana skin (soft)	30g	100g	130g
Lemon (normal)	40g	145g	255g
Cabbage (tough)	75g	170g	295g

Findings Obviously it was easier for the hook to penetrate the softer items than it was the tougher ones. But it is interesting to note that it took about twice the pressure to hook into the tougher cabbage than it did the softer banana.

If you consider this test in conjunction with the earlier bolt rig test, you will see that just to prick the barb home takes between 30g and 75g of pressure, depending on the type of fish you are trying to catch. The medium- and soft-mouthed fish would be pricked by most of the leads in the earlier experiment, but if you are fishing for tough-mouthed fish, the bolt lead you choose is demonstrably vital.

The amount of pressure required for the hook to penetrate past the barb is more than any 3oz (85g) bolt rig can give you, even in the case of soft-mouthed fish, indicating that a heavier weight should be used in this scenario. However, this does not mean that a hefty strike is required to bury the hook home: the effects of the baitrunner and the pressure that it exerts on the fish must also be taken into consideration. We did in fact attempt to conduct experiments with regard to this, but the number of variables was too great to record. This aspect depends on the type and model of reel, together with the setting of the clutch or the baitrunner. Generally, however, remember that the baitrunner also plays a part in the hooking of a fish, as well as the lead and the strike.

To bury the hook to the bend took between 130g and 295g of pressure, and this would only be achieved by a strike or the effects of the baitrunner, as just mentioned. Further consideration of this will be given later in this chapter.

Conclusions We hope the findings of our experiments will help the reader to understand the pressure required to hook a fish. There is quite a difference between a soft-mouthed fish and those with tougher mouths, so again we can only stress the importance of finding out about your quarry, as this will help you make a decision as to the tackle you should use. In addition to hooking the fish, the results can be applied to playing it, too, because if the hook was easier to

get in, it should in theory be easier to pull out. Care should therefore be taken when playing a fish with a soft mouth.

The experiment also indicates the importance of having a super-sharp hook for pricking purposes. Our hook was brand new, and use would have affected its hooking capabilities. Thus a slightly blunt hook might result in the loss of a fish because more force is required to penetrate the flesh. However, you must always balance this with the fact that a fine wire hook may pull out of soft flesh more easily than a heavier gauge model.

The Method of Hook Attachment

How important is the way you attach your hook to your hooklink? Many people might say that it is not that significant, as it is the hook itself which is crucial. Before the bent hook and the line aligner we might have agreed, but having seen the effectiveness of the bent hook when it was made public in the late 1980s, we immediately realized that there *was* more to effective hooking than just tying on the hook. For ethical reasons the bent hook was soon banned on many waters, and anglers had to think of an alternative: this was the line aligner, and there is no question as to its success. The knotless knot is also a favourite these days as it combines the effectiveness of the line aligner with being able to present a hook with no tubing or bulk in it.

In spite of the good results obtained by many using the line aligner or knotless knot set-up, there are still anglers who refuse to make use of this effective weapon. We decided, therefore, to experiment by comparing three methods of hook attachment in order to see which was most effective. However, we were immediately faced with the problem as to how to do this without using an actual fish. Most people use the finger test to experiment with the effectiveness of their rigs, but in our opinion this is next to useless: the effect of gravity on the bait will almost always turn the hook, and the bait would never hang straight down from the mouth of the fish in the way it does from the hand; moreover the water pressure would also have an effect on the behaviour of the bait whilst inside the mouth of the fish. For this reason we decided that the test must be conducted under water. We set-up a simulated carp mouth by lining a plastic glass with the skin of a banana; when submerged, this was a fairly good alternative and much more realistic than the finger test.

To get as accurate a reading as possible, we held the hooklink and simulated a fish backing off with the bait in its mouth. We also simulated the fish turning with the bait in its mouth, as opposed to just backing directly away from the hook. Each experiment was repeated twenty times with each set-up, an average was taken, and the information recorded in Table 8.

Problem To evaluate the hooking capabilities of the following methods of hook attachment:

- Line aligner;
- Knotless knot on its own;
- Straight attachment (palomar with hair tucked back through eye).

Method A tank was set-up, and a simulated carp's mouth constructed from a banana and a glass. Three rigs were tied by different methods (*see* above), but all were made of the same hooklink material and utilized the same sized hook and bait. The hairs were all the same length and left the hook at the same point, and the bait sat just off the bend of the hook in all instances.

The baited hook was placed into the simulated mouth of the fish. The end of the link was then held as if attached to a lead, and the glass was moved backwards to simulate a carp backing off with the bait in its mouth. The exercise was repeated twenty times and a recording taken of the number of times the hook penetrated the flesh of the banana skin.

The exercise was repeated, but this time instead of moving backwards away from the bait, the glass was turned to simulate a carp picking up the bait and turning as it moved off.

The whole exercise was then repeated three times with each method of hook attachment and an average figure obtained.

Equipment used For this experiment we used the following equipment:

- Water tank
- Glass
- Banana skin
- Hooklinks of Kryston Silkworm 10lb b.s.
- KN size 8 pattern 1 hooks
- Four 18mm boiled baits
- Rig glue
- Hooklink of 25lb Silkworm.

Variables The way the rig is set-up is the first variable. Our three rigs were identical in length, hook size, hair length and bait size. Any variation here would have given different results.

Braid material will also affect the results, as we found in the course of the experiments when we changed the braid. For example we were quite surprised at the ineffectiveness of the knotless knot (*see* later) so we set-up an identical rig but used 25lb Silkworm instead of 10lb Silkworm. This made a difference to the results, as did the addition of some glue to the 10lb b.s. hooklink near to the hook (*see* findings).

The simulated mouth is obviously one area that may affect the results, and the real thing may give a completely different conclusion. However, this method is much more realistic than the finger test.

Results Table 8 indicates the effectiveness of the hooking arrangement and shows the number of hook-ups for each attachment.

Table 8. The number of hook-ups for each hooking arrangement.

Attachment	Backing off	Turning
Line aligner	18/20	19/20
Straight	6/20	5/20
Knotless	10/20	8/20
Glued 1in (2.5cm) of link	14/20	12/20
25lb Silkworm	16/20	14/20

Findings It is clear that the line aligner was substantially more effective than the other methods, hooking up an average of eighteen times out of twenty on the backing off exercise, and nineteen out of twenty on the turning exercise. This was at least three times as effective as the straight set-up and 80 per cent more efficient than the knotless set-up when backing off. When turning, it was over twice as effective as the knotless set-up.

The knotless set-up was the second most effective method, being about 40 per cent more efficient than the straight set-up. However, we were concerned at these results because we have used the knotless set-up extensively and have found it to be quite effective in our fishing. The whole idea of the line aligner is that the line emerges from the underside of the hook and causes the hook to turn when it is pulled over the lip of the fish. This was not happening with the knotless knot while using 10lb b.s. Silkworm, because the braid is so fine that it did not have the thickness to turn the hook. In short, the braid was so thin, that it seemed as if it was coming straight off the eye of the hook. With this in mind we arranged an identical set-up but used 25lb Silkworm instead of 10lb and on repeating the exercise the results improved dramatically: instead of ten hook-ups when pulled straight, the rig was now effective in fourteen out of twenty tests and its success in hooking up while the

fish was turning was also improved, from eight to fourteen successful hook-ups out of twenty.

This left us with a problem. What if you are fishing in a scenario where a fine braid is required and you don't want to use a line aligner because it will make the hook more obtrusive? We then referred back to the 10lb Silkworm rig and applied some rig glue to the link nearest to the hook for a distance of an inch (2–3cm). We then formed it into the position where the link left the eye at the same angle as it would do if a line aligner had been fitted. After the glue had dried, we then repeated the test and found that in each scenario the performance of the rig had increased dramatically by over 100 per cent. However, the results demonstrated that the rig would still only hook up just over 50 per cent of the time.

The position in which the hook took hold was also interesting: when the knotless and the straight set-ups were used, it took hold in what would be the bottom lip and the scissors. The line aligner did likewise, but on a number of occasions instead of taking hold in the lip, it caught and hooked about an inch (2–3cm) inside the mouth, thus giving a much better hookhold.

Conclusions Always try to use a line aligner. They have been around long enough now for everyone to know how to tie them, and the

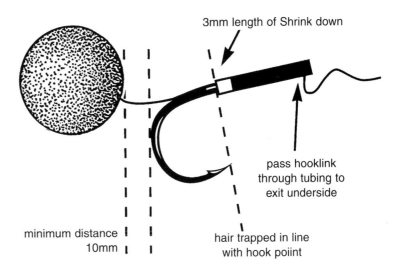

3mm length of Shrink down

pass hooklink
through tubing to
exit underside

minimum distance
10mm

hair trapped in line
with hook poiint

Fig 47 Line aligner.

results we found have just confirmed what we already knew. The line aligner set-up is infinitely better than the other two, and as near as you can get at the moment to a perfect hooking set-up. They can be used with most rigs and are effective with supple braids and stiff links alike.

There may be occasions when the addition of a length of plastic tube to your hook is the last thing you want. For example, when we fish over a clean sandy bottom in clear water we may abandon the use of tubing in an attempt to make the hook less conspicuous; however in this situation we would always use the knotless set-up, and will glue the link as well. If you are keen on using fine braids, bear in mind that they do not possess the turning properties of thicker braids and the addition of glue will help them to turn.

The Effect of the Clutch and the Strike

We have seen from previous experiments that sometimes the force of the lead is not enough to hook the fish properly. Traditionally the hook was always brought home by striking, but the effect of bolt rigs over the last few years has meant that the need to strike the hook home and therefore the quality of striking, was not what you might think it should be. Some anglers dash to their rods, lean over and strike the hook home with the force they would use if they were piking and had to strike a treble through a mackerel fillet at 100yd (90m). However, always remember to apply only the amount of force to the strike as is required for your fishing situation: too hard and you will only serve either to pull the hook out, or at the very least increase the size of the hole so the hook will probably fall out later in the fight anyway; too little, and the hook will not take proper hold and the fish will be lost.

Before striking, always consider the following:

- How far out you are fishing: you will need to gauge the strike to take up the slack line as quickly as possible to connect with the fish. The greater the distance, the more stretch in the line and the firmer the pressure required, but do consider the amount of slack line out there before whacking the rod in the air. If you

were fishing a tight line and the fish is taking line, there will not be much slack to take in and the force required will be less.

- How fast and in what direction the fish is moving. If it going directly away from you and taking line at a rate of knots from the baitrunner, the likelihood is that it is already hooked. Bear in mind how strong the clutch on your reel is set, as this will exert a great amount of pressure on the fish and the hook itself. The drag of the line in the water will also affect the amount of pressure on the hook, so more often than not, if a fish picks up a bait at distance and is taking line off the reel, it is already hooked.
- If the fish is coming back towards you, don't panic! Many anglers say they hate drop-backs because they rarely connect with the fish, but this is ludicrous, and there is no reason why you shouldn't connect with a drop-back. Simply gauge how fast the fish is travelling – you can do this by watching the speed with which the bobbin drops – lift up the rod and wind in the slack until you feel a contact with the fish, and give a firm but not too aggressive strike.
- If you are fishing slack lines and the fish is in the margins, you will need to strike the hook home, but be very careful when you do this, as the fish is likely to make an extreemly fast and powerful dash for freedom. Always ensure that the clutch on your reel is set correctly to below the breaking point of the line just in case.

We were interested to see just how much pressure was exerted at the hook end during the strike. Unfortunately we could not conduct this test under water so the results are not that realistic, but they will give you an idea as to the forces exerted on the hook during the strike. The experiment was conducted at a distance of 50m, although the pressure will be less if the distance between the hook and the rod is more than this. Furthermore a large proportion of the power of the strike will be used to lift the line out of the water, and also the line itself will act as a shock absorber because it stretches under pressure, thus reducing further the pressure felt at the hook.

Table 9. Striking at a distance of 50m.

Time of strike	Pressure
Immediately, on lifting the rod	1.1lb (0.49kg)
With rod at full curve	2.75lb (1.25kg)

Results The pressure felt at the hook can be seen from Table 9.

Conclusions First, there will be extra pressure exerted upon the hook from the baitrunner (if used) even before the rod is lifted. This pressure may be enough to hook the fish in itself, but once the angler lifts the rod and commences the strike (that is, when the rod tip starts to bend and the line is tightened to the fish) up to 1.1lb (0.49kg) of pressure is exerted upon the hook. Remember though, that the effect of the line being lifted through the water has not been taken into consideration and will lessen the force on the hook. The pressure of the strike increases until the rod reaches its test curve just past the vertical position (in this case 2¾lb/1.25kg on our Pursuits). If the rod is pulled back any further than this, the pressure increases according to the action of the blank, but the results will vary depending on the test curve and action of the rod you use.

Distance is the major factor when it comes to striking, as the longer the length of line between the rod and the hook, the more powerful the strike will need to be to lift the line out of the water and also to compensate for the stretch of the line.

Overall Conclusions on Hooking Arrangements

Probably the most important observation we made was that the way you connect the hook to the link is vital to success. The line aligner is without question the best method of attachment, and you should only deviate from this set-up if you really have to. It may be slightly more tricky to tie than the other methods, but it is well worth the effort. In addition, the force needed for the hook to penetrate the flesh of the carp's mouth varies according to the type of fish in the lake you are fishing, so always try to find as much about the

carp and their environment and feeding habits as you can. This will help you make the correct choice of tackle for the situation you are in.

Finally the strike and the baitrunner of your reel are also there to help you. If you use them correctly they will serve you well, but the wrong method of strike and of setting the clutch will only be a hindrance and will lose you fish. Choose wisely and make all these points form a part of your strategy.

The Sensitivity of the Set-up

It is vital to know when a fish has picked up your hookbait. In making such an obvious statement we might almost seem to be insulting the intelligence of the reader, but the plain fact is that while most anglers appreciate the need for a sensitive set-up, few make their own as sensitive as they could do. How many times have you seen someone get a single bleep, and ignore it or blame the wind? Alternatively, how often have you seen someone get a pick-up and express surprise when they strike into it because the carp is some distance away from the area they cast the bait to? If these scenarios sound familiar to you, then your own set-up requires some attention – it needn't be so insensitive that the fish can move a number of metres before you even get an indication that you have had a pick-up. Several things might cause this lack of sensitivity, but there are numerous ways of tweaking your set-up to make it register even the slightest action at the important end. Always consider the following:

- The angle of your rods and lines;
- The sensitivity of your alarm;
- The type of indicator you use;
- The way that you use that indicator;
- The use of backleads.

The importance of a sensitive set-up cannot be stressed enough, and we are convinced that a lot of anglers are not catching the fish they should because they are just ignoring pick-ups, or worse still, they don't even realize they have had one.

During the World Carp Cup 1996, we caught three fish that did not give us substantial positive indication. We use this term loosely, because any indication that you have which tells you there is a fish on the end, must be positive. In this context we will take positive indication as meaning a positive lift or tightening of the line that will register on the indicator and bobbin. (If you class positive indication as a scream on the alarm, or line being taken from the baitrunner, you have lost the plot somewhere). Those three fish in the World Cup gave a single bleep, a double bleep and one just gave a tip knock, but our set-ups were so sensitive that this could only mean one thing and upon striking the rod, we were proved correct.

In that competition, only sixteen teams out of fifty caught fish, although many stated that in spite of not having had any runs, they had experienced a couple of bleeps here and there. Did they miss out on fish? We will never know – although we *were* certain that those carp would be on edge as a result of all the noise around them, the pressure of 200 lines in the water, and all that bait being piled on top of their heads. Can you blame them for feeding cautiously? We think not.

The Effect of Angles on Indication

One of the surest ways to cut down the sensitivity of your set-up is to create angles between the hook and the alarm and indicator. By 'indicators' we mean the hanger, swinger and bobbin used to indicate a run. Electronic audible bite indicators are described as 'alarms'. Angles can

be created in both the line and the rod set-up, and both will compromise sensitivity quite dramatically. As an aside, we have actually seen it written that the most sensitive way of fishing is with the rod tip in the air, and quite frankly we are amazed at this statement. Fishing with your tips in the air reduces the sensitivity substantially, and unless you are going to stay up all night watching the rod tips for knocks, we would advise that you only adopt this method if you need to overcome another problem. For example if the fish are line shy in your lake, you can either pin the line to the lake with the help of a backlead, or you could raise the tips in the air to keep as much line out of the water as possible. Similarly, if there are snags and bars in your swim, or the margin in front of you has a large amount of weed in it, the tips-in-the-air method will help to overcome this problem. Finally, if you are fishing a heavy lead, it can be a deadly tactic to lift your tips in the air and tighten up the line so that the tip of the rod bends towards the lead. When the carp picks up the bait and shifts the lead, the tip will spring back, and this is often enough to hook the carp and send it bolting off on an impressive run. Other than these scenarios, the only function that tips-in-the-air will serve, is to reduce sensitivity.

Ideally you should level the rods out on your buzzer bars and pod so that the tips are pointing directly at the hook. This might mean having the butt of your rod higher than the tips in some situations, but it will increase sensitivity. Although the current trend is towards multi-rod set-ups,

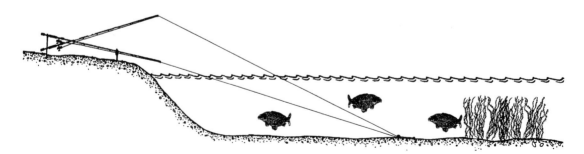

Fig 48 Cut down those angles as much as possible.

another way of increasing sensitivity is to splay the rods out on separate rests so that the line is running in a straight line from the reel to the hook. If you are using buzzer bars and not fishing directly out in front of you, when a fish picks up the bait and moves off, the tip of the rod will absorb some of the movement thereby reducing the sensitivity of your set-up. Sometimes this situation is unavoidable and if this is the case, make sure that you pay special attention to your rod tips: if you get even the slightest knock, hit it, because it may be a pick up.

As an interesting exercise, we simulated a scenario where a rod would be cast out into a swim 4ft (1.2m) deep. (The test was conducted in air not water, so although the ratio will be the same, the test was much more sensitive in air because the drag effect of the water was not present.) Once the rod was set-up and the lead in position 50m away, we angled the rod tip so that it pointed directly at the lead. We then measured both the distance the lead could travel and the pressure in grams that it took to cause the indicator to rise by 1in (2.5cm). We then lifted the rod tips to an angle of 30 degrees and repeated the experiment. As expected, the first set-up was the most sensitive, and it also took less effort to move the lead. This should be borne in mind when considering the hooking effect of the set-up.

Table 10. The effect of the rod angle on indication.

Rod angle	1in (2.5cm) indicator lift
Pointing at bait	60g per 4cm movement
Tips at 30 degrees	70g per 7cm movement

Results From Table 10 it is clear that when the tips were pointed at the bait, the lead could be moved some 4cm before the indicator lifted 1in (2.5cm), whereas with the tips in the air the lead could be moved 7cm before the indicator lifted 1in. This indicates that at a distance of 50m the first set-up is nearly twice as sensitive as the latter.

Before applying these figures to your fishing, remember that the experiment was conducted in air, not water. From Table 12 you will see that in water, at a distance of 70m, even with no backlead, the fish can move the lead 15cm directly away from you before there is any indication on the bank.

As far as angles within the line are concerned, these too are most important as they affect the sensitivity of the set-up. Such an angle could be caused by a natural factor such as the line passing over a snag or bar, or alternatively by the angler choosing to use a backlead. The subject

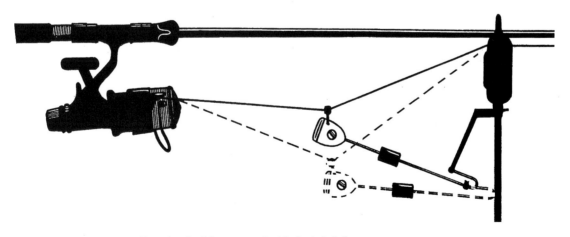

Fig 49 Always be aware of how far the fish can travel with the bait before even a 1in (2.5cm) lift is registered at the rods.

EXPERIMENTS

of backleads deserves a chapter in its own right, but whatever the reason for the angle in the line, it pays to reduce it, or if possible, to cut it out completely.

General Sensitivity Tests

Almost everything you do to your set-up will affect how it picks up an indication that something is happening at the business end. We next look specifically at the effectiveness of backleads and how they should be used correctly, and generally all the other ways in which the sensitivity of a set-up may be improved. As a starting point we set up yet another experiment. As far as we are concerned it is vital that we know immediately, or at least as soon as practically possible, when a fish has picked up the bait. Inevitably the fish will be able to move a short distance before a pick-up is registered on the bank, but the important thing is to aim to get this distance as short as possible. When you read the results of the experiments with backleads, you will no doubt be surprised at the distances fish can move in certain directions without us even knowing that they are there.

Our experiment this time again involved the use of a rod set-up at 50m. Once more the tests were conducted in the air, and not under water, so adjustments must be made for this deficit. (We will see in later experiments that the effect of water is to increase the distance moved by up to four times over a 70m distance.)

The rods were set up as they would be on the bank, fishing into a depth of 4ft (1.2m) they were angled so as to be parallel with a flat bank, i.e. not pointing directly at the lead, nor into the air. A Delkim T×2000i alarm was used on a sensitivity setting of two, and a Gardner Rangemaster bobbin without any weight was used to register the indication. (We wanted a bobbin as opposed to a swinger-type indicator because we feel these give a truer reflection of what the line is doing, they don't have to rise or fall in an arc.)

The lead was taken out to a measured distance of 50m, the line was tightened and the bobbin set as it would be in a normal fishing situation, with a drop of 4in (10cm). A set of scales was then attached to the hook, and the lead was pulled backwards as if a fish was running in a direct line away from the rods, until different levels of indication were given at the rod.

In order to test the pressure taken to cause a tip knock, we then lifted the tips back up to 30 degrees and the experiment was repeated to get the tip to move without making the indicator move or the alarm sound. The results can be seen in Table 11, though remember to add the effect of water to the results in reality.

Conclusion From this information we can conclude that even with the most sensitive of set-ups the fish can move a short distance without the angler realizing there is anything wrong. This test simulated a fish swimming directly away from the angler on a tight line; if it moves away at an angle or kites, the results are worse still from the angler's point of view. Sensitivity could be increased in a number of ways, such as improving the alarm, or using a different indicator. The alarm adjustment is self-explanatory, but the correct indicator system to use requires more thought.

Which Indicator to Use?

At one of our slide shows, an angler came up to ask our advice on some problems he was encountering. He was using Solar Quiver Loc indicators, but was finding that he was not getting very positive indication. This puzzled us, as

Table 11. General sensitivity tests in the air. A KN Pursuit 2¾lb t.c. rod was used at 50m casting distance.

	Tips in the air (tip knock)	Single bleep	Indication lift 1in (2.5cm)	Indication to top	Line off clutch	Screamer
Distance	2cm	2cm	5cm	18cm	20cm	25cm
Pressure	45g	25g	30g	50g	65g	70g

144

Solar indicators are excellent and we had not heard of any real defects with them that would mean they would fail to give the correct indication. On further investigation it transpired that the angler in question had cut the length of the indicator arm down because he fished his rods low to the ground and also because he thought they looked better (?). The lake he was fishing was quite well known, and the fish had seen a bit of pressure over the years. He was fishing at medium distance and the only indication he could get were a couple of bleeps. Some of these he hit and found that he would be connected to a fish, whereas others he would leave and either nothing would develop, or there would be nothing there on the strike. We considered that he was using the wrong indicator for the job as the customized arm was too stiff. The fish would pick up the bait and as it moved off, it would feel the pressure of the indicator and drop the bait. We advised him that in this situation, he should either go back to the original lightly tensioned arm, or change his indicator for a lighter one and fish it with quite a long drop.

Matching the indicator to the situation you are fishing is an important factor with regard to sensitivity, and one which you cannot afford to get wrong. Too many anglers use the same indicator everywhere they go and in whatever situation they are fishing, be it at distance or in the margins. Sometimes you can get away with the same indicator for a lot of your fishing if you adjust it properly according to the situation, but if possible, invest in another set to cover all eventualities. If you can only afford one set, consider the Wasp, which we have been using for a number of years now and which we find covers almost every situation. Springer-type indicators which double as swingers, such as the Wisp and the Quiver Loc, are also very good and superb value for money; a set of these, as well as a set of hangers such as the Gardner Rangemaster, will cover most eventualities and in fact all you will need to think about then is which one you should use in what situation.

As a rough guide, we would use the following indicators in the given situations.

- **Margin fishing and light lead:** As light an indicator as possible, with a long drop between the rod and the bobbin to allow the fish to move off without feeling any resistance.
- **Medium range, open water fishing:** Either a swinger or a hanger type set-up on medium tension and weight. The tension and the weight should be adjusted depending on the weather conditions and also the size of the lead used.
- **Open water, short to medium range, slack line:** A swinger set-up with no weight on the arm, and a long drop.
- **Tight line fishing to reeds and island margin:** A springer or a swinger set on medium to high tension and weight to register drop-backs. The fish will kite along the margin or drop back towards you, so you need to set your indicators to show this.
- **Long range:** A heavy indicator and high tension to keep the line tight and to register drop-backs. Position the indicator at the top of the drop, on a tight line in a clip. It must be heavy enough to show a drop-back and also to keep the tension in the line over a long distance.

The Effect of Backleads on Sensitivity

Backleads are, without question, a great tactical advantage in certain situations. They assist in concealing the line from wary fish by holding it on or near to the lake bed, and they also help to keep it out of the way of danger and to avoid tangles if there are a number of anglers fishing the same area. They can even be used in certain situations to assist the hooking effect of the lead: for example, if you are fishing with a 3oz (85g) lead and you fit a 3oz backlead to your line and fish it quite close in on a tight line so that it is not touching the lake bed, when a fish picks up the bait and moves the lead, the backlead will drop, thus acting as a type of bolt rig by exerting more downward force on the hook. However, this method does quite seriously affect the ability of your alarms to pick up slight twitches, and normally only the screaming runs will cause the indicators to sound.

There are disadavantages to backleads: many anglers use them all the time without giving a second thought to the fact that they might be pinning

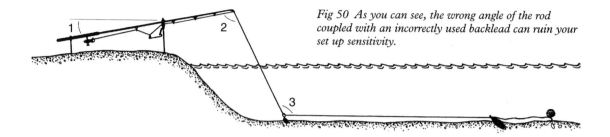

Fig 50 As you can see, the wrong angle of the rod coupled with an incorrectly used backlead can ruin your set up sensitivity.

the line down into obstructions such as weed or mussel beds; and as already mentioned, they do affect the sensitivity of a set-up even when they are used correctly. Use them incorrectly and they can have a drastic effect on any indication you might get (or not, as the case may be).

In order to test and illustrate the effects that backleads have on the sensitivity of a set-up, we carried out another experiment.

If you were carp fishing in 1993, you might recall an article that Simon wrote in *Carpworld* entitled 'Cutting down the Angles'. This related to backleads and also the other topics within this last section, but even after that thought-provoking article, many people still insist on using backleads incorrectly. This subject is a pet hate of ours, so to illustrate our point, the following experiment was carried out. It is also to try and educate those anglers who still insist on using backleads incorrectly.

Problem To test and record the effects of backleads on the sensitivity of a rod set-up.

Method For this experiment we needed the medium of water to ensure that the results were as accurate as possible. We therefore secured the use of a local authority paddling pool close to our homes to carry out the tests. Unfortunately we were only allowed enough time to conduct this particular experiment at the pool – we would dearly have liked to have conducted all our other experiments here but that proved impossible.

The pool itself was only 3ft (90cm) deep, but this was sufficient for our purposes. We set the rods up as we would in a fishing situation, and the hookbait was then taken out to a measured

distance of 70m. For the backleads we used two different weights of 1oz (28g) and ½oz (14g) and these were placed in two positions, directly under the rod tips in the margins, and the other a short way out into the pool. In order to get the backleads into this position, they were placed onto the line from the bank in the normal manner and the tip of the rod was then raised to let the lead slide down the line until it reached the water. The rod tip was then sunk and the line tightened as would be the case in a normal angling situation. At this stage we were approached by a woman who was out walking her dog, enquiring whether we had caught anything and what was in here, as her husband might like to visit. We did not have the heart to tell her the pool was a paddling pool. Wonder if he caught anything?

The next step was to simulate a take, and in fact we simulated four different pick-up situations, as follows: running directly away from the rod; running backwards towards the rods; running away at a 45-degree angle to the bank; kiting parallel to the bank. We repeated each simulated pick-up three times for each situation and calculated the average distance by adding all three together, then dividing by three. The exercise was then repeated for each of the four backlead positions, and then once again without any backleads on the line at all.

Variables The weather was calm on the day in question, so any effects here would have been negligible. The alarm sensitivity was the same throughout, so again there should have been no adverse affect here. The water being only 3ft (90cm) deep may have made a difference.

Table 12. The effect of backleads on sensitivity

Backlead and range	Running away	Away at 45 degrees	Kiting	Drop back
Heavy and medium	17cm	23cm	1,100cm	20cm
Light and medium	22cm	28cm	59cm	27cm
Heavy and close	26cm	61cm	174cm	27cm
Light and close	24cm	42cm	62cm	28cm
No backlead	15cm	20cm	38cm	19cm

Results The results are shown in Table 12.

Findings One of the first things we noticed was that whatever the backlead and wherever it was positioned, the sensitivity of the set-up was affected. Sometimes the effect was so great that a run would not be picked up by the alarm until the fish had moved a long distance. For an example of just how bad this effect can be before any indication is received on the bank, take a look at how far a fish can kite when a heavy backlead is used and slid out into the lake (by 'indication' we mean an audible sound from the alarms); this is almost certainly due to the fact that when the fish kites, it does so from the position of the backlead and not from the rod tip – the pick-up only registers when the fish has gone so far that the lead starts to move. So if you have encountered a pick-up while using a backlead and when you struck, the fish was a long way from where you cast the rod in the first place, this will be the reason why.

We discovered that the effect on sensitivity depended upon the way we moved off with the bait. If we moved directly away from the rods and the backlead was fished out from the bank, the effects on sensitivity were not that drastic; kiting or moving away at an angle had a dramatic effect, however, and the greater the angle, the worse the indication.

Drop-backs would register almost as well as takes moving directly away from the rods, and in the case of heavy leads, there was hardly any difference between the two.

Conclusions The best backlead to use in most situations was the light one. This was because it would still hold the line on the bottom out of the way, but it moved or lifted off the floor when the fish picked up the bait. A disadvantage is that the fish may be able to feel the weight of the backlead and might drop the bait as a result.

Another disadvantage of backleads is that they can pin the line down into such difficult obstructions as weed or a snag on the lake bed. Only use them if you really have to, when the fish are so line shy that they will not enter your swim if there are lines in it; and this case you could always rest the swim for a while to allow the carp to return. We have found this method to be effective on more than one occasion.

Yet another reason not to use a backlead is that the fewer angles you have in your line, the more sensitive your set-up will be. And if you have to use them, try to anticipate what the most likely take is going to be, as certain backleads work better in different situations. For example, if you are fishing up against an island margin, the likely indication is going to be either a drop-back, or the fish kiting along the margin. The best backlead to use in this situation would be a light one which you would slide out into the lake.

Overall Conclusions

Certain methods work better than others according to each situation; consider exactly what you are aiming to achieve, and how the situation might help or hinder you. By keeping your options open and applying the correct tactic to a given scenario, you will be able to gain the advantage in even the most difficult circumstances.

7 THE WORLD CARP CUP FISHABIL 1996

The World Carp Cup Fishabil 1996 was without a doubt an event with a difference. Never before had an angling match seen so much money spent on organization, nor had the sport of carp fishing ever received so much publicity. It was to be the first world championships of carp fishing, and the winners would be the team with the highest weight at the end of the contest. Radio stations and television companies from all over the world covered the outcome, and well over 20,000 spectators witnessed its happening. The event itself took place at the European Specimen Angling Centre (also known as Fishabil) in north west France, and lasted four days.

On paper, the match looked difficult for the fifty teams of two which took part in the competition: not only did anglers have to contend with each other, they also had to conform to tough rules and regulations, to draw for swims, besides battling against the hustle and bustle of the occasion itself – a very different scenario from the normal carp session for many. Both of the authors took part in the match as representatives for England, and for them, the outcome turned out to be the highlight of their angling achievements to date; it was an occasion when everything went according to plan and an experience which they will both never forget. Hopefully you will enjoy reading about their memories of that week as much as they did participating; but most of all, you will recognize some of the fundamental topics which need to be addressed when forming a strategy for success.

When a Dream Became Reality

On 22 May 1996 we set off from Britain for the town of Loscouet-sur-Mer, near Rennes in north-west France, to take part in the World Carp Cup at the world-famous Fishabil centre, a once river-fed water covering 50 acres (20ha) that had been sculptured into an 80-acre (32ha) angling centre towards the end of the 1980s. When we finally reached our destination the weather was extremely dull and overcast with a light rain; nevertheless there were still plenty of people rushing around outside the usually quiet Fishabil reception area. We checked in, and were greeted by the fishery manager Ludovic Dyevre who informed us that all participants in the match were free to do as they pleased until the next morning when the official ceremonies would begin; this meant that we had some considerable time in which to occupy ourselves for the rest of the day. We were very tense and excited about the event and we really did believe that we could win – most of the other contestants obviously thought they could, too; this conviction was certainly evident in one well known Essex angler who fishes France a lot, and who seemed determined to make his presence known with comments like 'Nash Bait Nil Points'. We chose to overlook the matter and laughed it off as just pure arrogance on his part; we prefer to let the rods do the talking.

Thursday Afternoon: Assessing the Water
Following a quick bite to eat, we decided to take advantage of the free hours by examining the lake and swims so as to know the best possible areas to select once the draw was under way. Although we had visited Fishabil on a number

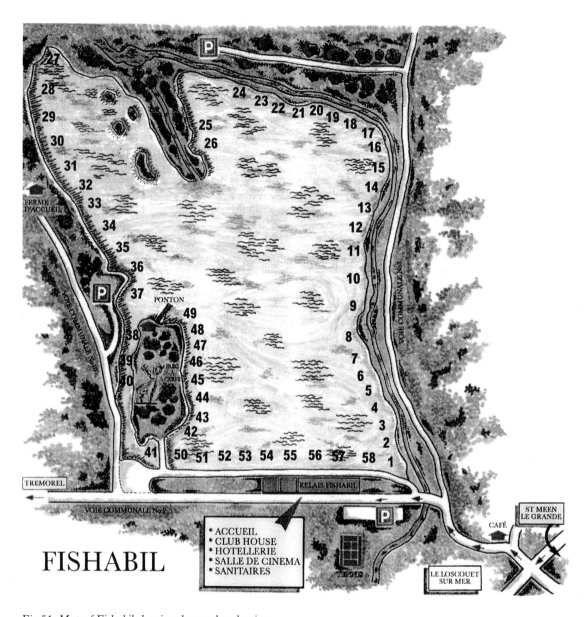

Fig 51 Map of Fishabil showing the numbered swims.

of occasions beforehand, we knew that swim selection would be a very difficult task due to the high stocking density which the lake possessed: not only would we have the draw to contend with, but the fish are usually very well spread, with only one or two areas holding large numbers of fish. It would therefore be a matter of finding the main bulk of the fish, and then hoping to be able to select a swim near to that area.

Experience told us that the fish would move on pressure, and for this reason our strategy was to opt for a swim where the main bulk of the fish would be at the beginning of the match. We considered the fish would be more vulnerable in the early stages than in the later, and the fact that the lake had not been fished by anyone for over a week meant that a good start was certainly possible if the correct swim could be chosen. In fact we had seen this pattern occur many times before at Fishabil during the *Carpworld* trips to the water, which trips involved thirty or so anglers fishing for almost eight days. At the beginning of the trips, the action would usually start off exceptionally well for one or two areas of the lake, but once the fish had become accustomed to the volume of pressure, the whole lake would normally begin to fish towards the latter half of the trip. The World Carp Cup was to last for only three days and nights however, and so it was quite possible that during such a short period, the water would not produce the widespread captures of which it was capable. The first couple of hours would therefore be crucial for the competitors, as thereafter the fish would begin to sense danger and move to the safer areas of the lake.

Our observations on the Thursday afternoon identified carp moving just off the north bank swims of 16, 17 and 18. We also noticed numerous fish moving in the normal no fishing zone where the island swims of 44–49 had been installed for the purpose of the match only. Anyone who has visited Fishabil in the past knows that this area is always full of carp. There are also one or two snags present along the island, and along with the island channel, these often act as the main 'safe' havens for the fish. Having visited all the swims individually, we decided to give each a rating of one to four, with four being a good choice and one a poor option. We also considered a handful to be chance pegs, as these covered the areas where fish might be held up in good numbers or where they might move to during the course of the match if weather conditions or pressure dictated. These swims were given a separate rating, to be selected if all our first choice swims were taken.

The weather on the Thursday was very changeable and it looked as if a wet forecast was in store. The wind had been blowing for a couple of days from the south-west, and following a quick call to the MET office we discovered that low pressure was indeed to set in for the rest of the week. The forecast of low pressure and south-westerly winds certainly made the north bank swims of 16, 17 and 18 look tempting, but the island swims of 44–49 had to be the better option due to the added bonus of the snags and the fact that they were not normally fished. From the island swims there was also a good chance of reaching the centre of the lake, another favourite 'safe' area of the fish. Thus our list of preferred swims at the start of the match read something like this: 47, 46, 45, 48, 49, 17, 16, 18, 37, and then came the chance swims of 24, 23, 41, 40, 39, 38 and 27.

The pads swim 24 at the far end of the north bank also looked tempting; it was here during the same week of 1995 that Simon banked over forty fish in two days during one of the *Carpworld* trips. It is always a successful swim at Fishabil when the frogs are spawning and the sun is shining, but an element of timing is required if you are to make the most of the opportunity. The low pressure and strong south-westerly winds meant that it was too much of a gamble as a top choice swim, however, so we rated it as a chance area which we would only select once the favourite swims had disappeared. It was our intention to win this match, and we had to assess every possible detail.

Friday Morning:
The Opening Ceremonies

Friday morning and the opening ceremonies soon arrived; a special marquee had been erected in the former deer park area of the island for both the opening and closing ceremonies, and on display here were some of the best cars in the world. The organizer Raphael Faraggi had acquired the backing of the leading car manufacturer Ferrari for the match, an achievement which clearly demonstrated the scope of the publicity the event had attracted. We were soon ushered into our seats by the officials, and following the formalities - which seemed to last a lifetime – the long-awaited draw for swims took place. The atmosphere in the marquee was incredible, with everyone tense and on edge. Michel Mahin, the President of the FFPC

The crowds gather for the opening ceremony.

(French Federation of Carp Fishing), was the draw master, and eventually our team number was pulled out in thirtieth place.

The draw was conducted on a first come, first served basis, rather than a swim being allocated to a team. This meant that anglers could choose where they wished to fish (from the vacant swims) once their team number had been pulled from the hat. Being so low down in the draw, we were not surprised that the island swims nos. 45, 46, 47, 48 and 49 had all been selected, but were amazed to find that the north bank swims nos. 16, 17 and 18 were still available at this point. We could hardly believe it – either the other anglers had not seen the fish in front of these swims, or luck really was on our side. Needless to say, it was along the north bank where we focused our attentions, but common sense told us that swim selection should not be dictated by the location of the fish alone. One of the main rules of the match was that a fish would be disqualified if it ran into the lines of an opposing team. It was therefore essential that our swim offered a good chance of avoiding this problem by offering a wide space between itself and any next door posts. We also wanted a good chance of reaching the centre of the lake where we expected the fish to move once the pressure started. With all these reasons in mind, swim no. 17, on a slight point, was chosen.

Friday Afternoon: Setting Up

We arrived in our swim at the slightly late time of 3.55pm, and did not have a great deal of time to set everything up before the start. We immediately set about rigging up two rods and baiting them with 20mm Kevin Nash 'S' mix boiled baits, specially made to our own specifications so we could bait at long distance should there be a strong facing wind. They were rock hard and included the excellent bio-plasma additive as well as a subtle flavouring of the now famous tangerine, and were dark brown in colour to help them blend with the lake bed at Fishabil and make them look natural in appearance. By the time the rods were out of the rod bags, the shot signifying the start of the match was fired.

There was no time to start casting a leading rod around, as most of the other teams were doing. Besides, we considered that this approach might spook any fish in the swim at the time; as mentioned earlier, we were sure that the team which established an early start would be the one in the running. Rob's buzzers were quickly poked into the ground, and his first rod, consisting of a single bottom bait hookbait, was cast in line with the end of the former deer park at a distance of approximately 80yd (73m). Although we had a strong headwind, the 80yd range was easily reached by Rob with his Kevin Nash 12ft 2¾lb SU Pursuit rods. These were

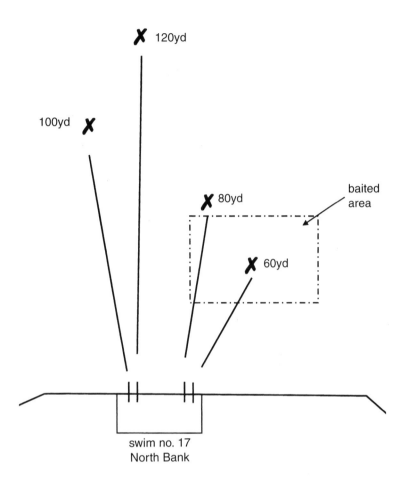

Fig 52 The World Cup winning swim strategy.

combined with Daiwa PM 7000 reels which were loaded with 8lb KN Power + line and an 18ft length of 25lb Kryston Quicksilver as a shockleader.

We were both allowed two rods each, and very shortly Rob's second was out of the bag and ready for action. Again armed with a single bottom bait, this rod was cast to the right of the other one, but this time at a distance of 60yd (55m). Once again, no feature finding or freebies were introduced into the swim: we knew fish were out in front of us and the last thing we wanted to do was to spook them away. Most of the other anglers on the water were baiting up and feature finding at this point, but we held back and made the most of the fish we had in front of us; our game plan was to scatter four hookbaits across the swim at varying distances

of 60, 80, 100 and 120yd (55, 73, 91 and 110m) for the first evening (*see* Fig 52) and then bait up at close range just before dark with boilie and KN squid ball pellet at close range. There was no point in firing out loads of bait while the fish were in the swim – this would only have informed them of our presence and put them on immediate guard; we wanted to make the most of the situation we had, and not ruin it by following the same path as all the other anglers. Besides, despite the high stocking density, Fishabil is quite a rich water which provides adequate natural food for its stock; it is also a water which is affected by angler pressure. The fish in our swim were feeding, but we had no idea when this feeding had commenced or when it would end so we had to select a strategy which met this scenario.

Friday Evening: First Success

At 4.20pm Simon had finally finished delivering the tackle to the swim, and no sooner had he started to unpack his rods than Rob's left-hand rod at 80yd (73m) was belting off. The alarm had not been turned on as we were still trying to organize ourselves, but thankfully the screech of the baitrunner was enough to give us an indication. The rod was soon bent into the test curve by Rob and very quickly a crowd began to gather. First came the judges, then the public and then the media – Tim Paisley was avidly clicking away with his camera, and we just prayed that the fish would stay on. It was all most exciting! In fact the fish didn't put up much of a fight, and was wallowing on the surface and ready for netting in only a matter of minutes. It looked a certain twenty-pounder and was a good sign that carp were out in front of us – and sure enough, a fish suddenly surfaced just to the left of the mark where Rob had only a few minutes previously cast his left-hander. Things were certainly starting to look promising. The fish was weighed by the bailiffs and was recorded at just over 20lb. What a start: not only the first fish for us, but the first of the contest.

The rod which the fish had just come to was quickly re-baited with the same tactic; and Simon was also ready to fire out his two rigs to the left of the swim.

Choice of Rig

The rigs we had decided to use for the match consisted of the set-up shown in Fig 53.

Fishabil contains a wide range of fish descending from different races: our records had told us that there were Aischgruender, Galician, Dinkelsbuehl, Ukraine Frame and Royale races of carp present, as well as a good head of grass carp. Rigs therefore needed to be carefully chosen, and certainly had to be adaptable to suit the wide scope of different fish which we could catch. The hooklink selected was Kryston Super Nova, a material which would lie flat on the clear and ultimately featureless lake bed. We wanted a natural appearance for our hookbaits, as a pressured fishing match like this would probably result in the fish being much more suspicious than normal. It was also our opinion that with one hundred different anglers competing in the match, there would be a wide variety of rigs being used, and we wanted ours to be as simple and as effective as possible. Bottom baits were chosen ahead of pop-ups, and small hooks of size 8 were also used to help avoid detection by the fish. The hook pattern chosen was the extremely sharp and strong Kevin Nash no. 2, and the line aligner set-up was applied to the rigs as we wanted to maximize their chances of hooking those fish which might only mouth the baits. The carp in Fishabil can be wary at the best of times, and with the disturbance of the match we expected them to be on full guard during the three days. (For those of you who are unfamiliar with the line aligner, its use provides increased hooking capabilities by causing the hook to rotate and search for a point to prick home – *see* Chapter 6.) We decided on tight hairs

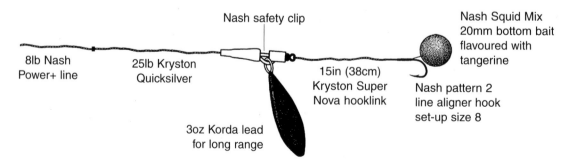

Fig 53 Our choice of rig for the contest. Simple but effective.

and a long link of 15in, as previous sessions at Fishabil had shown that hook pulls were a frequent occurrence due to the shy feeding nature of the fish. A shorter hair and longer link would help to achieve deeper and better hooking, besides which it would be more easily adaptable to the various races of fish present.

By approximately 5pm we were looking more organized: Simon had erected his bivvy and had cast out both his rigs; his rods were the same model as Rob's although 13ft long and combined with Daiwa SS3000 reels, and he was fishing them to the left of the swim at distances of 100 and 120yd (91 and 110m) (see Fig 53). Fishabil does not produce a great deal of fish at distances under 60yd (55m) in pressured conditions, and the fact that there would be a great deal of disturbance on the banks made fishing the intermediate stretches of 60 to 120yd an obvious choice. Simon's rigs also had single 20mm bottom baits and 15in Super Nova hooklinks; he too avoided introducing free offerings.

Evening Action

The south-westerly wind was blowing hard into the north bank and at 5.10pm Simon happened to notice that his left hand rod at 100yd (91m) had come out of the clip and the line was locked up tight. In his hurry he hadn't turned on his alarms or baitrunner, and so without further ado, he quickly picked up the rod and leaned into a hard-fighting fish. It was a chance strike because no indication had sounded, but he was certain that only a fish could have pulled the line from out of the clip, in spite of the strong wind. Sure enough the rod hooped over, and the battle was soon under way. It was a very dogged fight and at first he thought that he had hooked into a grass carp – he has landed some decent grassies in the past which fought in a similar manner to this fish – though he was not entirely sure. After ten minutes or so his initial thoughts were proved incorrect, and a bronze-coloured common carp revealed itself from the murky water of Fishabil. For such a small fish it gave a good account of itself, and it felt fairly heavy under the tip; basically it just hugged the bottom

until after a couple of minutes it suddenly popped up about five yards from the bank. As it was netted there was a round of applause from the group of onlookers. The fish was weighed at 16lb and three photographs were taken by the officials, as was customary.

The time was fast approaching 6pm when we were back with all the rods out in place. It would soon be dusk and we wanted to put some bait out before darkness closed in. Just as we were sorting out the spoding rods, Simon's right-hand rod at 120yd (110m) burst into life – it was a take which just came out of nowhere and roared off without any prior signal whatsoever. The fish did not put up much of a fight, however, and after about ten minutes we landed another chunky mirror to take our running total to 26.2kg. Things were certainly looking good for us at this stage as only one other fish had been out to another team. The fast start was just what we had hoped and planned for, and as we had expected, the fish were now beginning to sense danger – the first capture came at 80yd (73m), the second at 100yd (91m), with the final-pick up at 120yd (110m).

Baiting Up for Friday Night

We now needed to overcome the carps' caution by trying to coax them back into casting range, and therefore decided to introduce some bait for the night. It seemed obvious that the fish would become more confident under the cover of darkness, the noise from the day having died down. The rod fished at 60yd (55m) was thus re-baited and cast to the centre of an area baited with fifty boiled baits. The rod at 80yd (73m) was also re-baited, and this was fished just over the back of the baited area on its own. Two hundred Nash squid ball pellets were scattered over a broad area covering the 60–80 yard range and this was expected to attract feeding fish into the area, while not overfeeding them.

The ball pellet is a relatively new concept, a practical form of introducing a food signal into your swim without over-baiting. It has been designed specifically for the carp angler and can be baited with the use of a throwing stick at

A powerful Fishabil carp surges off towards the lines of Lagabbe and Cantin.

distances over 100yd (91m). Mistakenly, many anglers believe it to be just an attractant, while it is in fact a nutritional food source made from the finest ingredients available; when submerged in water, it will break down to leave a crumb-like effect on the lake bed. It is the brain-child of Clive Deidrich, and can be manufac-tured so that it breaks down to a crumb in as quick a time as five minutes, or as long as five days if necessary. The crumb will be left in small piles on the lake bed, and these may be eaten by the smallest or largest of creatures. It can also be taken by a carp before it has broken down, in which case it will act just like a boiled bait.

The pellet we were using for the match had been designed to break down in thirty minutes, as we believed that a quick breakdown would assist the situation because we did not want to over-bait in any way. They were also coloured black, as we had requested, to make them less obtrusive. Our reasoning was that there were so many baited areas in the lake that the fish were spoilt for choice, and we wanted ours to be com-pletely different. We hoped that the strong food message would trick the fish into believing that there were copious amounts of food for them to feed on, whereas there would only in fact be the hookbaits and the fifty or so scattered free offer-ings. The aim of the latter was to keep the fish interested and on the hunt for more – we had reasoned that if we held back on these and only introduced pellet, the fish may lose interest in their search and this would result in a shorter feeding spell, or worse, the fish moving onto the baited areas of those fishing either side of us. Obviously we wanted to promote feeding activ-ity as much as possible, since fish which are feeding are more susceptible to capture than those which are not.

Our capture records told us that the fish had now moved out into the centre of the lake. The two left-hand rods in the swim, controlled by Simon, were therefore kept at 100 and 120yd (91 and 110m) on single hookbaits because we antic-ipated that the fish would move closer into the swim during the night to feed on the baited area. At this point they would still be feeding

cautiously, but we wanted to cover as many options as possible – there was no point in cov-ering just one area. Also we thought that the pulling power of the baited area might have been too strong for some fish, and we wanted to increase our chances of catching both the hungry and nervous fish among them. Thus as the fish moved closer to the baited area, we hoped the single hookbaits might trap those holding back which might be sampling rather than feeding.

It was the sampling rod at 120yd (110m) which went screaming off at lam, causing Simon to leap from his bivvy and tighten down to a fish which did not want to stop. Twenty yards (18m) of line was immediately pulled off the reel. It looked as if it might have been a big fish, but after the initial run, we found that it was a crazy Fishabil carp on the retrieve. Fifteen minutes later it was in the margins where it was still fight-ing but ready for netting. It was a mirror and certainly not big, but it was fat nevertheless, and close to, if not over, 20lb – on the scales it went just short of 21lb and looked set for a bigger

Another one bites the dust.

weight in years to come. It was returned to the water no worse for wear, and the rig was re-baited and once again cast out towards the horizon. We were marking our lines at the distance required and simply lining up the horizon with the location of the feeding spot during daylight hours; all we had to do during the dark was overcast the marked line and clip up at the required distance, retrieve and then cast. The hotspot could then be reached time and time again in the dark. A very simple but effective method, which no one else seemed to be using.

Friday Night Action

As night set in, we were expecting the action to die off for a few hours; there seems to be a distinct pattern at Fishabil whereby the fishing always appears to slow during the first few hours after dark. We have absolutely no idea why this is, but our suspicions were proved right as we did not receive another pick up until the early hours of the morning. The fish, a Galician mirror, weighed in at 21lb and came from Rob's 80-yard (73m) rod at the back of the baited area. We sensed that the fish were now coming closer in, and shortly after returning the fat mirror to the water, a pick-up from Rob's 60-yard (55m) rod in the middle of the bait proved this to be so. It was a lovely looking fish too, all 24lb of it.

The light was now beginning to push through and we decided to hold back on the bait for the time being. We also decided to keep the levels to a minimum during the day, as we considered the noise from the loudspeakers and crowds would probably have a deleterious effect on the fishing; it was now the weekend, and despite the damp conditions, a large crowd was expected. Our running total at 10am on the Saturday morning was 56.3kg and we were now almost 40kg ahead of any other team.

Saturday: Sitting it Out

Observation of the lake during the first few hours of Saturday morning identified considerable numbers of fish moving in the centre of the lake and out of casting distance. A large crowd was also beginning to build up. Raphael had

certainly been right in his pre-match estimation of a big crowd – we had seen nothing like it before at a fishing contest. Most of them were curious visitors or holiday-makers just browsing, and were amazed at the levels of technology being used to catch carp; a species which to many French citizens is considered a pest. They were also surprised at the number of fish now showing in the centre of the lake. Unfortunately however, no matter how hard we worked, there was nothing we could do to tempt the fish into gracing the bank for the cameras. We just had to sit and wait. Sometimes carp fishing is just about time and in such a situation, no matter how hard you try, there is nothing an angler can do to make the fish feed. Forget the latest rigs or bait – all you need is patience.

Just before midday our patience paid off and the distance rod at 120yd (110m) gave a single faint bleep on the Delkim alarm. Without hesitation Simon swept the rod up towards the sky to feel a carp battling on the end. It had been an extremely delicate indication and a sure sign that the fish were not in their usual mood. The carp decided to kite left immediately, and at 120yd all Simon could do was apply heavy side strain to try and pull it back in an arc. Thankfully the fish did as it was told and we were able to keep it under control, as if it had reached our neighbours lines it would have been immediately disqualified. It was coaxed towards the landing net, and we let out a loud cheer as it went down on the score sheet.

Until our last fish, we had been catching one every two to three hours since the start of the match – in fact we could have set our watches to the exact period when a take would have occurred. The landing of this fish came approximately six hours after the last, and it came at just the right time, because we were beginning to think that the action was drying up. The pressures of the match were certainly bringing some negative ideas into our minds even though we were still well in the lead.

The weather changed considerably at about midday on Saturday: the sun started to shine through, the wind died off completely, and the lake became flat calm by 3pm in the afternoon. This was exactly the opposite of what we wanted. Fish activity in the centre of the lake had almost ceased as well, and our heads were beginning to droop. Not only were the fish no longer showing out in front of us, but we had also had no runs for a few hours. Word spread round the lake very fast regarding catch reports, and news was filtering through that Audigue and Kronenberg in swim no. 24 had landed a monster grass carp of 29lb 4oz, as well as another fish of 18lb. They had also lost a couple of fish during the day – but all things considered, the situation was certainly starting to look good for this team in the pads bay. Some of the English bailiffs had visited their swim and were reporting to us that there were literally dozens of fish in the bay around this area. The weather was now getting quite warm, and our anticipation of a possibly good result from the pads was starting to look like a reality. Thankfully, from our point of view, the warm weather did not hold, and as had been forecast, the wind soon picked up and it began to rain.

For the next few hours everything continued to be very quiet out in front of us. We just sat in the rain watching the water and discussing our own tactics and those of the other competitors. We consumed endless cups of tea during the afternoon, and finally about half an hour before dark decided to bait up the short range area. We were introducing the usual fifty boiled baits and two hundred or so ball pellets each evening; our intention was to apply a further fifty ball pellets after each pick up from this area.

Saturday Night: On the Edge of Despair

At 3am we received our next pick-up. Once again we had been up all night and not had a wink of sleep. The take came from the 80-yard spot very shortly after Rob had just re-cast this very same rod – for reasons which were instinctive and nothing else. The alarm was screeching out its signal and Rob was quickly on to it, signifying a contact, when all of a sudden the tip sprang back and the fish was lost. Our hearts sank, and when the rig had been retrieved, we saw that the hooklink had

snapped one inch from the swivel. Following examination, we concluded that the braid had wrapped around the swivel of the lead, probably on the cast, and had snapped during the initial contact with the fish. We quickly re-rigged the rod, adding a short length of protective silicon tubing, and cast it back towards its original mark at the back of the baited area.

No sooner had Rob put the line in the clip than the rod at the centre of the baited area went belting off. The fish certainly seemed to be on the feed now and they definitely had a liking for the Nash squid mix. Rob picked up the rod, wound down – and immediately looked dejected, because the line had tangled around the indicator and parted upon connection with the fish. Of all the things which could only happen during a world championship! Once again, however, there was no point in sitting there with a glum face; we had to put it to the back of our minds and not let it get to us. So in an attempt to bolster confidence, Simon kept commenting that at least the fish were back on the feed; with this, the rod was quickly re-rigged and cast back out.

Even so, our morale was very low now. Some instinct told Simon that he should reel in his rods and re-cast them both again; he had not received a pick up for a few hours and believed that a re-positioning of fresh baits may be necessary. The lake bed at Fishabil is very muddy, and on occasions it is possible for the hookbait to become masked; we were not pulling back after the cast either and the rigs may well have been lying awkwardly. Not only this, but sometimes you can just sense when the pattern of action has altered – this was one of those occasions, and something needed to be done. Having reeled in and re-baited with the single hookbaits, Simon wound up the distance rod to a maximum and let it fly towards the horizon mark. The wind was still blowing strongly, and it needed all the effort he could muster to reach the fish. The rod at 100yd (91m) was also re-cast, and then we sat back to make a cup of tea. Neither of us was tired, as the adrenalin was still high – never before had we felt so much tension while in a fishing situation. But we settled back and tried to forget about it as much as we could.

Less than five minutes later, a single bleep came from Simon's right-hand rod at 120yd (110m), then an unbroken warble from the delkim. The re-cast had certainly paid off, and Simon commenced battle with what felt like a heavy fish. It is always possible to recognize the bigger fish, as they go where they want to in a steady kind of manner. There was no head shaking or half-hearted pulls with this carp – just sheer power from its weight. Like most of them, it decided where it wanted to go and it went, and as it set off to the left there was nothing Simon could do apart from apply heavy side strain and pray. One of the other rules of the match was that anglers had to play all fish from within a designated box which surrounded the swim, and this meant that walking along the bank to achieve a better angle on a fish was illegal. So all Simon could do was hold the rod out at right-angles towards the lake and keep praying. But unfortunately the fish would have none of it, and it kept going left at an alarming rate; in a matter of minutes it would almost certainly clip the lines of the team next door. Bleep, bleep, went Lagabbe's indicator, and off went another fish as the hook pulled.

We were acutely disappointed; it was as if we had been built up to expect the fulfilment of our dream, only to be let down as we neared the final stage. However, just before daybreak we were rewarded with another couple of pick ups on the short range rods which we refused to lose. Thankfully, both of us kept our composure at a time when we needed it the most.

Sunday: the Competition Hots Up!

The start of Sunday was very different from the previous morning, the wind was blowing strongly and the rain coming down continuously. Nevertheless the crowds were starting to gather at the European Specimen Angling Centre, and it was very pleasing to see carp fishing receiving such excellent attention. To a certain degree it was quite nerve-racking fishing in front of such big crowds, who seemed fascinated by everything the anglers did – we were even videoed while cooking the dinner!

At mid-day we received our next pick-up at 120yd (110m), evidence that the fish were still out at long range during the day. The fish gave a scrappy account of itself and splashed water everywhere; Rob was soaked in the process of netting it, but he did not let it worry him because it was a nice-looking, low 20lb mirror. Rob's two lost fish from the previous night had both come to the baited area, and judging from the last few pick-ups, it was now obvious that the fish had definitely moved further out once again. There was a bonus to this mid-day fish, too: it came to Rob in the middle of a radio interview with event organizer Raphael Faraggi which was being broadcast all around the lake; there was a huge crowd around us for the occasion, and this catch certainly demonstrated the excitement of carp fishing to the many spectators.

By now our nerves were on edge as the end of the match was coming ever closer. The French competitors Freddie Remetter and Christophe Conrath were catching very consistently, and it seemed that every time we glanced across the lake towards their swim there were crowds of people surrounding them and they had bent rods; at one point, both their swim and ours had large crowds gathered around. Once knowing there was nothing happening in our swim, we picked up the binoculars to take a closer look at them and were surprised to see that *they* were also looking at *us* through their binoculars! We gave them a quick wave, and they returned the gesture – it was all good fun, and evidence of the excellent sporting atmosphere of the match. At the end of the day on the Sunday, Freddie and Christophe had landed a further two fish and were certainly pushing for first place; all they needed was a couple of decent fish and they would have been breathing down our necks. We were still in the lead with 87.2kg, but Freddie and Christophe were not far behind with 44.4kg, and although our position might have sounded like a convincing lead Freddie and Christophe had removed a snag from their swim and were in fact moving up the leader board at an alarming rate. Besides this, Fishabil being what it is, we knew that anything could happen at any time.

Lost Fish, Losing Confidence

Our next take was a flyer, and it occurred at 3am on Monday morning, a time which was proving to be the beginning of the night-time feeding spell. It was a belting take on the single hookbait at 100yd (91m) range. Simon leapt from his semi-dormant trance and leant into the rod. As soon as he hooked into the fish, he knew it was big. It immediately went on a run to the left, and there was nothing Simon could do with it except let it go. He tried to put on side strain, but the rod was soon at its test curve and his arms were beginning to ache as it maintained its powerful surge. It just kept going. Bleep, bleep, bleep went the alarm of Lagabbe and Cantin, and the fish was straightaway disqualified by the two bailiffs watching over our shoulder. Again we were acutely disappointed as the fish can only have clipped their line very slightly – so lightly in fact, that neither of them even woke up! Another fish lost, and the loss was even harder to take on this occasion because after about ten minutes of hard fighting we managed to bank it and found Simon had been right in believing it was a big one: on the scales it went to 30lb 12oz exactly! Had it not been disqualified, it would have taken us to well over 100kg for the match. Just as we were returning the big mirror to the water, we heard a screaming alarm coming from the island post of Freddie and Christophe. Out came the binoculars, and even in the dark it was possible to make out what was happening on the island, as all the swims had lights behind them. Unfortunately, on this occasion we could not see a great deal and so we had no idea of what was going on in swim number 47. We were both extremely nervous at this point, and were beginning to fear that we might even lose the competition on this, the very last day. Both of us were so fatigued as a result of complete lack of sleep that we dropped off for a while during the last few hours, so neither of us knew whether Freddie and Christophe had caught since dusk. What we did know was that they had been catching consistently the day before and that they had had another take during the short twenty minutes we had been up during the night. To say that we were shaking was an understatement!

Monday Morning Finale

The last morning finally arrived, and we were up early trying to find out the state of play. Thankfully, from our point of view, we learned that Freddie and Christophe had landed only a couple of fish during the night, and so we were still well in front. The night had been relatively quiet all round the lake, apart from a nice common of 13.4kg for the team in swim no. 40. As the end of the match came closer, the nervousness and anticipation of possibly losing at the last hurdle started to fade away. We had led since the first half hour, and it really would have been agonizing if we had lost in the last.

Our anxieties were needless, however, because at 10.30am the left-hand rod burst into life and Simon hooked into the last fish of the match. Once again the crowds started to gather and cameras to click, and at long last we knew we had the match won. Once again this fish was picked up from long range, and it was interesting to note that over the three days of competition there had been a distinct pattern to the action. Thus during the daylight the fish had been coming from long range and during the night from both long and short range, from which we were bound to calculate that – hardly surprising! – they were definitely disturbed by the occasion and the pressure. The final fish was brought to the net easily by Simon, and for the record it weighed a few ounces under 20lb. What a relief: with only half an hour left it was impossible for us to lose. When the gun went off signifying the end of the match, we all experienced a fantastic feeling. Everyone rushed to congratulate us, and it was a time neither of us will ever forget. We had *won* the World Carp Cup of 1996! Obviously we had intended to win, but in fact thinking back, we would not have felt let down with a high placing – as it was, we could now go home feeling more than proud of our achievement.

Rob cracked open a bottle of champagne and we soon drank it without a care in the world, oblivious to the fact that our names were being called over the loudspeaker! The closing ceremony had been brought forward in time, and we had to pack up in a matter of minutes – it would

We were in the lead, the radio stations arrived, and just to cap it off, Rob duly landed a lively, 20lb plus mirror.

We knew we had it won!

The £20,000 World Carp Cup was handed over and we sang our hearts out to the National Anthem.

have been very unconventional to have had a closing ceremony without the winners! We were not the only team to be late, however, and at the entrance we bumped into Freddie Remetter and Christophe Conrath who were just arriving. All of us were highly enthusiastic about the last three days of competition, and congratulated one another on our results. 'Nash Bait How many points?'

We could still not believe our success. People we had never seen before in our lives were coming up just to say 'Well done' – it was an amazing feeling. The presentations then commenced and the third and second placed teams were given a colossal applause as they made their way to the podium. And next it was our turn! The national anthem started to play and we were called forward to the front of the auditorium, our dream realized. As we arrived on the podium we took off our hats and sang our hearts out to the National Anthem. The £20,000 World Carp Cup and the huge cheque for

100,000 ff was presented to us by Michel Mahin and the President of the International Sports Fishing Federation, Fortune Jaguelin. In fact the prizes we received paled in comparison to the sense of achievement we felt. Fishabil had been very kind to us, and we felt we owed it so much: the memories of the whole event will rest with us forever. We caught the first fish, the last fish, the most fish, as well as the biggest, even though this was disqualified, and we look forward to the next World Carp Cup when we hope that we can relive our dream all over again! A big thank-you to our sponsor Kevin Nash for all his help and to everybody who made the event such a fantastic occasion for the sport we all love.

Table 13. Top ten angling teams in the World Carp Cup, Fishabil 1996.

Position	Team	Country	Swim	Weight (kg)
1	Hughes/Crow	Great Britain	17	96.1
2	Remetter/Conrath	France	47	57.2
3	Guillain/Alvarez	France	46	57.1
4	Tibermant/Giancola	Belgium	44	42.9
5	Bonazza/Campello	Italy	40	33.4
6	Schaeffer/Olinger	Luxembourg	9	28.7
7	Audigue/Cronenberg	France	24	26.8
8	Schmidt/Exner	Germany	49	17.0
9	Weemaels/Weemaels	Belgium	48	15.1
10	Tetro/Rommers	Netherlands	45	11.4

8 CARP: THE NEXT GENERATION

The import of carp from overseas has for a long time been a topic of discussion among carp anglers world-wide. For many years now, fish have been brought into Britain from places such as France, Poland, Italy and the Far East; indeed, many of these have made their way into a number of inland waters around the world. Although many have been brought in illegally, there have also been a number of legal stockings, and these have provided anglers with a variety of exotic species of carp which are set to turn the future into an interesting period for our sport. The outlook in Britain alone now looks completely different from the past, and anglers are already focusing their attentions away from *Cyprinus carpio* and towards such species as the grass carp, the koi carp, the ghost carp and the big mouth buffalo, as well as other exotic fish such as the silver and bighead carps.

In the final chapter of this book we will take a closer look at some of these fish and give you an insight into their background, behaviour and characteristics, as well as some of the considerations which are worth examining when specifically aiming to catch such fish. We hope that you learn something from it, and most of all we hope that you enjoy reading it.

THE CHINESE CARPS

The Grass Carp

The grass carp (*Ctenopharyngodon idella*) is widely known as the 'love carp' among French anglers (*carp l'amour*) due to its place of origin (the River Amur) and its large scales and attractive appearance. It has the characteristics of a large chub, and has grown to proportions of well over 20lb (9kg)

in Britain and to even greater sizes abroad. We are not sure what the actual world record is, but we know for certain that grass carp have been caught on rod and line at 80lb (36kg) in Poland, and netted at over 140lb (63kg) in the Far East. The fish is not a species which is indigenous to European countries, and is more suited to its natural habitat of the large northern and southern China rivers (hence its long, lean, streamlined body shape). As mentioned above, it originates from the River Amur, and the wild species is very often referred to as the 'white amur'. It first reached Eastern European countries in the 1960s and due to a successful artificial fertilization policy, it was soon dispersed around Western Europe. It is a fast-growing mid-water carp which will feed at all levels of the water column, and will tolerate a variety of environmental conditions.

As with most cyprinids, the grass carp grows larger and more quickly in warm climates, and according to scientists, at a temperature of 77°F (25°C) it is capable of eating its own bodyweight of food in a single day. This does not mean that a 'grassy' of 20lb (9kg) may suddenly increase to 40lb (18kg) overnight, of course: it is referring to younger fish of smaller weights which are extremely active and require nourishment to sustain lost energy and expedient growth.

Diet for Grass Carp In its early years, a grass carp will generally feed on animals such as zooplankton, but once it grows to a size of over 4in (10cm) its diet becomes almost uniquely herbivorous (mainly plant-based), usually consisting of the macrovegetation such as small aquatic plants; it will not consume all varieties, however, and of those which it does eat, preference will be given to some more than others. Understandably, the larger the fish, the more proficient at grazing on plants it will be, and for this reason the bigger fish may have a broader dietary span than smaller ones. Plants which are freely eaten by all sizes may consist of duckweed, stonewort, Canadian pondweed, starwort and small-leafed pondweeds. The grass carp also eats grass, and many fish farmers produce excellent fish flesh at very low cost through the use of this feed. In fact, such farming systems are responsible for the name 'grass carp'.

Although the grass carp may be used as a source of weed control within lakes, heavily choked waters will usually require treatment with herbicides rather than introductions of fish to control the problem. Not all weeds are freely eaten by the fish, either: hornwort, milfoil, water moss and large-leafed pondweeds are among several varieties which are not a favourite meal. Water lilies are another less desired food as they are too tough, although larger fish with well developed pharyngeal teeth do consume broken lilies – the number of bigger fish which are often caught from around lilybeds at some venues is an excellent example here. The grass carp is known to eat weed at temperatures as low as 41°F (5°C), but effective weed control in fisheries is very rarely achieved at temperatures of below 59°F (15°C). Within Europe, weed control is therefore hard to predict because fluctuating water temperatures and weather conditions will always affect feeding and growth patterns. It is also very rare for grass carp to spawn in the wild in temperate climates, as not only are most single sex stock, but the environmental conditions in lakes and rivers in this region of the world do not meet the necessary criteria.

Tactics for Grass Carp As far as tactics are concerned, you are very likely to catch fish using your usual carp fishing methods. Nevertheless, it may be an idea to try and change them if you wish to be more selective. Thus on a warm day, the grass carp will normally be found feeding on the higher water vegetation as well as the filamentous algae, so it may be worth trying a bait which can be found just below the surface (*see* Fig 54), or one which is popped up straight off the lead.

Bottom bait fishing will also need special consideration if you wish to be more selective. The main area of focus should be on the length of the hooklink, as the grass carp feeds in a completely different way from normal carp: it has a chub-like mouth and needs to up-end at a greater angle, and having observed fish feeding on the bottom at several venues, we believe that when the fish levels out, a very short link tends to straighten before the hook is set. This is because the fish tend to feed in a rather jerky manner, and they level out several inches above the bed of the lake – these two characteristics would almost definitely cause baits on a link of 6in (15cm) or below to have poor hooking capabilities. It is doubtful whether these characteristics

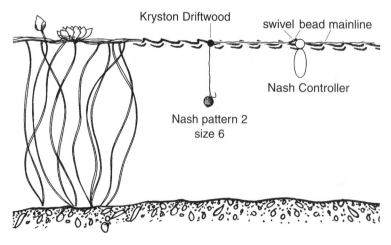

Kryston Driftwood

swivel bead mainline

Nash Controller

Nash pattern 2
size 6

Fig 54 Suggested method for grass carp on warm days.

Fig 55 The natural bottom-feeding process of the grass carp.

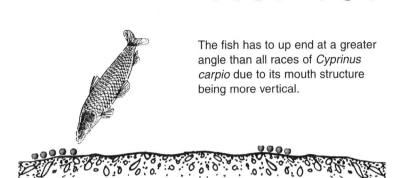

The fish has to up end at a greater angle than all races of *Cyprinus carpio* due to its mouth structure being more vertical.

will be the same on all waters, but they are points certainly worth considering if you are aiming specifically to catch grass carp.

Bait for Grass Carp These carp have been widely caught on the numerous carp baits available today and it would be very hard to select one type as being better than another. As regards boiled baits, we have caught the majority of our grass carp on fishmeal-based baits, with Nashbaits 'Sting' mix being the most successful. We have no idea why our results have been so, but there does seem to be a definite preference amongst grass carp for 'Sting' as compared to other fishmeals. This is not a free advertisement, but genuinely a finding which we have experienced in our fishing.

Behaviour Be prepared when you hit into one of these fish, as they are amazingly powerful and have the ability to pull the rod out of your hands if you are not careful. As far as the actual fight is concerned, they can pull yards of line off the spool and give you a terrific battle – or they can be completely the opposite. If a fish comes in without a fight, it is more than likely to go crazy when it is on the bank, and having lost a 20lb fish because it jumped out of the landing net, we suggest that you do not leave the fish unattended in the net while you arrange your weighing gear and so on!

Grass carp are not tolerant of long periods out of the water, and they should always be returned as soon as possible. They are very fragile and

under no circumstances would we recommend that you sack one.

Popularity The media have taken a distinct liking to the grass carp, and this has provoked a growing interest in it amongst carp anglers: already some are specifically targeting this fish before all others. France in particular is a country where a small band of anglers is now focusing on the grass carp only and it certainly looks like a fish for the future.

The Bighead Carp
The bighead carp (*Aristichthys nobolis*) is a popular food species specifically bred for cultivation in the aquaculture industry. In the correct environment they grow quickly, and they can reach weights in excess of 100lb (45kg) quite easily.

Appearance The fish has a strange-looking head, hence its name, and its bottom lip is very much longer than the upper one, and slightly upturned in appearance. Other characteristics of the fish are the golden-yellow coloured flanks and the small, sail-like dorsal fin. The strange oval-shaped and upturned mouth is designed for feeding on the fish's main diet of macroplankton.

Diet Macroplankton are the bigger particles of plankton held within the aquatic environment such as colonial algae, blue-green algae and zooplankton such as rotifers and small crustaceans. The bighead is therefore classed as a mid-water

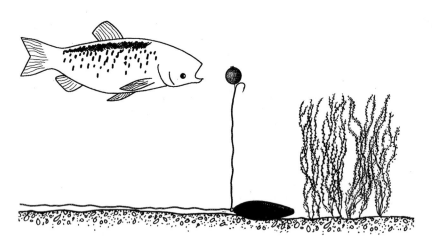

Fig 56 Suggested set-up for a mid-water feeder.

species because it will spend the majority of its time at this level, gently swimming around taking large gulps of water and filtering it through its well developed gill rakers. To a lesser degree, the fish will feed within the upper and lower levels of the water column also and due to this, it is possible to catch the fish on a wide variety of tactics.

Tactics The bighead is susceptible to capture via bottom baits when the plankton levels in a water are low (from September to March). However, consider carefully the length of the hooklink when pursuing bigheads on the bottom, due to the shape of the mouth and the way in which it feeds when there. A long link of 15in plus is best, as it enables better hooking to occur inside the mouth; a short link may tend to slip out when the fish starts to level out after lowering its head towards the lake bed. The best method for bigheads, however, would have to be based around the fish's main feeding area, in mid-water. Thus a popped-up bait straight off the lead around the mid-water depth would be our choice (*see* Fig 56) and indeed, this is the method which many of the Chinese anglers use to catch the species in their waters.

Distribution As we move into the late 1990s, the bighead carp is not widespread around sports fisheries, but we feel it will become widely distributed in the future because it is able to use a specific level of the water column. It also grows well and fairly quickly, a very desirable attribute for managers and anglers alike. It can produce eggs quite easily, but it does not spawn naturally in lakes and ponds, and is more suited to its natural environment of rivers.

The Silver Carp

The silver carp (*Hypophthalmichthys molitrix*) is a fish which is growing in stature as far as its sporting capabilities are concerned. In recent times it has been caught in a number of different countries by anglers, including places such as China, Bulgaria and Poland. It is a hard-fighting fish and one which can reach sizes of above 100lb (45kg) in weight.

Appearance and Diet The silver carp is very deep in the body, and most of the large fish start to gain their weight in this part of their anatomy. It has a very long intestine which can measure in excess of fifteen times the length of the body. Like the bighead, it has an upturned mouth and a sail-like dorsal fin, and its diet is very much plankton based. Nevertheless, the two fish differ in appearance and in dietary needs: the silver carp feeds mainly on the phytoplankton of a water body such as the unicellular algae; and in appearance its flanks are silver in colour and its

Crowie with one of his many 20 plus grassies.

fins a blood-red colour. The gill rakers for the silver carp are also considerably more defined than for the other Chinese carps.

Tactics and Behaviour The tactics for catching silver carp should be similar to those for catching the bighead carp. Silvers will also be more likely to feed on the bottom when the plankton levels within a lake are at their lowest. Like the grass carp, the silver carp originates from the River Amur in China; it has the unusual habit of tail-walking and leaping clear of the water during combat.

Other Chinese Carp

The two final members of the Chinese carps which are worth mentioning are the black carp (*Mylopharyngodon piceus*) and the mud carp (*Cirrhina molitorella*). Of the two, the black carp is the sports-fisherman's favourite, and in the right environment it has been known to reach 150lb (68kg). The mud carp, on the other hand, is not a growth fish and does not reach a very large size. Both are classed as benthic feeders and show a preference for food items such as molluscs and decaying vegetation. The black carp is a long fish, with dark or black-coloured fins and flanks. They are attractive to look at, and a very hard-fighting fish. Angling tactics should be the same as those used for the common carp.

ORNAMENTAL CARP

The Koi Carp

The koi carp – also known as the nishikigoi – is extremely well known around the world as a fancy fish, and is widely bred for ornamental purposes over and above anything else. In recent years, however, the koi has slowly become a much sought-after sports fish and one which anglers have great pleasure in targeting. For example in Britain there are a number of 20lb koi in certain lakes around the country, and these fish have become well known to anglers – on the right day they can be easily spotted swimming around their waters. Koi have become a target for anglers for a number of aesthetic reasons, but mainly because they are so different from the others and thus offer more of a challenge – rather like catching the biggest fish in a specific lake.

History The koi originates from the Far East, and more specifically from the Yamakoshi district of Niigata Prefecture on the island of Honshu in Japan. The term 'koi' means 'carp' in Japanese, but it has become famous in Western countries as a term signifying ornamental fish. All koi are said to be descendants of *Cyprinus carpio* – known as 'ma-goi' to the Japanese – and they are famous for their bright and unusual colours as well as their high value for particular specimens.

Values Prices for koi can vary enormously, and fish can be bought and sold at both cheap and expensive rates; generally speaking, however, those fish with exact patterns, colour intensity, soundness of conformation and/or a famous genetic background (ie descendants of the Emperor's fish) fetch the highest prices. Some koi have been bought for as much as £250,000 each, and fears are widespread about such valued fish dying whilst in transit to their new owner's home.

Despite what many people say, the koi seen in today's coarse fisheries will probably be valued at the same price as the commons, mirrors and leathers which we regularly catch. No sensible fishery manager would purchase a koi of high value and stock it into a sports fishery, especially as fish theft is rife nowadays.

Breeding Koi have been reared successfully all over the world, although the main market for the fish lies within Japan. A single female is capable of producing approximately 100,000 eggs per kg of bodyweight, although a great many will be infertile if the brood fish was susceptible to certain hormones used to enhance her colour pigments. Many of the eggs will also succumb to disease because the koi is not very resilient, especially when compared with the common carp. Nevertheless, many fish do reach excellent weights, albeit at a slower rate than the *Cyprinus carpio*, and it is possible for them to spawn successfully in the wild, in the mild temperate regions of the world.

The rearing of koi has been linked to the cross-breeding of the common carp (*Cyprinus carpio*) and the common goldfish (*Carassius carassius*), but even with the advanced technology of modern times it is difficult to pinpoint the exact background of the different races of koi which have become widely accepted among fish breeders. Many of the different varieties have been developed over the last fifty years, and indeed, these are still being added to today. There are said to be over one hundred different koi varieties in circulation, although a basic set of thirteen is generally used to classify fish. Each variety is genetically different from any other,

This ghost koi fell to a HNV.

and thus the genetic situation is very complex. Certainly some strains breed true to specific features, but the prospects for cross-breeding are excellent and this is why the number of varieties is being added to constantly.

Appearance Fish come in all shapes and sizes, as well as in a variety of colours; including yellow, blue, red, orange, black, white or a mixture of any of these. Space restricts us from listing all the different varieties here, besides which there is no point investigating the topic at any great depth. For this reason, if you wish to further your knowledge of koi carp, then we suggest you peruse a decent book specifically targeting the species – there are plenty in circulation. However, we have listed some of the main types which you may come across at today's fisheries (*see* Fig 57).

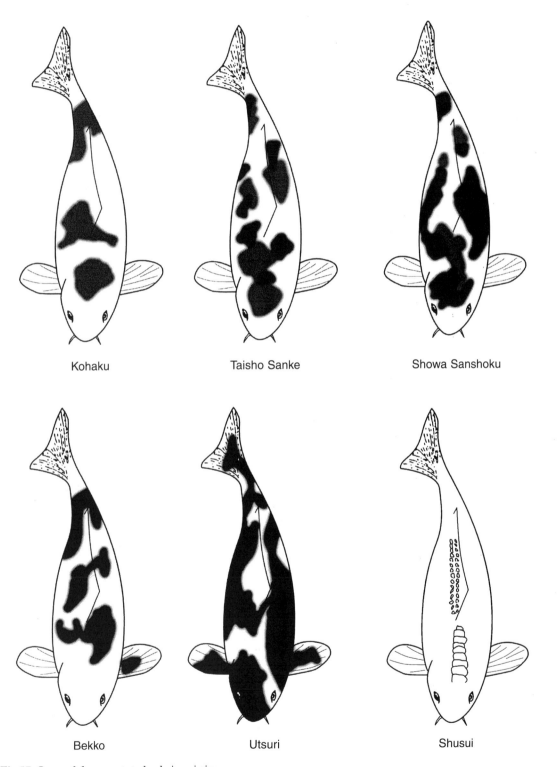

Kohaku   Taisho Sanke   Showa Sanshoku

Bekko   Utsuri   Shusui

Fig 57 Some of the more popular koi varieties.

Diet The diet for koi is very similar to that of *Cyprinus carpio* (ie omnivorous classified), and when introduced into an inland fishery they fall into the category of bottom-feeding species. This said, koi will quite happily feed on food items found both in the mid-water region as well as in the upper layers of the water column. Basically, they will utilize the most abundant food source available to them.

They have been known to grow to large proportions of 50lb (23kg) or more, and to live for longer than one hundred years when kept in captivity; but in the wild, it is not possible to say exactly how well they will respond, as records and research regarding this are scarce at the present time.

Fishing Tactics The angler's tactics for specifically targeting koi should be no different from those he uses for common carp. Get to know the fish within your lake, and try to observe them feeding as much as possible. Examine their body shape, and design your rigs around their feeding characteristics. For bait selection, it may be an idea to use a high nutritional value mix. The reason for this is because many koi are raised on such a diet when in captivity to ensure that the body shape and colours are maximized; moreover many of the koi we see in our waters will be stock fish, and not naturally produced in the water environment where they are held. A bait of high nutritional value will usually have been fed artificially to the fish at some stage of its life, and it may quickly become accustomed to its value as a food source when introduced into a lake after a period of time.

Other than using his observational skills, there isn't a great deal more the angler can do to improve his chances of catching koi carp. Just enjoy their beauty – and make sure that you don't make a mess of the photographs when you catch one!

Ghost Carp

Similar to koi carp, ghost carp have also become extremely widespread around inland fisheries over the last few years; probably the most famous within carp angling circles are those held in Withy Pool in Bedfordshire, England. However, there are plenty of others distributed all around Britain as well as in France. It was in France that Simon caught his biggest strain of ghost, weighing in at 21lb 8oz.

Appearance Ghost carp, also known as ghosties, are distinguishable from koi by their shiny scales which are silvery in colour and very often bluish in appearance. When viewed from above, the true ghost carp has the shape of a skull marked on its head in a greyish colour, and it is this which is normally used as a form of identification. Among fish breeders, the ghost carp is well known for its growth rate, and it ability to overwinter extremely well.

Behaviour and Tactics The endurance of the fish almost certainly has something do with the fact that it is an offspring of the female common carp, albeit crossed with a Sanke koi male. Again, similar to koi carp, there are several different strains in circulation, and all can be caught by techniques identical to those which may be used for common carp.

The Big-mouth Buffalo

The big-mouth buffalo fish (*Ictiobus cyprinellus*) has been in the press a great deal in the 1990s due to the capture of some truly enormous specimens in the north of America. It was widely reported within the pages of *Carp Talk* by Chris Ball that a huge 88lb (40kg) buffalo had been caught in November 1993. The lucky angler was Tony Crawford, who landed the fish from Lake Wylie in north Carolina; apparently it was 46in (115cm) long and 40in (100cm) around its girth.

Plenty of other big buffalos over the 60lb (27kg) mark have been reported in America, so it is no surprise that they are becoming more widespread around Europe as their name becomes established among fishery bosses. They are a bottom-feeding species which are dark brownish-red in colour. In fact their growth rate is said to be no different from *Cyprinus carpio*, and rivers in this region, and especially in the main channels. Angling tactics should be no different from those used for common carp.

The Indian Carps

The Indian carps make up the third major carp group, the others being the common and the Chinese varieties. As the name suggests, these fish are widespread throughout India, and like the other forms of carp they are primarily used as a food source. There are several different varieties amongst this family of fish, with the main types being the rohu (*Labeo rohita*), the mrigal (*Cirrhina mrigala*), the catla (*Catla catla*) and the calbasu (*Labaeo calbasu*).

These four cyprinids have similar characteristics, although their eating habits and morphology are distinctly different. Within India they are called the major carps, although at the present time they have yet to become widespread around the Western side of the world. For this reason they are not yet known as a popular sports fish within the developed countries.

Diet and Behaviour The catla is probably the most known and desired type; it is more rounded in shape, and is also renowned for its surface- and column-feeding abilities. Such a species generally feeds on zooplanktonic organisms such as the protozoans and crustaceans. Algae also makes up a considerable proportion of the diet, as well as rotifers, molluscs and decayed macrovegetation. Similar to the catla, the rohu is also a column feeder and therefore susceptible to capture on the bottom every once in a while. Nevertheless, a popped-up bait off the bottom would have to be the most effective method. The mrigal and the calbasu are classed as bottom feeders, where they prefer to stir up the benthic matter in a similar sort of fashion to the common carps.

Of the four different fish, a variety of the catla known as the boulenger (*Catlocarpio siamensis*) is the largest: this fish can reach 5ft (1.5m) in length and 120lb (54kg) in weight. All fish prefer to spawn in the shallow floodwater zones of the rivers.

The big mouth buffalo.

and it is thought that the large weights some have reached in America probably has something to do with the absence of angling pressure.

The big-mouth buffalo should not be confused with the small-mouth buffalo (*Ictiobus carpio*) which is also widespread throughout Canada and the United States. The two are distinguished by the large oblique and terminal mouth of the former and its more slender-looking pharyngeal teeth. It is not a carp as such, but a large powerful fish which is carp-like in appearance, possessing a blunt head and a moderate-sized eye. It occurs from the Hudson Bay drainage throughout the Mississippi system to the rivers of north-east Mexico and the Gulf Coast. It is found in almost all the main lakes

9 SPECIFIC STRATEGIES

A book about strategic carp fishing would not be complete without a chapter detailing some suggested strategies for particular scenarios. Although we have looked at a few strategies in Chapter 1, we will now look at our favourite methods for approaching certain situations. All waters are different and each requires a specific strategy at a specific moment dependent upon conditions, but generally speaking you will find that the strategies we detail here will prove to be excellent starting points for your own lakes and rivers. Use the information we have listed in the

right context, but do not depend on it all the time. Remember, it is you who is to blame for a lost fish or a blank session, and so make sure that you apply one hundred per cent effort to your selections before putting them into practise.

Big Fish Selection

Selecting big fish from a water requires a great deal of hard work. Not only does the time factor play an all important role, but very often the

Simon got his big fish selection right with this lump.

numbers game also comes into the equation. There are literally hundreds of different ways of catching a particular big fish from a water, with stalking being probably the only sure way of achieving this feat. For us though, a concentrated area of bait in an area that the bigger tend to prefer, is one of our favourite methods. This strategy is an attempt to mimic a natural feeding area, such as a bloodworm bed, by providing a high concentration of bait within a small area. It is especially successful if small baits of 14mm or less are used, and we have found that the bigger fish often prefer to feed over this type of strategy than a normal boilie/stringer method.

The strategy involves baiting a circular area of exactly 2yd (2m) radius with two distinct concentrations of bait, that is, an inner and an outer circle, the inner one being more concentrated than the outer – quantity is dependent on the population and size of the carp in the lake you are fishing. One hookbait is fished right in the centre of the inner concentrated area of bait, the second in the lesser concentrated outer circle whilst a third one is fished just off the edge of the outer section on its own. The idea here is that the outer hookbait is strategically placed for the larger fish, which are sampling very cautiously on the edge of the baited area. This is something that we have observed on numerous occasions at pressured waters. Very often the big, wary experienced fish will hold back and observe others before getting their heads down. In such cases, they will normally be picking up the occasional bait before making their decision to move off or feed heavily. When they do feed on the central intense area of bait, the hookbait in the lesser baited outside area will pick up the fish first, with the hookbait placed into the centre of the inner baited circle being taken once the fish are really heavily on the bait.

Short Visit to an Unknown Venue

Short visits to unknown venues must be the hardest way of carp fishing. The carp angler is fishing blind and therefore needs to make the most of his time spent at the lakeside. In such a case, we always make a quick reconnaissance trip around the water and try to gather as much information as possible. If the trip uncovers some valuable information then we will on most occasions follow this. However, if there is no-one at the lake to talk to or the other anglers are being a bit secretive, we apply the 'multiple area' strategy to our fishing. This involves fishing all three hookbaits, or however many rods you are permitted to use, to as many different areas as possible. Basically, we spread the rods about to try and cover as many features as we can. This does not just relate to the areas in which we place the hookbaits, but also the depths in which they are placed. We have found on numerous occasions that the carp may be feeding at a specific depth across the whole of the lake, and a bait placed at this depth in most of the likely looking areas will produce fish. Our opinion on this phenomenon is that quite often macroscopic animal activity is affected by the penetration of solar radiation to a certain depth, and that the fish may be feeding on these animals; a fly hatch in the spring is an example. If the lake you are fishing has a wide variety of features, then use these to your advantage by covering each with a rod. This is the strategy we used at Borwick Lake to great effect (see Chapter 1).

Normally in these situations we fish single hookbaits or stringers comprising no more than three baits, but on occasions we introduce feed in the form of Ball Pellet to the swim (usually ten pellets per rod). Rigs are comprised of 8, 12 and 15in Kryston Super Nova or Silkworm hooklinks in the 15lb breaking strain. These are fished in different areas and form the basis of our strategic decisions; that is, if we start getting hook pulls or aborted takes we will alter our strategies accordingly. Should we receive any action then we analyse the situation and decide whether or not to fish more than one rod to an area. However, before we actually decide to increase the amount of rods in an area, we must first receive substantial evidence to do so – at least two takes in one area is needed.

This method has proved a very effective strategy for hunting down the location of the fish on

This double was part of a 'fourteen fish in a night' catch from an overnight session to a water Rob had never seen before.

most occasions, and very often we work as a team to increase our chances of locating the better spots to fish.

Weedy Waters

It is very difficult to generalize carp fishing in weedy waters as never have we come across two weedy venues that are the same. The type and densities of weed varies in all waters, but if weed is present in your venue, then the carp will certainly be not far away. In our experience, carp absolutely adore weed and the profuse amount of food items it holds. The first piece of advice we give anyone regarding weedy waters is not to be intimidated by them – with the correct strategy selection, fish can quite easily be extracted from weed.

One effective method is to fish in the weed itself, as on most occasions this is where the fish are actually feeding. Normally, we use single hookbaits when approaching weed, as the abundance of food already present limits the need to introduce any freebies. However, if after a period of time the fish are seen not to be interested in the hookbait, it may be necessary to introduce some feed. In this instance, we would opt for a small particle-sized food source such as Nashbaits Micro Mass or just crumbed baits. The reason for this is that the natural food items are of a similar form to these in that they are small and present in abundance (e.g. crustaceans, snails, etc.). Feed is presented via a bait boat if possible or via a PVA bag (*see* Chapter 5) so as to ensure that the bait is concentrated to a small particular area similar to the natural environment.

PVA bags produced this mid twenty from the very weedy Motorway Pond for Crowie.

Hookbaits are, on most occasions, pop-ups presented on buoyant hooklinks such as Silk-worm in the 15lb strain, and hooks are the Nash pattern 2 in at least a size 6 to allow for a hard battle if the need arises. Mainline must be tough and our favourite is Power Plus in 15lb breaking strain, although this varies depending on the distance we are fishing – we select a lower strain with a Quicksilver leader if we need to cast long range. The reason we use Power Plus is mainly down to its durability, but also the fact that it is part stretched and fine in diameter, thus reducing the amount of stretch in the line which the fish has to play with (we usually fish locked up tight). The line is kept from the water as much as possible by fishing the rod tips in the air, and we never use backleads. We always select a lead which can break free from the line as it is normally this which is the cause of fish becoming snagged in weed. Whilst fishing Hull and Districts Motorway Pond in 1997, Simon witnessed fish lost in the weed due to the lead snagging up.

Not wanting to lose any fish in this way, Simon decided to wade in and net a fish which was snagged. The fish was moving quite freely, whilst the in-line lead he was using was snagged solid. Nash In-linner leads soon became his choice and as a result of this change he landed numerous other fish shortly afterwards. Using the In-linner method, the lead falls off the line allowing the fish to swim through the weed without getting caught up in it.

Gravel Bars

Although gravel pits possess a wide variety of different features, it is the gravel bars upon which we will focus our attentions here. Gravel bars are excellent features to fish to in that the carp will favour them greatly for social, safety, as well as feeding reasons.

The first piece of advice we recommend is to plumb all around the bar as much as possible and get to know it like the back of your hand. Gravel bars vary in size as well as make up and there are certain to be silt as well as firm around them – use this information to your advantage. Besides this, gravel bars also offer numerous depths which may be attractive to the carp as well as to the angler. To maximize our chances of success, we normally spread our hookbaits around the gravel bar to increase the likelihood of locating the area in which the fish are feeding. The rigs are spread along the bar whilst being focused at different features. We try one rod on the top of the bar (if depth allows), one at the side in the gully and the other on the facing or far side. The rod fished at the top of the bar is normally one of the side rods to ensure that this line is kept as discrete and as far away from the others as possible, whilst the rod

A chunky gravel pit twenty for Rob caught off a small gravel hump at 50yds.

fished at the facing or far side is placed according to the direction of the wind; it is fished at the leeward side where the food will deposit. Rigs are governed around buoyant hooklinks to keep them away from any sharp objects, and hooks are always checked before casting to ensure they have not been blunted in any way. We usually use strong mainline of 15lb plus breaking strain coated with Granite Juice for all gravel bar scenarios, and we always possess some square or flat baits to prevent them from rolling down the face, or faces, of the bar.

Deep Lakes

Carp can survive adequately in deep lakes despite what some scientists would have anglers believe. If the swim you are confronted with offers an abundance of different depths and you are unsure of how to approach it, then our choice would be to fish at varying depths just as you would for varying features in a shallow lake. Make the depths your features by fishing small clumps of bait to as many areas as you can. If your swim varies in depth from 1–70ft (30cm to 20m), and you are permitted the use of four rods, then try these at 5, 10, 30 and 50ft (2, 3,

10 and 15m). It is unlikely that the carp will be at the 70ft depth, but if they are, you will start picking fish up on the 50ft rods after a period of time. The fish will come up to the shallower regions eventually, as they will not find the deeper water the most comfortable for feeding due to poorer food deposits compared to the shallow areas. We experienced this scenario whilst fishing Cassien in 1996, and we found that after twenty-four hours or so, the fish which were in the deeper areas of the lake, began to make their way up to the marginal areas to feed.

Open Water/Large Lake

Since the latter half of the 1980s we have both fished a number of large lakes where there is a need to bring the fish to the angler. On occasions, it is just not possible to reach the fish at a practical range of fishing so we have needed to bring the fish closer to us by creating some sort of food feature. This scenario is very much the norm on some of the large reservoirs of France, and indeed, it is in that country where we have put this particular strategy into action. The strategy involves creating a large circular baited area

Indiana Dyevre with a big venue twenty.

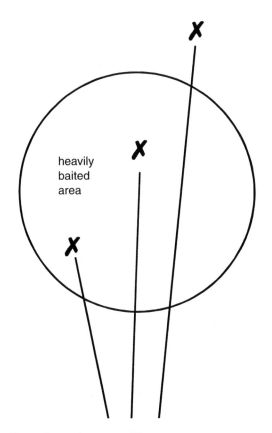

Fig 58 Featureless water. Big water strategy.

off the bait. This rod acts as a roving rod and is intended to intercept any fish prior to them reaching the baited area – this basically tells you that the fish are on their way. The other two rods are fished in the baited area itself, with one fished into the centre and the other fished in the outer part. Bait is topped up according to catch rate at the centre of the baited area.

The particular bait chosen is normally focused on high attractors and additives and low cost. The idea is to mimic a food source and make it so irresistible that the fish need to feed upon the bait, and thus draw them into your swim. A standard soya/semo type bait is our choice on unpressurized waters, and this is combined with an excellent attractant flavour, such as strawberry. An ideal mix comprises the following:

6oz (170g) White semolina
6oz (170g) Soya flour
3oz (85g) Red Factor birdseed
1oz (30g) Lactagold (Calf milk replacer).

We add to this 5ml of Strawberry EA flavour and 10ml Minamino.

Snag Fishing

One of the biggest mistakes that many anglers make when fishing to snaggy areas concerns the matter of bait application. Although tackle selection is high up on the list of mistakes here, applying bait to the snag itself has to be the worst mistake an angler can make. If the fish are well within the snag, they are very unlikely to come out if there is an abundance of free food within!

We normally bait some distance from the snag itself and fish hookbaits on the closest side to the snag, thus ensuring that the first baits the carp come across are the hookbaits. For such instances, a very accurate baiting tool is essential, and our favourite, besides a boat, is a bait rocket of some description. Simply attach one to a spod rod and clip your line up at the correct distance

fished at a distance where you anticipate the fish will patrol or where you expect it to be possible to attract them. The size of the baited area and the quantity of the bait used is dependent upon the projected biomass of the fish – we have made baited areas ranging from 2yd (2m) in diameter and a couple of pounds (1kg) of bait to one of 50yd (15m) diameter comprising approximately 65lb (30kg) of bait. From our experience, the bigger the water, the larger the baited area we consider using (the larger the area, the more hookbaits are fished to it as well).

The general strategy for this type of scenario involves spreading the bait around and fishing as many different hookbaits to the area as possible. In the case of three hookbaits, one of these is fished to the far side of the area and somewhat

A winter snag produced this Waveney fish for Simon.

by casting as close to the area as possible using the reel's line clip for assistance. Apply the bait away from the snag and cast the hookbaits over the back.

After a period of time, the fish are certain to become wise to this strategy, and so regular introductions of bait when you are not fishing will assist greatly here. Don't forget to make sure that your tackle is up to the job and capable of extracting the fish from the snag should they find its sanctuary. Strong line with limited stretch is excellent, and this should be combined with some Kryston Granite Juice for added protection. Hooks of a heavy wire type are our preference to give extra control whilst at the same time limiting mouth damage on the fish, and a snag bar set up with a tight clutch is used to stop the fish setting into the snag.

Small Waters

On this occasion, we will define a small water as being no bigger than 5 acres (2ha) and one which is similar in nature to one of the old estate lakes, which means it is surrounded by trees with very little angling pressure. Such waters are significantly affected by anglers and noise, and

for this reason, we always opt for a surprise kind of strategy. Stalking is our chosen strategy and we make sure that we are kitted out with a tackle bag encompassing all sorts of different tackle implements. If the water is fairly turbid and the bottom fairly silty, as is normally the case with these waters, a simple float set up fished lift style is our first choice. This is combined with a natural type bait like a water snail or tiger nut.

If our experience is anything to go by, the least prolific strategy to use at this type of venue is a standard buzzer bar method alongside static baits. If we did fish this type of method here, however, then we would opt for minimal noise from the bankside, simple rigs comprising 12in (30cm) buoyant hooklinks, light leads, particle type baits, backleads where possible, and fine diameter line. Baits would be dark in colour, small in size, and we would probably look to devise some sort of pre-baiting campaign. We would also encourage the use of camouflaged gear and clothes and try to set up with as minimal amount of disturbance as possible. The margins of such lakes are often an excellent starting point, as very often, there will be an abundance of cover to be found in these areas which the carp will prefer, so keep well hidden and well back; rods included!

Estate lakes: Silence Please.

Pressured Situations

This one is quite a simple scenario to address, as our choice is always governed by the actions of the other anglers. Basically we opt for a strategy that is very different from that used by the others – if all others around you are using fish-meals and the fish have been hammered on them in the past, then try a semo, milk or bird-food bait. The same is true for rigs. If everyone is using short rigs and the fishing is hard going, then try extending the link somewhat.

Information is the key to success on a pressured water, and for this reason, it pays to make regular visits and keep in regular contact with the other anglers. Only the thinking anglers are successful time and time again in pressured situations, and this is why a knowledge of a wide scope of strategies is an excellent armoury to possess. There is no substitute for experience at this type of venue. Certainly, getting on a going

bait and following the crowd can be successful on occasions, but a regular practitioner of this type of fishing will soon become stuck for ideas and will possibly be only a one-hit wonder!

Pressured water carping seems to have a stereotyped method of approach which the majority of anglers follow. This involves short hooklinks, heavy leads, popped-up hookbaits and lots of bait. In this case, we try longer links of 15in (45cm) with a sinking link (our preferred choice is Kryston's Super Nova). This is combined with a running lead set up and a standard bottom bait straight out of the bag. Basically, we try to make the set up look or appear to be as natural and as simple as possible. Bait for such a water should be a high-quality mix like Nash-baits S mix combined with a subtle combination flavour such as Scopex and Strawberry. This should be used at a low level of 1–2ml per pound of dry mix and is included just as a label for the bait. We do not, however, try to over-complicate

Cassein: a pressured water but everyone else was fishing in the North or South Arms.

matters on the bait front by including an abundance of different flavours. Most complex base mixes work very well on their own, and you don't seem to see many people using that tactic on the pressured waters. We usually use the bait in low quantity to start with and increase it depending on the success rate. We also opt for backleads at this type of water and camouflaged leads in an attempt to make the rig and line as discrete as possible.

Highly Stocked Venues

We have all experienced those waters where there are plenty of fish in the venue, but they are very finicky feeders. For example, small waters like Birch Grove and Cuttle Mill have a very high stocking density for their size, but neither can be classed as easy waters. In fact, the opposite is the case, and both venues are difficult due to the amount of angler pressure they have seen over the years. Small, heavily fished, but highly stocked venues can be the most difficult to beat as the fish are very rig shy and will not feed without caution. It is increasingly difficult to induce the greed factor with these fish, and they will more often than not pass and re-pass over your baits plenty of times throughout the session without sampling even one bait. Beds of boilies are almost useless in these situations, and it is for this reason we adopt a completely different strategy to induce these fish to feed.

The ball pellet in its fast dissolving format is ideal to place a food message into a swim without the danger signal that a bed of boilies gives off, and by really piling in the pellet we create such an intense message of food that the carp just cannot ignore it. By 'piling in the pellet' we mean up to 10lb (5kg) over an area of normally 15ft by 15ft (5m by 5m). This may amount to about 1,000 ball pellets to which we add a small number of boiled baits to give the fish something to eat. The pellet stimulates the carp into a feeding frenzy, and because there are usually a large number of carp present, there is an element of competition. The fish hunt around the area for food items, and by introducing only a small number of boiled baits to act as the food source (perhaps fifty baits within this baited area), when a carp does actually locate one of the freebies it will be taken without caution as the fish will fear that another carp will be along to snatch its prize from it. If the fish are very wary of boiled baits, we only use a very inconspicuous boilie and pellet combination such as black squid. We have been instrumental in the production of black baits since we had such a

good result with them in the World Cup, and as a result of this there are now a number of black baits available on the open market.

Conclusion

These are some of the strategies that we have put to good use over the duration of our carp fishing lives. Remember that the strategies worked for us in specific situations, and that they may work for you in a similar situation.

The whole ethos of this book is to try to get you to analyse the situation that you are fishing, and apply your mind to every aspect of your approach from the swim that you fish, through the bait that you use, to the type of lead that you choose. To be a consistently successful angler you must consider everything in detail. You can be lucky some of the time, but consistent successful carping has very little to do with luck.

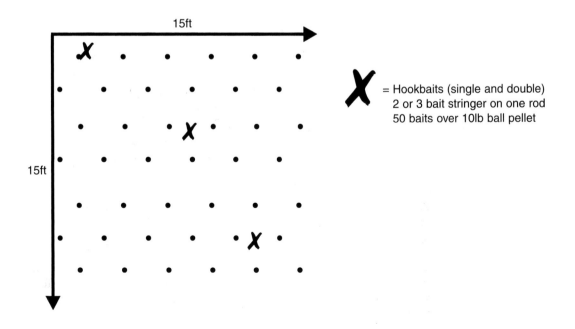

Fig 59 Alternative bait strategy.

Carpe Diem

GLOSSARY

Alleles Alternate forms of genes.

Biomass The mass of animals or plants in a given area.

Chromosome A microscopic rod-shaped structure that appears in the cell nucleus.

Column Feeder A fish which feeds at all levels of a water body.

Fecundity A count of ripe eggs in a female fish.

Gene A unit composed of DNA forming part of a chromosome by which inherited characteristics are passed from parent to offspring.

Macrovegetation The larger plants in a water body.

Morphology The form and structure of anything.

Operculum The bony type gill plate of a fish.

Osmosis The diffusion of liquids through a membrane until they are mixed.

Otolith An opaque coloured bone situated in the ear of fish which forms concentric rings of daily growth.

Recessive A gene that has a characteristic which will only be passed on if the other gene has the same properties.

SSS Single sitting satisfaction.

Taxonomy The classification of plants and animals into groups based on their likenesses and differences.

INDEX